New Flows in Global TV

DATE DUE

This book is for James Moran

New Flows in Global TV

Albert Moran

intellect Bristol, UK / Chicago, USA

First published in the UK in 2009 by
Intellect Books, The Mill, Parnall Road, Fishponds, Bristol, BS16 3JG, UK

First published in the USA in 2009 by
Intellect Books, The University of Chicago Press, 1427 E. 60th Street, Chicago,
IL 60637, USA

A catalogue record for this book is available from the British Library.

Cover designer: Holly Rose
Copy-editor: Sue Jarvis
Typesetting: Mac Style, Beverley, E. Yorkshire

ISBN 978-1-84150-194-9

Printed and bound by Gutenberg Press, Malta.

CONTENTS

PREFACE

In 1992, I was fortunate enough to visit Grundy House in Sydney with Stuart Cunningham and Marie Delofsky. Stuart and Marie were there to interview Ian Holmes, Grundy World Wide's president, as part of the research that would result in the book *Australian Television and International Mediascapes* (Cunningham and Jacka 1996). I had previously interviewed Ian Holmes as part of earlier research work on Australian television drama production but had failed to keep up with the company's international developments, first in the area of program distribution, and more recently in the area of format adaptation. Like others, I was conscious of the process of program copycatting whereby television program ideas from elsewhere metamorphosed into Australian productions and vice versa. However, I was surprised to learn in the interview with Ian Holmes that this kind of content exchange took place under regular business arrangements rather than by some kind of mysterious osmosis.

Over succeeding years, I have continued to connect with the phenomenon of the TV format industry and culture. Besides various journal articles and book chapters, I have authored, co-authored or co-edited several book-length studies of the social and business dynamics of television format programming. In 1998, the University of Luton Press published *Copycat TV: Globalization, Program Formats and Cultural Identity* by Manuel Alvarado. Together with a team of researchers in Asia and the Pacific, led by Michael Keane, I co-edited the book collection *Television Across Asia: Globalisation, Industry and Formats* for Routledge/Curzon. In 2006 this was followed by the handbook *Understanding the Global TV Format*, co-authored with Justin Malbon and published by Intellect. The following year saw the appearance of *New Television: Globalization and the East Asian Imagination*, published by Hong Kong University Press and co-authored with Michael Keane and Anthony Fung.

Clearly, there is much more to be said about the subject of TV program formats. An inventory for further inquiry might include the dynamics of the trade; its impact in the domain of production and reception; the meaning and consequences of the processes of localization that it engenders; its place within international television and media developments; cross-border comparisons of program adaptation; its consequences for a 'television after TV' or even 'the death of television' scenarios; conceptualizations of what occurs in TV program remaking; and theory building to do with adaptation including TV format remaking. At the same time that such a research program can be envisaged, there are signs of a burgeoning interest in the overall subject of TV program formats on the part of experienced and newly emerging scholars. The next two years will see the publication of two important collections of essays: *Global Television Formats: Understanding Television Across Borders*, edited by Tasha Oren and Sharon Shahaf for Routledge; and *Localizing Global TV*, edited by myself for Intellect. In addition, Michael Keane and I are editing a theme issue of *Continuum: A Journal of Media and Cultural Studies* entitled 'Cultural Adaptation', which will also be made available by Routledge under its journal-to-book publishing arrangement with the UK-based Taylor & Francis.

New Flows in Global TV should be seen against this background. In 2003, I was fortunate to meet and become fast good friends with Bill Grantham while he was teaching in the Law Faculty at Griffith University. We discovered common origins in Dublin as well as subsequent degrees in English literary studies. Bill is the author of the seminal study of French film policy, *'Some Big Bourgeois Brothel': Europe's Culture Wars with Hollywood* (2000). Somewhere in there, he found time to pursue a career as a television journalist working for such trade papers as *Variety* and *Television Business International*. The idea of a study of the global TV industry had already taken root and Bill generously shared his extensive knowledge of the trade fairs and exhibitions with me over several days. In 2004, I visited the MIPTV trade convention in Cannes as part of fieldwork to do with the international TV industry in general and the TV format business in particular. *Understanding the Global TV Format* was a first down-payment on that research cycle. The present volume represents a subsequent phase of the same work. Meanwhile, a business biography of Australian television executive Reg Grundy, now in progress, will complete this program of work. Grundy used to refer to the practice of TV format adaptation in terms of an 'international parochialism'. Clearly, there is a lot more to be said about such a subject.

ACKNOWLEDGEMENTS

The research and writing for this book were supported by an Australian Research Council grant awarded for the project 'The Culture of International TV Format Flows' (DP0667066 2006-9). I am grateful for this support. I would also like to thank my home institution, Griffith University, which for over 30 years has given me the opportunity to undertake investigative work relevant to understanding how the media fit into the human landscape. The idea of this book first took the form of an unknown reviewer's comments in regard to a publishing submission on a rather different topic; those thoughtful suggestions led to the present volume – I am most grateful.

Various people have helped me along the way. Bill Grantham deserves a particular thanks for his generosity in sharing his extensive knowledge of the TV industry trade fairs. While I have not had a full-time research assistant on the project, nevertheless many have contributed in a part-time capacity or have assisted me with specific tasks and requirements. I am most grateful to Elizabeth Davies, John Davies, Tom Graham, Cory Messenger and Kate Moran, who have all aided me in this research journey. In the latter stages, Sue Jarvis has been wonderful with her copy editing and other inputs. Teresa Jordan has drawn the maps. Melanie Harrison and Sam King at Intellect Books have been most supportive and patient. I would also like to thank Holly Rose for providing the design for the book's cover.

My biggest debt, however, is to my wife and family. Noela has been a rock of support and encouragement, and at times an unsuspecting sounding board. James has been encouraging, even if he believes that fame and fortune might await the writing and publication of a textbook. Kate has been very responsive to my continuing demands on her time and patience. My grateful thanks go to them and to those mentioned above.

1

ISSUES

The choices TV programmers make about what gets made reflect more than their attempt to please audiences and tap the cultural Zeitgeist. Behind the creative task of bringing programs to audiences, TV is a business. That matters because the way TV conducts its business has a direct impact on the process by which programs are selected, financed, and produced. Reality TV may have captured the attention of audiences, but it also looks good on the books and balance sheets of those whose business is television (Magder 2004: 133).

Introduction

Back in 1920, French filmmaker Abel Gance wrote that the time of the image has come (Wollen 1968). The proposition was extremely prophetic of the cultural and social world we face in the new millennium. Never have picture and sound been so apparently abundant. The Age of Television continues apace with a spiralling multiplication of visual content of all kinds, delivered not only through older 'first-wave' and 'second-wave' screen technologies but also through 'third-wave' technologies such as the computer and the mobile phone (Turner and Tay 2009). At the same time, television itself is claimed to be entering a new phase, where it is increasingly deterritorialized (Morley and Robbins 1995; Morley 2000). The newer technologies such as satellite and digitalization, driven by larger political, economic and social agendas, have seen television enter a post-broadcasting phase (Griffiths 2003). The modern age is, to quote the title of a recent collection of essays on the subject, 'television after TV' (Spiegel and Olsson 2004).

At the same time, it is worth recalling that television has always been characterized in terms of this kind of abundance. In his classic pioneering study of US broadcasting history, Barnouw (1970) titled his volume dealing with US television *The Image Empire*. Meanwhile, *Tube of Plenty* was his name for a subsequent composite volume based on the two-volume history (Barnouw 1992). Whether we accept that the abundance is recent or dates back further, the matter remains the same. Excess is a feature of delivery, so the task at hand in thinking about television in the present is to study this phenomenon of exchange. In fact, television itself has been much analyzed in terms of two sectors. At one end of the process, the medium is grasped as a site of reception and audience activity (Jensen 2002). How viewers watch programs and what they make of them can tell the researcher much about the society and the times. Meanwhile, at the other end of this communication chain, the institution of television is understood in the light of organization, production and programming. To the extent that the business of distribution is recognized at all, it is assumed to be a facilitating service that joins the other two sectors together, the connection that links the beginning and end of a program's journey from inception to broadcast (Wright 2005).

This is, however, a mistaken view of the situation. Distribution is the master element in the circuit across the field of television (or any other media, for that matter). In a classic study of the US motion picture industry that appeared in 1944, Huettig explained that, although drawn to studying the US industry at its glamorous point of motion picture production – Hollywood – it turned out to be much more important to do so from the financial centre of New York where distribution was organized (Huettig 1944). This remains the case with television. Distribution helps to organize the supply of program content and the production of that content, and it dictates the terms under which the consumption of that content takes place. Distribution regulates markets and orchestrates supply to those markets. It is at the very centre of the communications process.

Flow and the 'spatial turn' of communication studies

This book, then, has to do with television program distribution. It is especially concerned with new streams of program content in television across the world. The issue of what characterizes program content will be addressed shortly. For the moment, however, the emphasis has to do with inquiry into the distribution sector. This study deals with the subject under the label of new flows in global TV. The term 'flow' has been a favourite term for characterizing key features of television content. For almost 40 years, researchers and teachers have stressed the four-letter 'f' word not least because of the apparently irrefutable ontological status that the concept has acquired in relation to television study and understanding. The term 'flow' has been a favourite one in the analysis of program scheduling ever since the early 1970s, and it has a strong underlying presence in two seminal studies that have become classics in the field (Williams 1974; Nordenstreng and Varis 1974). Coming to the medium after prolonged researching in the field of literature, Raymond Williams suspected that television viewing entailed a different form of attention than did film viewing. The distinctiveness of the former appeared to lie in a ceaseless stream of apparently heterogeneous images and sounds, a trend that was especially evident in television offerings he encountered in the United States (Williams 1974: 62–75). Nordenstreng and Varis's television project was markedly different and more 'scientific'. Sponsored by UNESCO, their study was also more international, concerned as it was to trace the movement of television program exports on a world scale. Coincidentally, the term 'flow' was used in the two studies. Subsequently, both inquiries have been challenged in different ways in recent years (Thompson 2004; Sinclair, Jacka and Cunningham 1996; Tunstall 2008). Nevertheless, it is still possible to recognize that the term 'flow' has a useful methodological dimension in our understanding of the institution of television. The idea of flow is a valuable one because it joins verb and noun together. It unites carriage and content. Flow may be thought of as movement, as the activity that pushes an entity from one place to another, creating or using a channel or stream. Flow may also be imagined as an object, as an entity or content that undergoes such a displacement. In other words, the idea of television flow can be seen to join the notion of transportation with that of communication.

Carriage and content in the apparently new era of global television are the objects of study in this book. Of course, media have always had a spatial dimension as well as a communicative one – even if that relationship was loosened with the coming of wired and then later radio telegraphy (Czitron 1982; Carey 1989). Electronic media have tended to obscure the physical dimension of communication, and the term 'flow' is useful in reminding us of the spatial aspect of transmission. The term is also valuable in suggesting the textual or semantic dimension – the message component – of television. In short, as two Nordic researchers have pointed out, television mediatizes space just as it spatializes media (Folkheimer and Jamson 2006).

This geographical idea has taken on a particular saliency in the recent present, with what has been called the 'spatial turn' of media studies (Aksoy and Robins 2000; Shiel and Fitzmaurice 2001; Hay 2001, 2004). This approach is one that emphasizes the physical and material dimensions of media, whether as institution, process, representation or object of consumption. Applied to television, the method is concerned to ask about the place and location of what Hay has called the televisual. Hay writes:

> The importance of a geographical understanding of television lies in recognizing that television always has been produced for, has circulated across, and has been engaged at particular sites. Consequently, what is understood as the 'televisual' has never been a discrete object but a set of practices and or attributes – always attached to, situated within, and dispersed across different environments (Hay 2004: 976).

Hay's own background lies in the discipline of geography, and his recent work signals an awareness on the part of some geographers at least that studying the physical dimensions of communications can constitute a significant contribution to cultural geography and a geography of communications (Storper 2002; Stober 2006). For the most part, however, geographers have been slow to initiate inquiry into the material dimensions of communications (Stober 2006). This has not been the case with media scholars (Jansson and Falkheimer 2006; Ek 2006). Instead, in recent years there have been signs of a reawakening and a renewal of a long-standing tradition of media inquiry that stresses the centrality of place. The expanding engagement with the spatial dimensions of communications probably began with Innis (1950) and McLuhan (1962), accelerated with scholars such as Williams (1974), Anderson (1991) and Carey (1989) and became a major focus of analysis with such writers as Morley (2000), Couldry (2000, 2003) and McCarthy (2000).

Spaces of television delivery
Even beyond this growing concern with place evidenced by media researchers, there are more pressing reasons for inquiring into the distribution of contemporary international television.

Three justifications can be mentioned. The first is immediate and practical. While particular analyses exist concerning the export of programming from one national territory to other parts of the world and their insertion into local programming schedules in such studies as the international circulation of *Dallas* in the 1980s (Silj 1988), Australian soap opera exports in the 1990s (Cunningham and Jacka 1996a) and overseas sales of UK television programming in the new millennium (Freedman 2003; Steemers 2006a, 2006b), these are all concerned with an older and familiar form of program content. By contrast, *New Flows in Global TV* is a pioneering investigation into how the kinds of exchange associated with less familiar and more novel forms of television programming work. No other volume has concentrated on placing world distribution at the centre of its inquiries into global TV. This study does exactly that as a means of getting a firmer grasp on contemporary dynamics of the cultural, economic and social exchange that takes place at the centre of world television.

A second reason for this investigation is more conceptual. It has to do with the perceived recent globalization of culture and communications, including television. McLuhan anticipated a media global village, and particular screen institutions such as Hollywood are now said to be global if not planetary (Olson 1999; Miller et al. 2005; Cooper-Chen 2005). Certainly, recent years have seen a sharp growth in the study of international media and communications. The fact that television markets are now increasingly multilayered, existing at local, regional-national, national, world-regional and global levels (O'Regan 1993; Straubhaar 1997, 2007; Chalaby 2005a), creates the opportunity and the necessity of many different forms of market investigation. Multi-regional and multi-national comparisons of different media phenomena are one such type of analysis. The present investigation constitutes another kind of inquiry. It concentrates on global-regional and global-national connections in the distribution of television programs. In short, the study seeks to contribute to the ongoing understanding of the phenomenon of globalization, particularly as it operates in the domain of television.

The third justification for this study is methodological. An engagement (or re-engagement) with geography studies highlights the methodological flexibility of media and communication inquiry. The latter is a field of study and not a discipline. However, in its short history it has been prepared to draw on more established disciplinary outlooks and research strategies from the humanities and social sciences. Media and communications are constantly changing in their technologies, their output and their relationships with sites of power and influence, so it is necessary for new research approaches, novel investigative techniques, exceptional insights and procedures derived from other disciplinary areas to be incorporated into the field to help investigators extend their purchase on the realities with which they deal.

Global television
The phenomenon being investigated in this volume is the worldwide system of television circulation. I have postponed specifying what might be meant by the phrase 'global television' up to this point, but it is necessary to do so now.

Is global television synonymous with a television globalization or a globalized television industry? Is it better addressed using a more neutral term such as 'transborder television'? Are we in an era of post-broadcasting television? How does present-day international television fit into this domain? To answer such questions, it is necessary to take bearings on the state of television at the present time (Parks and Kumar 2003; Spiegel and Olsson 2004; Straubhaar 2007). Five different but interconnected spatial levels at which various television systems have operated are important. These have already been identified as the local, the national-regional, the national, the world regional and the global (O'Regan 1993).

The five levels are interconnected, even if they can also be thought of separately. Like the waters of the high seas that here and there go under particular names such as the Irish Sea or the Pacific Ocean without ever losing their liquidity or mobility, so television in any place has always existed at various interrelated levels. Of course, the strength, connection and significance of these levels have differed considerably over time. During the first seven years of television service in Australia, for instance, television was predominantly a local metropolitan affair, with transmission and reception limited to a particular radius in the state capital cities (Moran 1998, 2005; Moran and Keating 2007). The development of a cable landline infrastructure encouraged the emergence of a regional-national system alongside this local system, and eventually a more completely national system. Australian television is also cross-border and transnational, showing itself to be part of several world-regional television systems. Linguistically, it is a member of an Anglophone media region. Culturally and politically, it is part of both a European cultural region and a British-diasporic territory (Tunstall 2008). Geographically, Australian television can even claim to be a (weak) component of an Asian-Pacific mediascape (Cunningham and Jacka 1996b).

Chalaby (2005) has identified four of the five levels recognized here. He calls the last, mega level of television 'global television'. However, it is worth recalling that an older term, 'world television', is also an appropriate label for such a configuration (Straubhaar 2007). Television at this level has certainly grown over the past 80 years. Skeletally present before and after World War II, when audio-visual broadcasting was being inaugurated amongst the wealthiest, most advanced nations of the West, global television or world television is now an increasingly visible and powerful component of the total accumulated system of television across the planet. Equally, though, one should always bear in mind that this growth occurs alongside changes in the visibility and power of the other levels of television. The planet's television is also marked by different spatial arrangements, as is the case with those systems existing at the other levels.

Chalaby (2005) identifies four interconnected components of this planetary system that are complexly integrated and changing (2005: 14–17). First, there is the media industry component, itself composed by seven giant transnational corporations supplemented by other multinational organizations with strong regional sales or those with global reach specializing in niche markets. Clearly, a body such as BBC Worldwide is such a player, even if it belongs to a second tier rather than to the first. Second, there is a technological infrastructure in the shape of worldwide communication networks that include cable, satellite and the internet; this infrastructure facilitates and maintains the operation of these organizations. Additionally, there is the news and entertainment content and associated data and services that circulate through the system. Finally, there is the global regulatory regime that includes various international bodies, technical and trade agreements, and legal decisions and ordinances.

Such a scheme is rudimentary, and various other interconnected sectors might and should be mentioned. One such domain, for example, is the vital matter of television and media labour, with matters such as employment, worker association, new technology, skill and craft in constant flux and contestation (Miller et al. 2005; Wasko and Erickson 2008). In fact, a fifth interconnected component should be added to Chalaby's quartet model of global television. This has to do with what Waisbord (2004) has called the growing 'interconnectivity' across the sector of global television that witnesses an increasingly common, transnational and transcultural adoption of practices, outlooks and goals among the giant corporations and the many smaller organizations that facilitate their operation, including their human infrastructure of directors, managers, executives and assistants. This milieu provides the cultural glue that helps to hold the system of worldwide television together and facilitates its operation.

Chalaby's own particular focus of interest has to do with transnational satellite television as it operates in five different geolinguistic world regions: Europe, Latin America, Greater China, India and the Middle Eastern Arab world. This development was contingent on the emergence of a new technology that has considerably outstripped the geographical reach of cable landlines. First developed for military purposes, satellite has facilitated the increased spread of television channels across national boundaries to other geolinguistic territories in the same region over the past twenty years. Transnational satellite television is certainly an important component of the complex evolving jigsaw of world television, but so too are other developments. One of these is especially important for this study. The TV format program can be approached in terms of the content and related services that Chalaby identifies as the third of his four interrelated components of the global television industry. Here, there is a need to recognize not only a more familiar form of television program content, but also a more recently distinctive form that now complements the latter.

Forms of programming
These two kinds of television content can be identified as canned and format programs (Waisbord 2004). While these forms or modes ultimately serve the same function of delivering information and entertainment to television audiences, nevertheless they operate differently. They display variations in organization, circulate their commodities in two different systems of distribution, make quite different assumptions about television production and audience reception, and disclose two different histories of evolution. The first form of the canned program is familiar, the second rather less so.

A canned program is one that has been broadcast and recorded for transmission in another time and place. What was crucial for its development has been the appearance of a succession of recording technologies – kinescoping, filming, videotaping, digital warehousing and personalized electronic delivery – which has facilitated programs being warehoused for later rebroadcast. The canned program takes its name from the early material container or receptacle in which the recorded content was physically stored and transported to its place of subsequent transmission.

Historically, this system of program content development first appeared in US network television in the late 1940s and early 1950s (Barnouw 1968, 1992; O'Dell 2004). The canned TV program is a product of the national level of television, even if it spills across borders when licensed into other national territories. As new national television services subsequently came on the air in other parts of the world over the next two decades, well-established program producers were advantageously placed to license canned programs for rebroadcast elsewhere. And if the language in a particular territory happened not to be English, then the finished programs could be dubbed or subtitled into the local *lingua franca*. In turn, this international market situation allowed several national television services to become large-scale exporters of canned television programs to other television nations. The most notable, of course, was the United States, but other important national export systems have included the United Kingdom, Russia, Japan, Brazil, Mexico and Egypt.

However, by the 1990s the world picture of canned program production and export had become more complicated. Thanks to new technology, deregulation and privatization, broadcast channel capacity across the planet had increased markedly (Moran 2005). National broadcasters and production houses found that there was an expanding market for their canned programming, so world trade in content showed a marked expansion. The traditional centres of television output were now joined by many others, including India, Canada and Australia (Sinclair, Jacka and Cunningham 1996). The worldwide distribution of canned TV programming could no longer be described as a 'one-way street', but more closely resembled a 'patchwork tapestry' (Sinclair, Jacka and Cunningham 1996). The existing flow of programming had been joined by a contra flow (Thussu 2007).

In any case, the formatting, adaptation and remaking of programs in other territories had become an important additional means of helping to generate the television content demanded by the expanding world system. Format program television had undergone a different kind of development to that experienced by canned program television. This variation happened in part because of the commodity form of canned television. A TV format is a complex, coherent package of industry knowledge that is licensed to facilitate the making of another version of a program in another television market (Dawley 1994; Fiddy 1997; Purcell 2001; Daswani 2002). Thus the devising and development of the program can occur in one place before a package of know-how is assembled, so that the program can be put together again in another territory. Its new audience may have a different language and culture than that of the program's original broadcast audience; however, format program circulation is not dependent on physical technology in the way that canned program distribution is. Instead, format information and know-how come in the shape of a set of services designed to help in the production of the program elsewhere.

The business model for this kind of enterprise is that of service franchising. Service franchising is the arrangement whereby a business service is licensed out to a franchisee who, in return for the payment of a fee, is given careful and systematic access to a range of assistance that in turn enables the franchisee to offer a commodity to the public at large (Dicke 1992). The franchise industry underwent a dramatic expansion in the United States in the early post-war period so that it is no surprise to discover its increasing attraction to television producers from the 1950s onwards. Nevertheless, it has only been since the late 1980s that the TV program format has become more and more visible in international TV program exchange (Moran and Malbon 2006). A brief outline of the trade's development over the past half-century highlights format programming's place in global or world television.

Format program evolution

Before outlining key stages of this development, it is useful to realize that the program remaking which occurs under the label of format adaptation is a complex process. It involves the orchestration of many different commercial and cultural elements rather than being a rudimentary, unvarying activity with simple ingredients and outcomes (Moran and Malbon 2006). The emergence of two different activities associated with this kind of program copying must be underlined. The first of these had to do with the business of remaking a radio or television program as a one-off process, with little or no thought given to the facilitation of further adaptations. However, once remaking is anticipated, a system and process can consciously be engendered to simplify and streamline the process of adaptation. In this second stage, which has to do with distribution, the activity of remaking is not left to chance but is consciously prepared for by deliberately modularizing the skills, knowledge and materials needed for adaptation. One can even envisage a third stage in this historical development. In such a phase, the process of increasing the adaptability of a program occurs not in isolation and by happenstance on the part of single individuals, but instead becomes an industry norm. A set of industrial practices emerges that is routinized and codified, with a series of institutional supports coming into existence while also drawing on developments in allied fields. The first phase of broadcast program remaking occurred from the 1930s onwards, with US broadcasting playing a central role. By then, radio systems in many parts of the world had consolidated nationally, but at the same time had significant international linkages. Hence, recent inquiry into the inter-war years has stressed various connections between the United States, the United Kingdom and Western Europe (Crissell 1996; Camparesi 2000; Hilmes 2003a, 2003b). These links frequently became conduits for the spread of program remaking know-how. By the late 1930s, for instance, Australian commercial radio had its own versions of several popular US radio network series in such genres as drama and soap opera (Moran and Keating 2007). In these instances, the knowledge transfer taking place was occurring between different national arms of a set of transnational companies. An additional element was added at least as early as 1951. That year saw two separate national organizations on different sides of the Atlantic enter into a licensing agreement concerning broadcast program knowledge transfer. BBC Radio paid a fee to Mark Goodson and Bill Todman, the devisors of the US game show What's My Line?, for permission to make their own version of the program for a British audience (McDermott 2004; Brunt 1985). Sporadic international borrowings under licence arrangements followed over the next twenty years. Generally, though, there was little thought given to increasing either the adaptability of an original program or its accessibility so far as foreign radio and television producers were concerned. The possibility of greater international distribution had not yet been grasped.

At the same time, there were signs of how program remaking might become a trade in its own right. The advent of the US daytime children's television program *Romper Room* (Hyatt 1987: 316) marks an important watershed in this development. This program first appeared on a local television station in Baltimore in 1953. Although the Baltimore version of the program was reasonably successful, its husband-and-wife creators turned down CBS Network's offer to buy the program. Instead, they franchised its business format to a string of local television stations across the country. The services bundled together in the format package included puppets and toys, inventories of games and songs, and training programs for program hostesses. By 1957, 22 local stations across the United States were licensing the format. Six years later, 119 US stations had their own *Romper Room*, each led by a college graduate hostess. By then, the format was being distributed internationally and included several versions being made in Japan and Australia (Hyatt 1987: 316).

Romper Room was distributed by a franchising agent going to individual local stations on a door-to-door basis. The method was time-consuming and laborious. So, despite this individual lead, this kind of pathway saw little traffic following. As far as the US television networks and their suppliers were concerned, the licensing of canned programs to overseas broadcasters was their core business. For the time being at least, distribution of format programming was mostly destined to remain under-developed.

There were, however, continuing signs that a possible market of customers might exist for this kind of franchising, even if – initially at least – they were not inclined to pay licensing fees. As late as 1980, overseas producers from such places as South America, Western Europe and Australia were visiting the United States to tape programs in hotel rooms that they would later imitate in their own home territories (van Manen 1994; Drummond 2000). Chapter 8 recounts how, in 1988, a public service organization in New Zealand had little compunction in copying a UK game show without bothering to inform the latter's format owner (Lane and Bridge 1990a, 1990b; Lane 1992). The genres undergoing international appropriation at this time were game show and other 'live' talk-based formats, and a legitimate trade in licensed formats was already underway. TV game show owners and devisors were increasingly involved in renting production knowledge for program remaking in other territories.

A third phase of television program remaking began around 1990, and continues in the present. This form of exchange has become one of the pillars of television program production across the planet. International branding practices grew significantly in the 1980s, and this in turn led producers to a more careful and systematic distribution of their program production knowledge and skill (Bellamy and Trott 2000; Moran and Malbon 2006). By 1995, several large European licence-owners had emerged, including BBC, Endemol and

Pearson Television (later FremantleMedia). As Peter Bazalgette has documented in detail, the watershed year of 1998–99 saw the appearance of three reality formats – *Who Wants to Be a Millionaire?*, *Survivor* and *Big Brother* – which were enormous successes in key markets including the United States, the United Kingdom and Western Europe (Bazalgette 2005). Reality TV had arrived with a vengeance. So too had TV format distribution as one of the main games in town. From this point on, program format developers would attempt to ensure the near-simultaneous remaking of their formats on a worldwide basis, not least to help thwart unlicensed appropriation. In the new television landscape, other more expensive forms of content, such as drama and current affairs, were increasingly displaced in favour of less expensive forms whose economies were, in part, based on the local remaking of global or universal formats (Brunsdon et al. 2001; Magder 2004, Moran 2005; Frau-Meigs 2006). Major new format distributing companies emerged; significantly, these were based in Western Europe rather than in the United States.

Program franchise trading has become serious business at the international round of television markets, most especially the MIP fairs held at Cannes twice a year. In 2000, a group of format companies came together at Cannes with a view to establishing an industry body, the Format Registration and Protection Association (FRAPA). The group is an international trade association. It also offers a mechanism for dispute resolution over formats, which is designed to help avoid costly legal proceedings. (Moran and Malbon 2006).

However, a number of legal battles to do with alleged program format appropriation have been fought over the past decade, and several of these are discussed in Chapter 8. The collective outcome of these cases has been the beginning of legal recognition of TV program formats as valuable intellectual property (van Manen 2003). Additionally, a small cadre of lawyers specializing in legal matters concerning formats have also identified themselves under the banner of the International Format Lawyers Association (IFLA), which they saw as the engine room of FRAPA (Coad 2007). As further signs of the coalescence and formalization of this element of the format industry, regular industry training courses and workshops have come into being and handbooks have also begun to appear (Moran and Malbon 2006).

Program remaking is now one of the mainstays of the modern cross-border system of television. This trade heralds a new era in the international history of television. Whereas cross-border exchange in canned programming is a phenomenon that has to be understood in terms of the national level of television (albeit on a worldwide scale), this is not the case with format programming. The format program business is not a manifestation of the border spillover of television, but rather of a kind of television without frontiers, without borders. With this kind of television, most licensors (although not all) recognize the need to customize a format to produce a program amenable or adaptable to local taste. As a commodity, the format is denationalized or universalized in such a way that a program made from it can successfully be customized and indigenized for audiences in particular national or local television territories. Given this disposition, it is clear that the TV format is a content component of the global television industry, belonging to category three of Chalaby's model referred to earlier.

The structure of the book

The aim of *New Flows in Global TV* is to furnish the reader with an analysis that identifies the main elements of international television distribution, most especially having to do with program formats. The analysis is concerned with the scale of this system as well as its organization. Accordingly, the chapters that follow investigate in detail the institutional arrangements associated with this circulation. Chapter 2 has to do with the actual markets for television that occur on an annual basis and are a must in terms of attendance for those in the business. These trade fairs or bazaars are regularly staged each year at times that are convenient for the principal attendees. Participation confirms membership of a kind of club that is the worldwide television industry. However, little critical literature exists regarding this kind of meeting or get together, so the approach taken is one of ethnographic description. This concentrates on the orchestration of time, space and ritual that is a central component of such events.

Chapter 3 concentrates on the market rhetorics that form the discursive landscape of both trade fairs and exhibitions, and the global television industry more generally. How does the trade talk to itself about itself? What does it tell itself? The chapter examines the dominant tropes and figures at work in this oration as a means of articulating the implicit sense of the business's own purpose and trajectory. All the same, the global television trade is more than the structures provided by such elements as marketplaces and trade talk. Therefore, the next chapter takes up the matter of human agency. Thousands of executives, producers, program devisors, broadcasters and others throng the market exhibitions and festivals, where they deal in the wares of this kind of modern bazaar. Various figures stand out as exceptional in their business dealings. Some of these warrant the description 'trade celebrities', and the chapter analyses the star personae of three such industry figures.

Chapter 5 is transitional between the worldwide television industry's hub and its rim, between what goes on at its metropolitan centre and what takes place in broadcasting's outlying provinces. The chapter itself has to do with the languages employed by the trade. The claim is that there are two linguistic realities operating in the domain of TV format programming so that there are two parts to the discussion. The first has to do with the Anglophone nature of the international television business. In home territories, on the other hand, TV programs acquired through market dealings undergo cultural recuperation. They need to look and seem familiar to home audiences. This recasting inevitably involves embedding in a local or national language (as well as in the native culture more generally).

The shift from the centralized places where programs are devised and marketed to the outlying territories where they are remade and broadcast highlights the geographical channels along which TV programs flow. Hence Chapter 6 investigates the routes that the format trade adopts, and is especially interested in the various national television markets that it services. Canned and format television programs are not the only elements to travel these business trails. Typically, the licensing of a TV program format to a particular territory will also entail on-the-spot consultative services provided by an experienced producer sent from head office. The chapter examines the work of such an ambassador, and especially the complex negotiation involved in the customizing or indigenizing of a program format for a home audience in a particular part of the world.

The next two chapters also deal with national and local television territories. The international nature of the global television industry means that producers are well placed to take over successful program ideas from elsewhere, even while owners are increasingly ready to litigate in foreign jurisdictions over what they regard as theft of intellectual property. Chapter 8 is especially concerned with the ongoing attempt to privatize generic appropriation of TV formats under supposed intellectual property protection law. Chapter 9, as a case study, focuses on one national market that is increasingly part of the global television industry. Australia constitutes a salient and valuable instance of how production in a national television industry is impacted by, and can in part become a branch plant of, a much, larger cross-border business.

Chapter 10 summarizes the argument of the book concerning the distribution of this commodity form of television. Having once been a business of the world, television is increasingly a world business. Taking the TV format program as its particular subject, this book maps out the significant dimensions of this relatively new form of cultural merchandising and the various movements, human and otherwise, associated with it.

2

PLACES

For all of human history, markets have been central spaces for transactions and encounters beyond commerce... In an early chapter of *Don Quixote*, for example, Cervantes recounts his fortuitous recovery and rescue of some 'old notebooks and documents' written in Arabic that turn out to be the rest of his great novel. The place for this monumental (fictional) discovery: the Alcaná (marketplace) in Toledo – Spain – a bazaar of such cultural diversity and plenitude that the author has no difficulty finding a translator who accepts payment of fifty pounds of raisins and three bushels of wheat 'to translate carefully and well, using no more words than absolutely necessary' (Thorburn and Jenkins 2003: 3).

Introduction

As this quotation reminds the reader, the notion of a market is an ancient one. Variations on the term 'market' include 'fair' or 'bazaar'. The physical event is constituted by the coming together of interested parties, traders, onlookers, tourists, and so on in a designated place for the purpose of buying and selling. It is worth noting that, in the etiology of the term 'market', the appearance of the noun preceded the emergence of the verb. The place defines the activity. In the case of television programming licensing, as Cunningham (2004) notes, this linguistic history is reversed. The business of selling and buying television programming probably began in the 1940s after the end of World War II, although the first marketplace events did not occur until around 1963. Up to the early 1980s, markets or trade fairs catering to the television industry were few in number, with only a limited volume of programming changing hands and only a modest amount of deals concerning finance and co-production taking place. Over the past quarter of a century, however, television markets have mushroomed in terms of number, frequency and size; this is due largely to institutional change associated with privatization, deregulation, new technology, multi-channelling and media convergence.

This chapter is concerned with locating the television market at the very centre of world trade in television programming, both in its canned and in its format forms. Markets are the hubs of the international television system, the still point at the centre of a dynamic, complex network that helps determine what local viewers or consumers access on their television sets, mobile phones and computers, and what they interact with in terms of viewing, public turnouts, phone voting, messaging, and so on. World television trade occurs at a series of well-defined times throughout the year, and at fixed places around the world. The biggest international trade shows happen in Las Vegas in January, Brighton in the south of England in February, Cannes in March and September, and Los Angeles in May. Like some of the grand marketplaces of the past, these trade fairs act as great business crossroads. They have their distinct geographies and histories, and these have a determinative effect on the culture and the dynamics of the TV trading that takes place at such bazaars.

The analysis of the fairs in this chapter is split into five sections. First, I survey the limited amount of critical literature that exists on the subject of television markets. This brief preamble is followed by a longer discussion of the advent and structure of the annual cycle of TV fairs and festivals, wherein buyers and sellers of licences for both canned and format programs come together. In the third part of the chapter, I take the MIPTV market at Cannes as a case study to provide a means of amplifying the general pattern already outlined. This analysis is based on participant observation there in late March and early April 2004.

Figure 2.1: Traders at a TV fair.

In fact, markets may be more important for symbolic and participatory purposes than for actual business dealings. Many aver that the markets are not good places to enter into deals, and that far more business arrangements are in fact brought to conclusion in the offices of broadcasters in far-flung territories than are finalized on the floor of the markets. The last part of the chapter examines this claim. However, even if the assertion is true, it still remains necessary to account for the markets. Why do they happen? Why do very busy executives, producers, broadcasters, advertisers, mobile phone companies and others come to these events year after year? In the concluding discussion, I suggest that these events are an important means for a global industry to engage in a form of cultural and business networking that maintains a physical, social dimension alongside a virtual one.

Critical reflection

Television trade markets have received little critical attention despite their historical longevity. As we shall see in the next chapter, there is plenty of coverage of this kind of event by the trade press at the time of its occurrence and immediately after. On the other hand, there is generally a paucity of more extended, reflective writings about this kind of commercial event. This is hardly surprising. After all, in the parallel domain of feature film promotion and circulation represented by the film festival event, there has been little follow-up to Neale's (1981) pioneering study of this international institution of art cinema. However, two book-length studies of film festivals are worth mentioning. These are not only interesting in themselves, but also help the reader to a more critical engagement with the phenomenon of television markets and fairs. The later volume is the more general and wide ranging of the two. It deals with a series of different types of film festival. Journalist Kenneth Turan (2002) provides a suggestive perspective on the film festival as an international event by grouping ten such festivals that are quantitatively different from each other. These are organized into three categories across a spectrum of commerce, politics and culture. Thus he considers a triangle of festival types whose primary function has to do with the business of film, commerce, geopolitical agendas, and aesthetic purposes respectively. Two last chapters deal with festivals that have failed and disappeared, and with the jury system for the judging of film awards. Undoubtedly, the best known of all the festivals with which Turan deals is the Cannes Film Festival, which began in 1939 after the model of the Venice Film Festival. The Cannes Film Festival currently operates for twelve days each year. Whatever its original cultural ambitions, it has long been a highly commercial event, catering as it does to film distributors and producers from around the world, most especially from Hollywood.

Meanwhile, Beauchamp and Bohar (1992) provide a valuable complementary case study by analyzing the operation of the Cannes Film Festival at greater length. This account is also aimed at a popular audience, but is solidly historical and sociological, while at the same time peppering its analysis with plenty of colourful detail and anecdotes. Among the subjects explored are: the history and layout of the festival venue, the Palais des Festivals; the competition system; Cannes as film marketplace; the presence of the Hollywood companies; the orchestration of publicity and fame; the jury system; and the awards ceremonies. While such a listing might suggest a degree of arbitrariness in what they choose to analyze, the fact is that Beauchamp and Behar's overall subject is precisely delineated and has to do with how the

Cannes Film Festival is now part of the distributing and marketing mechanism of the institution that is global Hollywood (Miller et al. 2005).

Television market scholarship has been more neglected. There are no monographs dealing with the subject of media fairs and festivals. Instead, what little analysis there is must be sought in journals and other specialist publications. Two analyses can be mentioned. The first is provided by a team of Canadian economists with a research interest in film and television marketing (Acheson and Maule 1989; Acheson, Maule and Filleul 1992, 1996). These researchers have undertaken a financial and managerial analysis of the Banff Television Festival held in that city in the province of Alberta each year since 1978. To that end, they have provided an interesting and useful analysis of the festival as an entrepreneurial venture where entrepreneurship is the business capacity displayed not by an individual but by a team that is responsible for the conception, staging, consolidation and continued operation of the Banff Television Festival itself. Hence, although the television industry personnel who attend such an event are considered in passing as the 'customers' of the team, the emphasis falls on the festival as a kind of business operation, and the authors are concerned with such matters as finance, management and structural innovation. Unfortunately, with this kind of middle-range focus, there is no room for more general observations regarding the larger circuit of international television festivals and fairs. Nevertheless, the analysis provides significant insight into the origin, development and operation of an important festival, and helps suggest how culture and commerce are intertwined in such events.

The most interesting analysis of the international television markets is provided by Stuart Cunningham (2004). This author brings a strong cultural studies perspective to bear on the subject of festivals and markets. Recent years, he suggests, have seen the development of important international television industries in a number of territories outside the United States and United Kingdom. Once, television distribution across the world could be described as a one-way street. Now there is more point in Tracy's (quoted in Cunningham 2004: 1183) characterization of world television as a 'patchwork tapestry'. In turn, the development of trade markets is a sign and a confirmation of the fact that international television is now truly a world industry. As part of the organization of that industry, there are a significant number of trade events and festivals differentially timed across the globe. Cunningham also sketches the principal participants in trade fairs as well as contrasting alleged buying behaviour by commercial broadcasters and European public service television operators. This differentiation allows the observation that the global television institution is a highly structured one in which power and influence are unevenly distributed. Even in the heady, distracting atmosphere of a television trade market, there are many intimations of these patterns of domination and subordination. Cunningham's suggestion is a useful means of introducing analysis of market origins and development.

Markets: Location and timing
Television trade fairs have been slow to develop, and have only reached their present strength in very recent years. Since the early 1950s, TV operators have looked to the international

Figure 2.2: The Mandalay Bay Casino Hotel in Las Vegas is the site of the annual NAPTE market.

trading of programs to help fill their broadcast hours. At first, much trading was done on an *ad hoc*, one-to-one basis, often proving to be cumbersome and inefficient. Deals were effectively done at the doors of television stations as overseas broadcasters came looking for wares. Beginning in the 1960s, various international television exhibitions, markets and festivals have developed, with the basic function of putting those who wish to trade in programming, finance, rights and so on in touch with those who deal in such wares.

Like all fairs, modern and ancient, television festivals bring together the two components of any exchange: sellers and buyers. Markets often extend preferential treatment to sellers, given that they in turn attract buyers (Grantham 2003). Trade fairs occur for various reasons. The markets are opportunities for those in film and television, as well as new media, to make different kinds of deals. TV program format exchange is only one of the many kinds of commercial transactions that occur at the markets, but nevertheless it is one that is rapidly expanding in economic and cultural significance.

These modern bazaars are trade events where the television business comes together physically as opposed to being an industry with an electronic internet presence and footprint. The exhibitions and festivals are not usually open to the general public; instead, the core attendees come from within television businesses across the world, and include broadcasters, production house personnel, regulatory authorities, public agencies that promote film and television, trade associations, firms involved in entertainment law, media representatives and journalists, and government consuls, ambassadors, and other public officials. The main players are producers, distributors and broadcasters, while subsidiary actors include government agencies, financiers, packagers and sales agents. Additionally, there are important secondary reasons for those involved in the TV format business to attend the fairs. As a recent note on MIPCOM's website put it, the industry is there at the market in order to 'buy and sell TV programs; develop long lasting business relationships for the months ahead; make new contacts; speed up negotiations; create partnerships; [and] keep abreast of important changes affecting the audio sector' (MIPCOM 2003). *Variety* gave a more informal sketch of this same bustle: '[F]ive days of immersion in a series of talkathons, keynotes and demos about convergence, user-generated content and how I, too, could become a star of sorts if I'd just unleash my own virtual fantasy self' (Guider 2007).

Although drawn from all corners of the world, nevertheless there are a disproportionate number of participants from the United States, the United Kingdom and Western Europe (Edmonds 2004; Griffin 2005; Hetsroni 2005). Over the years, there has been some variation in location, timing and scope of some of the exhibitions and markets, although the major ones have been very stable in terms of place and time. Just as Turan (2000) was able to divide film festivals into three major types, so it is possible to assign televisions bazaars to one of three categories: the showcase market; the trade fair; and the market festival.

Showcase markets

This kind of fair is organized around programs of showcase screenings where new television programming is premiered to overseas buyers, usually before it has been put to air in a domestic market. The event is like a film or television festival that serves a country, a region or even a single company. Recent showcase markets have included the European independent, Nordic, German, and French showcases. Nowadays, there are two really notable instances where sellers have the buyers come to them rather than both going to a neutral third space. These occur in Los Angeles and Brighton.

LA Screenings

The LA May Screenings are a marathon, ten-day event that takes place in Los Angeles in late May or even early June (Grantham 2003). It attracts broadcasters, cable operators and, lately, foreign online and mobile companies who sometimes arrive early to visit New York for scheduled business discussion with the top network executives. At the LA Screenings, the Hollywood studios and the networks unveil their new programs that will go to air in the United States beginning in the autumn. For foreign buyers, this time is a golden opportunity to check out the pilots for new programs and to lock up rights for different territories. The fair is a dispersed one, taking place at different venues around the city. Hence Disney likes to kick off its selling event with a Sunday evening 'International Upfronts' at the El Capitan Theater in Hollywood. Because the studios themselves are scattered around the Los Angeles area, a tradition has evolved whereby the companies coordinate their screening dates to avoid clashes. Meanwhile, the international buyers remain in central accommodation, many at the Century Plaza Hotel near Fox Studios in Beverley Hills. Buyers are bussed from their hotels to the different venues for premieres of the new season's programming. Sometimes, though, not even a pilot is available. This was the case in 2007 when only a two-minute promo for Disney's new spinoff series from *Gray's Anatomy*, *Private Practice*, was ready with the promise that there would be a pilot-screening launch of the new series at MIPCOM later in the year.

BBC

The BBC Showcase occurs even earlier in the calendar year. Here, the wares are entirely the output of one organization. The four-day showcase is held annually in Brighton in February. Begun in 1976, the event – organized by BBC World Wide – is the world's largest program market hosted by a single broadcaster. In 2003, for example, over 1,500 hours of programming including drama, entertainment, comedy, factual and documentary, children's and music was presented in the form of showreels and full screenings (BBC World Wide 2003).

Format licensing is another key component of BBC business so that the same year the Romanian, Dutch, Chinese and Indian women hosts of *The Weakest Link* were on hand for a presentation. The showcase also offers deals on new games and interactive services linked to digital platforms.

However, while a great deal of business is done at these two screenings in Los Angeles and Brighton, nevertheless it is the staging of the big markets at other times in the year that brings out both sellers and buyers in their thousands. Commerce becomes the only game in town – even if it has to do with the commerce of culture.

Trade markets

Business can also take place on neutral ground where sellers and buyers come together on more equal terms, often under the aegis of a trade association or a commercial operator. Where the showcase screenings are by invitation only, the trade markets are prepared to admit the public for the price of an (often costly) registration. Coincidentally, the major trade markets in television programming in the United States and Western Europe both began in 1963. The former now sponsors one trade market held in Las Vegas in Nevada, while the latter mounts two markets in Cannes in spring and autumn. This by no means exhausts the variety of trade markets held annually. Other commercial fairs serve such regions as the former Soviet Union countries and the German language territories, although these regional trade markets are not analyzed here. Instead, attention is directed to the major US and Western European fairs. Additionally, one other television bazaar serving Eastern Europe, which appeared after the downfall of communist governments in that part of the world, is also outlined.

NAPTE

The National Association of Television Programming Executives (NATPE) is easily the largest market and fair in the world, with participants sometimes numbering as many as 30,000 (Grantham 2003; NATPE 2004). Set up in 1963, NATPE is a non-profit US trade association or grouping that maintains its own permanent secretariat and hosts an annual convention that is also a marketplace (Grantham 2003). In the past, the exhibition has been staged in different cities in the United States, including New Orleans and Los Angeles. Since 2004, however, it has been mounted permanently in Las Vegas. The event occurs in January as both a convention for its members and as a trade market. The latter includes as many as 300 stands of major companies and others in the main exhibition halls. This annual get-together began as a forum for TV executives to interact and in order to provide a venue for the facilitation and interchange of ideas. As part of this legacy, NATPE remains dedicated to a market that is less expensive so far as attendance is concerned compared with its principal European rivals (Grantham 2003). Earlier, the event was a means of distributing television programming, though it now focuses on all forms of content and serves all kinds of platforms (Guider 2007).

The past few years have seen a downturn in the size and scope of NATPE, which recently has been contracted into a three-day event. The downturn undoubtedly reflects various industry tendencies, including company takeovers and mergers, a slump in advertising sales and a

Figure 2.3: The bustle of a trading floor at NATPE.

Figure 2.4: NATPE delegates in action.

peeling off of some market business from the exhibition floor to private hotel suites. Reportedly gone is much of the fanfare that once took place on the market floor, such as the appearance of TV stars and other costumed promotional activity. Additionally, NATPE's timing is somewhat unfortunate, with the US networks having only last year's new programming wares on offer (Grantham 2003). However, the event is still very significant in the international calendar. In recent years, for instance, Latin American companies have been using the trade market as a major opportunity to buy from and sell to each other. Hollywood remains the centre of the international television and multimedia industries in canned programming, so NATPE will continue to be a vital market.

MIP

This is the generic name for several trade fairs that take place in Cannes each year with the acronym designating the name Marche Internationale de Programme (World Market for [Television] Programs). The major twin fairs are MIPTV and MIPCOM; these occur in the first and second halves of the year respectively (Grantham 2003; MILIA 2004; MIPCOM 2003; MIPTV Magazine 2003). They are housed in the Palais des Festivals on the city's beachfront. While some television markets elsewhere are the initiative of trade associations or municipal or city authorities, these French markets are commercial exhibitions that regularly turn a handsome profit for their owners. Generally, they attract about half the number of delegates that come to NATPE, although attendees constitute a more genuinely global cross-section of media companies. The MIP fairs are about twice as long as NAPTE and their registration fees are considerably more expensive (Grantham 2003).

MIPTV began in 1963 as the brainchild of a local businessman. The early 1960s was not an especially favourable time to launch such a venture because television markets in many territories were quite restricted in their need for programming. However, Bernard Chevry's market soon caught on, as did his music market begun in 1967. Indeed, the latter's name, MIDEM – an acronym for the music market (Marche Internationale de Disc et Editione Musicale – World Market for Records and Music Publishing) – became the parent company, whose festivals included MIPTV. Two parallel events occur at MIPTV. The first is a meeting of important elements of the Francophone television industries, most especially that of French television broadcasting. The parallel event is the one better known to the international television industry at large. This is the television exhibition, which attracts about 15,000 participants involved in TV broadcasting, program production, distribution for TV, video and the Internet, advertising, licensing and merchandising, consultancy, service companies and new media. Format deals have become increasingly important over the last two decades, and are now one of the main activities at MIPTV.

MIPCOM was established in 1984 as a video marketplace, but soon adopted the same structure as MIPTV. Held in September, the fair is slightly shorter than its sibling. What really fuelled the speedy growth of this trade exhibition in the 1980s was the rapid expansion of channel capacity in television systems in many places, most especially Europe. Cross-border satellite television and cable television linked with deregulation and the introduction of

Figure 2.5: Promoting MIPTV, held at Cannes in 2007.

commercial broadcasting rapidly increased the need for more programming. Meanwhile, in the United States in the 1970s, the introduction of both the Financial Interest and Syndication Rules and the Prime Time Access Rules brought about a significant increase in the volume of television programming available. In practice, MIPCOM is much like MIPTV. Although usually one day shorter, there are substantially the same numbers of individual participants and companies attending, and the same number of deals are struck in the same areas. Although the Hollywood studios are on hand at MIPTV, in September/October at MIPCOM they have their new catalogues available so business is especially brisk.

DISCOP
Begun in 1992, the Discount Programming (DISCOP) market occurs annually in Budapest each year over three days in late June (DISCOP 2004; Grantham 2003). Its mission is to cater for the needs of emergent markets, most especially those in Central and Eastern Europe, Central and South East Asia, India and China. More specifically, the exhibition addresses itself to trade in TV programming and feature films, thematic channels, TV formats, telenovelas and interactive solutions. To cater to this range of interests, DISCOP splits its activities into four different sections: program showcase; new technology exhibition; TV formats market; and an industry conference. Under the Discop banner, it is also worth mentioning the first TV program format market that the group held in Lisbon in February 2001. The intention was to establish a festival entirely devoted to this newest area of international trade in television. The festival was not well attended and has not survived.

Market festivals
Over and above the trade exhibitions where the principal business is that of buying and selling, some television fairs are organized around two different kinds of meeting: markets, the trade fairs and festivals of workshops; and screenings of programs and television programming – either in competition or alone. The thinking behind this doubling is obvious: two attractions

should draw more participants than one. This has not always proved to be the case. Market festivals are actually few in number and are not important in the diary of the international television industry. Nevertheless, it is worth noting the two most significant of these events, the Rose d'Or and the Monte Carlo Television Festival (Grantham 2003).

The Rose d'Or
Begun in 1961, occurs over three days in May in Lucerne in Switzerland (http://www.rosedor.com). The founding idea was to create a forum where European broadcasters could fill gaps in their summer schedule by swapping light entertainment programming. Accordingly, festival competitions are organized around seven light entertainment categories .The Rose d'Or also functions as a competitive television festival of screenings and jury selections whose ultimate prize is the golden rose award. Nonetheless, the festival remains a minor event in the calendar of the global industry, attracting only a tenth of those who attend Cannes, with only token involvement from the United States and Asia (Grantham 2003).

The Monte Carlo Television Festival
Although initiated as the Monte Carlo Television Market and Festival in 1961, this annual meeting has recently vacated the area of the trade exhibition in favour of a television festival of screenings and industry-related events. Designed to lure business and other visitors to the principality of Monaco, the market and festival event was originally scheduled in February but was wound up because of lack of interest. Since 2002, a revamped Monte Carlo Television Festival has been timed for early July as a means of snagging early holidaymakers from the industry. The festival runs for six days, and features publicity-grabbing international awards, premiere screenings, panels and workshops. In addition, it also features a small amount of market-related activity such as a one-day workshop on TV formats in 2002.

Many other television exhibitions and festivals could be added to this list. Cunningham (2004) refers to a total of eleven such fairs. Like television production companies themselves, festivals and trade fairs come and go, rising and falling in terms of popularity and attendance. MIP Asia in Singapore opened its doors on the eve of the Asian currency crisis and shortly thereafter disappeared, although Reed will try again in 2008 with a new media trade fair, Amazia, in Hong Kong (Rhodes 2006). Meanwhile, the markets and fairs identified here are the principal ones so far as the global television industry is concerned. The annual round of markets helps define the television year for broadcasters and producers, including those active in the field of TV formats. Going to the markets is one of several ways in which the global TV format business maintains its worldwide reach. As the MIP website (http://www.miptv.com) suggests, attending the markets brings licensors and licensees into regular contact, builds and helps maintain business relationships, enables broadcasters and producers to spot new trends and developments, and draws nationally based industry figures into more international networks. The markets function as a kind of club, and club membership is maintained and exercised through repeated attendance at club events. What, then, are the principal institutional and cultural forms and practices in operation once these members come together? What is the physical and human environment of a market?

MIPTV: A case study

Over and above the larger pattern of trade events, there is a commercial dynamic at work at the more local level of the individual market. Matters of time, space, social ritual and custom are significant elements in the milieu of the television fairground. An analysis of MIPTV in 2004 is a useful means of outlining the culture of the television marketplace in more detail. Matters of timing, location, custom and activity serve as guides to such an event.

Time

Following the lunar calendar, MIPTV and MIPCOM at Cannes in March/April and September/ October fit into the international TV industry calendar as well as filling a preordained place in the annual diary of events in that city. Cannes is neighbour to both Nice and Monte Carlo. While the Côte d'Azure was a popular winter retreat for the ruling classes of Europe during the nineteenth century, the place was 'discovered' in 1834 when Lord Brougham, the then Lord Chancellor of England, was prevented from wintering in nearby Nice by an outbreak of cholera. Instead, his party found its way to Cannes, and subsequently the city became a favourite winter playground of the rich and upper classes. By the end of World War II, however, social patterns had changed. The aristocracy had been replaced by a more middle-class clientele, eager to spend summer on the water's edge. But hoteliers and city businesses still found it hard to find patrons in other months of the year. In 1939, the Cannes Film Festival began in opposition to the Venice Film Festival, and it resumed in 1946 after the end of the war. The festival occurs in June. In turn, the glamour and sophistication that it developed from the 1950s onwards has acted as a magnet to lure various other elements of the international entertainment and communications industries to Cannes for their trade and festival events. The hotels are also heavily booked around Easter because of that season's religious significance for Christians and Jews. The combined effect of these commitments was to nudge MIPTV, and later MIPCOM, towards spring and autumn stagings.

Nowadays, MIPTV and MIPCOM are sandwiched into a busy round of professional trade shows that Reed MIDEM, MIP's parent body, brings to Cannes. The latter organization is a division of Reed Exhibitions, the world leader in mounting some 460 public exhibitions and professional trade shows. In turn, Reed MIDEM is a major unit that specializes in fairs held at the Palais des Festivals (Rhodes 2005). These professional trade shows include MIPDOC, MIPTV, MIPCOM JUNIOR, MIPCOM and MILIA for the television and multimedia industries, MIDEM for music professionals, MIPIM and MAPIC for the property sector, and GLOBAL CITY for urban management specialists.

If MIP's timing is set by an interlocking set of institutional commitments, then its duration is suggested by other factors (Grantham 2003). As already suggested, apart from NATPE, MIP is the principal global event insofar as television marketing is concerned. The two events draw producers, broadcasters and others whose flying time is up to 24 hours. Hence, persuaded in part by the two-week length of the Cannes Film Festival, MIP is organized as a week-long event (one day longer in the case of MIPTV). At the spring and autumn markets, a great deal of business happens in the first three days, although many company representatives continue to pitch, make deals and talk to would-be clients and partners right up until the end of the market.

Fifteen or 30 minutes is the smallest unit of time during the working day. The pitch meeting is scheduled accordingly. Organizing these and other kinds of get-togethers between those in the television business is the appointments book or diary, a means of scheduling a large series of dates across the week with many meetings already being arranged at previous MIP events. This kind of cyclical round of get-togethers, appointments and further meetings is one of the many elements at work to persuade the trade to ongoing attendance at Cannes. Of course, matters of time cannot be divorced from those of space. The international scope of television is most apparent in the domain of formats. This latter technology brings about the global television program, drawing companies across the planet into a world business. Hence the geography of Cannes MIPTV, a microcosm of this terrestrial reach, is also worth mentioning.

Location
Cannes is a city of approximately 70,000 people with nearby Nice airport serving both it and Monte Carlo (Grantham 2003). It is reasonably convenient from a transportation point of view, with Nice being directly accessible from most major European city airports and with one transfer from the United States. The city has other advantages for a television-marketing event. There are none of the tourist distractions available in larger cities such as London and Paris. Instead, the emphasis is on convenience, with hotels and restaurants located within walking distance of the Palais des Festivals that sits between a beach and a small harbour, and adjoins The Croisette. Television business is the main business on hand, both in the daytime and in the evening. In 2007, attendance was counted at 13,224, companies participating stood at 4,553, exhibitors amounted to 535 while there were 3,797 other delegates and officials (Guider 2007).

Although some industry levelling-out is at work, rank and privilege are also present. Reed Midem, which organizes the market, takes over all accommodation in the area close to the Palais (Grantham 2003). Delegates have only a limited say in the quality and convenience of their accommodation. The more important the corporate attendee, the grander and more prestigious the accommodation made available. Some corporate players even eschew the commercial location itself in favour of conducting business in their luxury hotels or on hired yachts in the port. Their corporate stands are left to employees. These settings do more than register corporate wealth and power. They also function as private business offices, where privilege and confidentiality are more guaranteed than they are in the hurly-burly of the floors and halls of the Palais. Some of the largest and wealthiest of deals can be made in these surroundings.

Nevertheless, the principal setting for meeting and business dealings is the Palais. This is a large, commodious convention building, an asymmetrical giant wedding cake with all kinds of barred doorways, passageways, wings and rooftop courtyards that sometimes make it difficult to locate and relocate a particular floor and stand. Its carpeted front steps, manned by security staff, lead into further stairs and escalators that carry delegates to any one of five storeys from a crowded basement to rooftop wings and courtyard gardens. Each floor consists of various

Map 2.1: Cannes near the Palais des Festival.

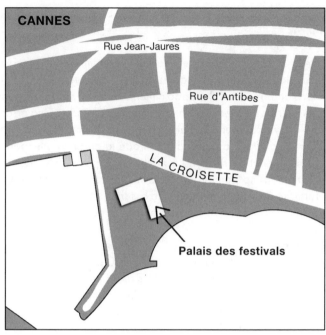

stands or suites arranged into blocks divided by alleys. These sites are available for hire for the week of the market, being assembled and stored by the Palais. Floor space rental is at a premium. In 2004, the Australian state government film agency the Pacific Film and Television Corporation (PFTC) occupied a basement space no bigger than a bedroom with a double bed, for which it paid approximately $2,500 a day. Larger, wealthier companies frequently pay a lot more for more generous amounts of space on upper floors. European format giant Endemol, for instance, was located on Floor 3 at MIPTV, where its stand included not only a front desk with armchairs for those awaiting meetings but also a suite of small individual meeting rooms. Very large displays and posters promoted a series of different Endemol formats, most especially *Big Brother*.

The meeting space is the microcosm of MIP's geography. The pitch meeting takes place around the smallest of circular tables with would-be buyer and seller facing each other. For the larger, more affluent and powerful media companies, these meetings can occur behind closed doors. Meetings are disarmingly public on lower floors, with the tables situated close to the pedestrian alleys and the passing throng.

There is bustle everywhere. Everything and everyone is very busy. MIP attracts another 15,000 to 20,000 people to the Palais and to the city, so this part of Cannes is very crowded. The stands, halls, theatres, stairways, eating areas and restrooms of the Palais, not to mention the adjacent Riviera area, the beachfront, the main avenue, the nearby cafes and restaurants and backstreet shops are a moving kaleidoscope of greeting, talk, dealing, pitching and gossip. While delegates are there to 'meet and greet', they are certainly at MIP to strike deals. However, while time and space are important, custom and style also play a central role in proceedings.

Ritual and custom

While it is business that draws together delegates from all over the world, nevertheless the cultural codes in play at the television market are striking and emphatic. Many conventions and decorums are particularly marked so that, without exhausting their meaning, we can underline several of the more striking. Take the matter of attendance and its frequency. One devisor/ producer mentioned in an interview:

> It's a case of networking. It's not good enough to go to the market once. You have to go to the market ten times before they say, 'Good to see you again – I've been thinking about what you said last market'. Because it's not going to happen straight away. It's going to take years for that person working at home to get something up (Overett 2002).

This sentiment was echoed by others, testifying to the perception that Cannes is as significant for the television industry – most especially those involved in the TV format trade – as great

Figure 2.6: Cannes hotels and Palais des Festival on the foreshore.

holy festivals and ceremonies are for various religions and creeds. Both function as a way of attending to what the membership believes is important, but also in affirming membership itself. Hence, while the onset of virtual communication – telephone, email and the Internet – have made much in the way of person-to-person business dealing unnecessary, nonetheless this appears to only heighten the need for physical contact and congregation in the global television business once or twice a year. MIPTV at Cannes and the other television festivals serve to reiterate and enhance this belonging.

In terms of this attempt at a thick description of the fair, there are a number of other elements that can bear sustained scrutiny. These include written documents at MIP, such as the *Trade Directory* issued each market, and the daily newsletters. The next chapter analyzes the latter resource as a means of tracing some of the discourses whereby the global television market makes sense of itself. Meanwhile, specific dress codes are also in place, most especially as these have to do with the business suit. Casual clothing may be an option while travelling; however, at Cannes the business suit – worn by both women and men – is one of the many signs of belonging. Equally, there are various other important objects. One of these is the diary, a pivotal tool as far as the activity of meetings is concerned.

Display, spectacle and hoopla are a regular part of the marketing taking place at a fair such as MIPTV. After all, traders are there to drum up business for their wares so that publicizing these

Figure 2.7: Packed auditorium at MIPTV for session on product placement.

is a regular part of proceedings. Hence the story is told of how, in 1993, the US documentary cable channel Discovery, for its first foray as a seller, brushed up its profile by dressing its stall as a movie set. Actors were employed to create live action scenarios around a World War II theme to coincide with Discovery's use of Normandy landing documentaries as its flagship programs (Cunningham 2004). Similarly, as we shall see in Chapter 4, an actor such as John Nettles can make a floor appearance and do a press conference as part of the promotion of programming offered by a particular distributor.

Even more important – indeed, the ostensible reason for being at a trade fair – is the matter of doing deals. As already indicated, these can occur during pitch meetings within the halls of the Palais. Related occasions such as the taking of lunches and dinners in nearby restaurants, as well as the cocktail party on the first night of the fair, are also important moments for business. According to Cunningham (2004), programming is frequently bought or rejected sight unseen, based on company reputation or distributor clout:

> Very broad, rough and ready. Generic expectations are in play, too, when it comes to making deals. Buying decisions not central to the schedule are often made on such apparently arbitrary grounds as program type. Conversely, there is a tradition among some European broadcasters of scrutinizing possible foreign acquisitions very closely. In such a situation, it is often extremely difficult for the new company, the offbeat project or the unusual format to find customers (Cunningham 2004: 1183–84).

Such an insight is certainly accurate in its own way. However, it tends to accept the market's own claims about the number and value of deals struck during any particular fair. This is frequently exaggerated by the market organizers for their own business purposes. Therefore, the last part of this chapter scrutinizes the degree of coincidence between the event of a trade market and the business of striking deals.

Markets and deals
On the face of it, making deals appears to be the principal function of television festivals. Selling and buying has traditionally been the business at hand at bazaars, fairs and markets, and screen industry get-togethers would seem to be no exception to the rule. A common industry perception – no doubt encouraged by the industry's own press and media coverage – is that a great deal of business does indeed get done. But how much deal-making actually occurs at a trading event such as MIPTV? The answer seems to vary considerably depending on the market power and track record of participants. For the small independent producer, broadcaster or others, bargains really are struck and some of these get reported in the trade press or on the market's website. Such activity helps support the sense that get-togethers such as NATPE and MIP are essential events for those in the industry wishing to do business.

Of course, valuable large-scale deals also get concluded at the fairs, and these in turn are publicized to participants. In 2004, for instance, Icon Animation from Spain and US channel Animania HD came together at MIPTV to announce a deal regarding the series *Lola & Virginia*.

Two principal executives were on hand in the Palais to announce the deal and to publicly sign off on it. This enabled the producer to 'close' the finance on the deal, but it also allowed for the industry promotion of the series and its broadcast. Closing the deal at Cannes was symbolic and ceremonial as much as it was actual. After all, the parties in question had been in negotiation for some time beforehand and had already decided to trade.

The television business is highly cyclical. Company representatives are based in particular places, and allocated specific countries and regions as part of their beat. Sales executives move around different territories across the world pursuing deals where canned and format programming are licensed, finances organized between parties, co-venture arrangements decided, consultancies put in place, and so on. This activity is constant and ongoing throughout the year, even if its culmination may be left for a media event at Las Vegas or Cannes. However, to actually close or complete a deal, a company must have its lawyers on hand at the market so that contracts being signed are legally vetted. In fact, most prefer to conduct such occasions both before and after the markets and leave themselves free to concentrate on other activities during the market. Part of this involves staying abreast of trends, eyeing off the opposition, catching up with who is doing what. In between manning their stands and speaking to customers, company executives typically will be involved in the launch of up to a dozen or more new canned programs and formats which have already been anticipated in earlier discussion and publicity flyers.

Indeed, several industry managers are of the opinion that the place to initiate and conclude deals is not on the floor of a market but in the offices of broadcasting executives and others. Graham Spenser, who has been a TV format sales representative in Latin America, put this point as follows:

> I lived in Buenos Aires, Sao Paulo and Mexico...We would sell formats on month-long trips, moving from producer to producer and country to country. It worked better that way. Some markets you needed to actually be there in front of people. Sometimes they come to you but nothing beats going to their home office and saying: 'What are you after? I've got this and this. Would it be of interest?' When you turn up in a country it's easier to get meetings than if you phone or mail them (Spenser 2006).

Paralleling this tendency to make deals somewhere other than at the markets, one might also recall the trading that may take place in advance of the LA May Screenings and the BBC Brighton Showcase. These events attract a significant number of important buyers who may represent different networks and channels in the same territory. This has the potential for a bidding war that would drive prices up. To counter this, these broadcasters will frequently employ agents or acquisition officers in Los Angeles, New York or London for advanced advice about upcoming programming and formats so they can strike early deals even before the screenings or showcase.

These exceptions aside, it is the case that a great deal of business is initiated, discussed, supported, continued and concluded in and around the different markets. The world television industry has a continuing reason for going to its various trade fairs. But even beyond the commercial reasons for being there, there are the cultural motives for attending these events. At the markets, the trade has a living, human presence. It is experienced as a community. Being a regular attendee is a crucial means of asserting membership of this group, of claiming commercial and social solidarity and kinship with those who might be ethnically, linguistically and culturally different. The international television industry is a global network, and the markets are a means of helping to support and bind this network together.

Summary
The annual round of TV markets helps define the world of the global television industry so far as broadcasters and producers, including those active in the field of TV formats, are concerned. Going to the markets is one of the several ways in which the world TV format business continues to maintain its global reach. As the MIP website suggests, attending the markets brings licensors and licensees into regular contact, builds and helps maintain business relationships, enables broadcasters and producers to spot new trends and developments, and draws nationally based industry figures into more international networks. In short, the markets function as a kind of club, and club membership is maintained and exercised through repeated attendance there.

But how does the trade, as manifested at the market, understand itself? What awareness does it have of itself as both a business and as a culture? What cultural resources does it employ to facilitate its activities? The next three chapters answer these questions. For the moment, the emphasis falls on the way that the industry talks to itself. Prophecy is the main fare that it offers its attendees. News of what is happening in the industry constantly gives way to more oracular pronouncement about what will happen. Soothsaying about the future is very prominent in this discourse. The television trade's rhetoric structures and promotes business frames of understanding. The next chapter examines the dominant tropes and figures at work in this discourse as a means of articulating the implicit sense of the business's own purpose and trajectory.

3

RHETORICS

Blue skies, smiling at me
Nothing but blue skies, do I see
Bluebirds, singing a song
Nothing but bluebirds, all day long

Never saw the sun shining so bright
Never saw things going so right
Noticing the days hurrying by
When you're in love, my how they fly
(Berlin 2007)

Introduction

As suggested in the previous chapter, the television market exists in a variety of forms. It is apparent in the halls of the convention centres and the individual stands of particular companies. It is also embodied in the many executives, producers, financiers, marketers, assistants and so on who throng the floors, stairs, passageways, cafes and amenities of the television trade fairs. Talk inevitably concerns the business at hand, with conversation forming some of the rhetorical glue that holds these different elements together. Written text is all around the delegates in the form of signs, pamphlets, trade flyers, screen titles, digital presentations, PowerPoint displays, and so on. Words and images form part of the dazzling mobile kaleidoscope that is the spectacle of the global television industry at the market.

Helping to structure and promote market frames of understanding at events such as NATPE and MIP is the television trade's rhetoric concerning its own business. How does the industry perceive itself? What is its view of what it does and where it is going? How does it make sense of its present and its future? Conversation, talk, gossip and chat represent one arena of discourse – even if the output is fleeting and ephemeral. Another important realm is that of the printed word. In various trade publications including the *MIP Daily News*, *Variety* and on the fair websites, the trade talks to itself about itself. Tracing the things it says and the way it says them affords further insight into the worldwide television industry. It also begins to dramatize the trade – if not the whole trade, then at least a significant part of it – something that will be taken up again in the next chapter. Meanwhile, the present chapter examines the dominant tropes and figures at work in market discourses as a means of articulating the implicit sense of the business's own purpose and dynamic. The overriding assumption is that, while a television market is characterized by many voices incidentally talking about this or that, there is an overall consistency of purpose and outlook; therefore, a common pattern can be traced, revealing a set of recurring themes and propositions underlying these utterances. Textual or discourse analysis provides a qualitative approach to social material or content whose study offers the possibility of achieving greater understanding of a particular phenomenon. It is useful to further contextualize the method and frame of reference of this kind of inquiry before embarking on an investigation of how the television trade communicates with itself.

Analyzing discourse

A cultural text is an organized system or network of elements that are seen to be interconnected and interdependent. At the micro level, a media text might be assumed to be a body of communicative elements with discernible boundaries between itself and the world. Hence, for purposes of understanding, a text might be a newspaper, a radio program, a film or a television program. At the macro level, a text might be a larger whole composed of a series of such micro elements – a group of films, a number of television programs, a series of newspaper reports, and so on. Historically, these outputs often constituted the 'mass' of the media so that new methods of analysis seemed necessary to deal with such a large-scale phenomenon. One such approach that emerged as a way of understanding such materials was discourse content analysis. This methodology emphasizes the systematic (scientific) measurement and compilation of results before interpretation takes place (Krippendorff 1980).

However, as Schroder (2002) has suggested, there is also a qualitative research tradition insofar as the analysis of media output is concerned. Such a research strategy draws on older traditions of inquiry in the humanities, but also finds reinforcement in recent departures in media and cultural text analysis. As a methodology, this approach is less concerned than quantitative content analysis with postponing interpretation before undertaking its measurements. Indeed, as Berelson notes (in Schroder 2002), qualitative analysis allows itself to begin interpretation as it goes through its material assuming that the material will cue interpretation in some way. This interactive dimension of the approach is important. Schroder offers a convenient outline and summary of discourse analysis as a means of investigating factual output produced by media or by processes of communication.

Three kinds of qualitative discourse analysis can be identified: critical linguistic analysis; critical discourse analysis; and conversation analysis and discursive psychology (Schroder 2002). The first and the third of these have an obvious disciplinary origin, and have not gained broad acceptance and adaptation in what might be called the interpretative community. Critical discourse analysis, on the other hand, has found much wider acceptance among media scholars – especially those working within a cultural studies paradigm (Schroder 2002). Here, the work of Foucault has been taken up as exemplary, investigating as he does he operation of power in its discursive forms as well as its social forms (Foucault 1972). However, as influential as it has been, Foucault's work constitutes a series of case studies rather than an explicit and consistent elaboration of method. In fact, in the domain of media and cultural studies, Fairclough (1995) offers one of the few attempts to outline discourse analysis as a research approach. Although he proposes a model that situates such an activity within the broader field of social practice, Fairclough limits his investigation to linguistic analysis. Schroder (2002) criticizes Fairclough's deliberate decision not to consider discourse within the broader field of its production, circulation and consumption.

The same restriction operates in relation to the market discourse of the television trade fair analyzed below, where the writing and the reading of trade fair marketing publications have been left to one side. However, as a general defence against the claim for a wider investigation, it can be suggested that the discourse certainly helps to set the general horizon of expectation for those attending the trade fairs and conventions. The discourses operating in such literature as the trade press and the daily news magazine available to convention delegates have an important agenda-setting function. Simply, above and beyond its ostensible subject of interest, discussion, quotation and explanation, this literature talks in a recurring way about a series of interrelated topics and issues that help shape the preoccupations and predilections of those attending the trade fairs. Delegates not only walk the walk but also talk the talk. It is to this market rhetoric that I now turn.

Tomorrow

If the fair, market or bazaar is ancient in its lineage, then it must also be recognized that the trade fair, exhibition, convention or exposition is a more recent variation of this older form. The forerunner to the latter type is the International Exposition held at the Crystal Palace in London in 1851. American social historian Robert Rydell (1984) has analyzed these as well as another variant of the type, the Century-of-Progress Exposition. He finds that, while these events have been laden with particular ideological baggage including imperialism and masculinism, nevertheless the single recurring theme that they articulate has been to do with progress. These fairs are replete with discourses of progress and prosperity – albeit ones encapsulated in different settings and representations. Artefacts in trade fairs and exhibitions offer ideological vistas of the present and the future, even if their specificity of display and spectacle initially seem only related to commerce and business. Tomorrow is eagerly anticipated in terms of promise and plenty.

The fundamental object of the television trade fair is the future. Attending the fair, entering into deals and business arrangements, and planning new ventures are some of the ways of getting a grip on what is still unfolding, unclear but inevitable. The television trade everywhere is plagued by unpredictability (Gitlin 1983; Bielby and Bielby 1995).

Much of the market discourse is concerned with making inroads into what is ahead, getting some kind of control, taking out some form of insurance. However, the underlying assumption turns out to be that the future is not radically unknowable, incalculable and dangerous. It is imagined for the most part in a more comfortable manner as an extension of the present, but bigger, better and brighter. This larger scale can add up to a revolution, a 'media and technology explosion' (*Daily News* 2004a). With this promise of more and more of the same, business optimism and trade confidence are recurring. A recent survey by eMarketer, for example, predicted to the 2004 trade fair at MIPTV that 'the US population watching TV on mobiles would increase from 1.2m to 15m by 2009' (*Daily News* 2004a).

These types of prophecy and vision abound within the trade fairs and exhibitions, although rhetorical addenda such as the above quantification attempt to mask the leap of faith as hard-nosed, business calculation. If numbers can have an incantory effect, then some of the terms in which the industry talks to itself can have a ritual rather than a clarificatory one. How else does one make sense of an utterance such as the following attributed to John Helmrich from International Broadcast Communication: 'One of the biggest challenges facing the industry is to develop an economic system that will allow us to construct a viable business model that will reliably deliver high quality programming in sufficient quantity to fire the engines of growth for these new outlets.' (*MIPTV Magazine* 2004c)

Particular delegates are singled out as visionaries or soothsayers who can see into the future and are generously ready to share this with their fellow delegates. These help set the discursive industry agenda, especially around what are taken to be key ideas and buzzwords. Hence it was reported that, at the Cannes MIPTV exhibition in 2006, Ashley Highfield's conference address would 'cover what digital content will look like and how the industry should prepare itself for the seismic changes ahead...Michael Jackson will also share his vision as to how entertainment and commerce will evolve on the internet...Takeshi Natsuno will explain NTT DoCoMo's plans for Mobile Television, as well as his visions for the convergence of entertainment and commerce...this year's "TV Reloaded!" conference program will focus on the convergence between telco and broadcast companies.' (Palais des Festivals 2006)

Even if the future seems likely to be suspiciously like the past, the world is changing or has changed for the better. Some of the industry's high flyers are now in a position to pass on these benefits to their viewing audience. Thus a key executive at the BBC could offer a challenge to other public broadcasters: 'Creatively a new world of possibilities has opened up allowing the BBC to experiment and challenge digital audiences.' (*Daily News* 2004b) From all parts of the media landscape of the future, the same conclusion is reached. The future offers change and improvement, but this is reassuringly familiar. Hence Tanya Gugenheim, Zone Vision's senior vice-president, explained: 'I think things are really changing in the global channel market. We are starting to see the acceptance of international programming concepts on US cable channels.' (*Daily News* 2004c)

Further buoying this optimism is the fact that some parts of the industry have already set up camp in the future, and confirm the rosy forecasts of what is ahead. Thus Ashley Highfield from

BBC New Media and Technology could report that: 'Last year we entered into an agreement with Rainbow Media where an increasing MPEG4 rollout and the 2006 soccer World Cup in Germany will provide an impetus for the arrival – at long last – of a new age of HDTV.' (*Daily News* 2006a) Two particular shibboleths appear to underline this optimism concerning both the future and the business utopia it will sustain. The first of these has to do with Adam Smith's 'invisible hand', the apparent capacity of free market economic forces to generate growth of their own accord. Kon Kloeppel of CNN put the sentiment this way: 'Increased competition usually means everyone raises their game, which is good for the sector as a whole.' (*Daily News* 2006b) More usually, though, market growth is seen to have a less abstract cause. Instead of these general capitalistic forces, it is the insatiable viewer consumer that encourages the industry to continue to expand what is available.

The myth of consumer sovereignty is so central that there is an unflagging visionary optimism about the infinitely elastic capacity of such a viewer to continue to expand his or her consumptive capacity for content and technology. Hence an item in MIPTV's *Daily News* reported that: 'In [the] UK texting was given a big boost by the SMS-voting element in FremantleMedia and 19 TV's *American Idol*. 3G phones now offer audio and video downloads to cell phones ... for those who can't get enough TV at home. And similarly: 'The DVD consumer market is "exploding",' Mitchell said, 'but viewers do not just want VHS on a disc – they are demanding added-value features ...' (Anon. 2004f). Hence 'consumer empowerment, in terms of access to technology, is revolutionizing the way we live, according to MILIA keynote speaker Patrick Kennedy executive vice-president of Sony Pictures Digital Networks' (Daily News 2004a). Indeed, this apparently altruistic determination to service an apparently very demanding and therefore very sovereign consumer could even occur at the level of broad national deals. So market press reported Michelle Sie Whitten, Encore's president and CEO, recalling that: 'From the start we asked ourselves: "What do the Chinese want?" And "What's good for China?" as opposed to "I can sell you something and its good because we'll both make money."'

Finally, it is worth recalling that consumers are not only those anonymous members of the public at large who buy the latest technology, watch content on new interactive platforms, and so on. Rather, they also include delegates at the trade fairs themselves. The latter might be referred to as creating 'a window of opportunity for global content trendsetters to participate in the making of the next generation media' (*Daily News* 2004b). For such a group, the trade fair offers the opportunity not only to learn about television and new media's future, but also to be in position to take advantage of business opportunities.

Technological sublime

There is, then, a great deal of forecasting about the future in the literature associated with the television markets that verges on the visionary. Tomorrow is marked off from yesterday by a demand from the insatiable consumer for novel provisions, including new technologies and their new arrangement, new business strategies, new business deals, and the cross-shuffling of existing forms of content. Of these would-be departures, technology is king. New machinery developed by IT specialists, engineers and others can, for some market traders at least, be used as the most obvious symbol of the fact that the future has arrived and that it is time to take stock accordingly. In fact, youth has already plunged ahead into this technological sublime: 'The average teenager carries more technology on his back than NASA had when they put the first man on the moon.' (*Daily News* 2004a)

In this gesture of embracing a technological future, Sang-Gil Lee, executive vice-president of the Korean Culture and Content Agency, was reported as saying that: 'The most important question is who owns the technology. This is more important than who owns the content. The power will shift from the content distributors to technology companies. Broadcasting and mobile communications will merge, because they are both heading in the same direction. Both want to maximize bandwidth, mobility and interactivity because that's what the customer wants.' (*Daily News* 2004c) Meanwhile, Jana Bennett, the BBC's director of television – another media visionary at the same market – was just as rhapsodic about the technological cornucopia that lies ahead: 'Digital television is deepening the experience and raising expectations about what television can do.' (*Daily News* 2004b)

The industry is told of 'a brave new broadband world' (Palais des Festivals 2006). A MIPTV press release notes that: 'BBC Executive Board Member Responsible for New Media and Technology, Ashley Highfield's conference address will cover what digital content will look like and how the industry should prepare itself for the seismic changes ahead.' (Palais des Festivals 2006) However, even beyond this general wedding of technology with progress, particular machinery has the capacity to capture the imagination of the TV market insofar as the future generally and industry profitability are concerned. This has been the case especially with the mobile phone. For instance, Allan Gosling, CEO of Extreme Group, is cited as saying: 'A phone is a fantastic way to interact with viewers, users and people in general.' Claire Tavernier, senior vice-president of Fremantle Interactive, was equally enthusiastic: 'Now, as the number of phones that can handle video clips increases, we are looking at adopting the phone as an entertainment device.' (*Daily News* 2004d) The same chant was taken up elsewhere by Annette Bongartz, senior sales consultant for Germany's Convisual, whose opinion was: 'This market has been especially good for meeting independent producers. We really feel MIPTV is looking to the future and that mobile is an intrinsic part of that process. We find this market is a greater opportunity to meet people and connect with our international members.' (*Daily News* 2006c)

For others, however, the technological voodoo word was digital. Hence a MIPTV press release in 2006 enjoins delegates to 'exploit the creative potential of new digital platforms and maximize the interaction between audiences and broadcast TV' (MIPTV 2006). The following year, a *Variety* report could refer to 'the burgeoning interest in all things digital' (Guider 2007a).

On the other hand, if 'being interactive, multiplatform, digital … is the current name of the game' (Guider 2007b), then some are more cautious about embracing this technological sublime. Carmel Landy, director of mobile media for MTV Networks Europe, sounded a warning message contained in the fate of an earlier technology:

The opening up of the US market to texting and its more profitable brother, premium SMS, has opened up huge opportunities for content-providers. For the first time someone who dreams up a game or some other content has a potential global market only a click away. This, of course, was also true of the internet. But the internet never had, and still does not have, an easy way of enabling small content providers to be paid. Mobile phones have, thanks to premium messages. But there is still a huge marketing problem – telling people your product is there – and anyone who can conquer that will make a killing (Guider 2007b).

Similarly, Peter Cowley, Endemol UK's director of interactive media, was cautious about the chances of a rapid adaptation among the public: 'Even when penetration of video phones increases, it is going to take some time to get into the millions. We don't know where it's going but we feel it's right to start testing content…the market hasn't stabilized.' (*Daily News* 2004d)

Buzz
The tendency for pronouncements to become highly ritualistic and liturgical has been mentioned. Here, though, it is worth noting the terms that currently have considerable cachet as far as the industry's self understanding of the future is concerned. These buzzwords are not hard to pinpoint. Elizabeth Guider from *Variety*, for instance, has observed that at the trade market 'nothing here of any respectable dimension is just a TV show. The BBC project and others touted here are now routinely billed as "multimedia cross-platform brand experiences". They involve not just linear video, but all these other layers – embeds, podcasts, audiobooks, you name it – and perceived opportunities to make more money.' (Guider 2007c)

'Convergence' is one of the incantations repeated constantly. A business deal is described as a 'development of truly creative cross-platform talent, while also offering the TV industry the opportunity to discover the latest content innovations evolving from convergence' (MIPTV 2006), while another executive was explaining that 'today, we're constantly adding new dimensions', 'citing the ability to download a *Spider Man* game to a mobile phone as an example of today's burgeoning convergence' (*Daily News* 2004a). Meanwhile, 'interactivity' is another obligatory term in the marketplace. Peter Bazalgette, chief creative officer at Endemol, waxed lyrical about this development in 2006: 'Interactivity is a fascinating trend. We have only just begun to imagine how viewers/users will interact with entertainment in the future. With always-on broadband, 3G and interactive digital TV, this is no longer a passive business.' (Palais des Festivals 2006) Other favourite terms relating to new media technology also abound. Hence customers are invited to sample the new outlets on display: 'MIPTV's high-tech zone is worth a visit by anyone looking to migrate their content to new platforms.' (*Daily News* 2006d) In a more expansive mood, MIPCOM's *MIPTV Magazine* offers a glimpse of the future as follows: 'No movie is produced only for theatrical release any more, and soon TV will be produced with an eye on all the other windows and platforms of exploitation. It will certainly become the norm within the next two years to consider in depth how a format will work, creatively and technically, on all the relevant platforms, from mobile to PSP.' (*MITV Magazine* 2006; Newby 2006) In short, tomorrow's world has arrived and its name is convergence: 'convergence is upon us…new media platforms are coming into their own.' (Guider and Foreman 2007)

DAILYNEWS

MiPTV ■■■
International Television
Programme Market

MILIA
World Interactive
Content Forum

2

MOJTO BUYS BETA FILM

GERMANY'S Beta Film
will announce today in
Cannes that it has been
sold to television veteran
Jan Mojto's EOS Distribution.
The deal with Michael Jaffe,
receiver for the financially
stricken KirchGroup, gives
Mojto control of an international distribution company
with customers in 165 territories and partners in the US,
Asia and Europe, as well as
international rights to 15,000
hours of film. The parties
have agreed not to disclose
the purchase price or further
details of the transaction.
Mojto was hired by Kirch in
1977 as a screenplay editor
and rose to become direc-
tor of programming. He
quit to found EOS in 2001,

Jan Mojto

months before Kirch's
financial collapse.
Beta Film employs 25 people
and has particular strengths
in the Spanish, Italian,
French and Latin American
markets. Mojto has attracted
attention recently for producing large-scale historical
works, including a series on
Napoleon.
Jaffe said it was "particularly
gratifying that not only the
assets, but the entire company, as well as the jobs,
could be sold and their future secured". He added that
the sale represented "an-
other major step forward" in
realising Kirch's assets.

EC HEEDS PLEA FOR AD CASH

MARIJAN JURENEC, general
manager of Slovenia's
Produkcija Plus, interrupted a
crowded MIPTV session on
Brands And Integrated Product
Placement yesterday to make
an impassioned plea for
Europe's producers to have the
same access to advertisers'
cash as colleagues in the US.
The European Commission's
Emmanuel Joly had called
product placement "surrepti-
tious advertising... not compatible with EC rules in principle".
But Jurenec argued that the EC
should allow broadcasters to
find the funding they need.
Joly said the EC recognised
the industry's funding problems
and was about to consult on
the issues.

More in issue 3.

SUPERSTARS COME OUT FOR WORLDBEST FINALE

POP SUPERSTARS Lionel
Ritchie and Phil Collins arrive at
MIPTV today to take part in the
grand finale of the
Endemol series
Worldbest, which

takes place in the grand auditorium of the Palais des Festivals
(20.50), and is broadcast live on
France's TF1.
Representatives from 11
countries will be com-
peting in the event,
which will also be trans-
mitted live in Spain,
Russia, Canada and
Lebanon, and screened
in 25 other countries.

Lionel Ritchie   **Phil Collins**

CONFERENCES: BETTING ON BARTER

TODAY's MIPTV conference
programme includes panel
discussions on barter advertising and branded content
and sponsorships. The barter
advertising conference, which
begins at 10.30 in Auditorium
A, features speakers from
Mediacom Paris, EVP

Worldwide Media, LedaFilm,
Universal McCann and TWI.
Representatives from BCMA,
Discovery, North One
Television, Enteraction TV
and TWI will debate the
increased use of branded
content and programme
sponsorship at 14.30.

Figure 3.1: Front page of MIPTV's *Daily News*.

Back to the future

Great expectations, then, suffuse the rhetoric of the market. The move into tomorrow's world will be revolutionary, with rapid innovation not only in the area of technology but also in much else. New business models are also on the agenda. Consequently, in 2004 Ben Silverman could be quoted as proclaiming: 'I have always been looking for people who are not getting much value for the money for [sic] they are spending … There is a new media landscape that requires a new kind of studio that operates independently, but backed by a … company.' (*Daily News* 2004e) The same refrain was repeated elsewhere:

> We are looking at ways of ensuring that a windowing system acceptable to our existing clients is in place, so that they are happy to continue to acquire our programming when it is also available on a VOD basis in their territory. This will enable us to grow our existing broadcaster business, as the broadcasters themselves move into the VOD market. We see a profusion of new business models (*Daily News* 2006d).

Others were planning new strategies in the face of change and uncertainty in the screen market. Again, these were dressed up as bold new business initiatives: 'Steven Soderberg and Mark Cuban, the free thinking billionaire who owns a theatre chain, are going to start releasing in theatres, on DVD and on Pay TV on the same day. They can do this because Cuban owns the theatres.' (Edmonds 2006)

On the margins of the trade, however, there is frequently a deal of caution about where market change might be leading. Risk-sharing was still in vogue in 2004: 'As a content owner, it would not be in our best interests to take on the risk of developing the mechanics to deliver content. I'm looking for a third party.' (*Daily News* 2004d) Equally, older business practices were proving to be relevant and worth adopting: 'Barter is tarnished by an outdated image in which advertisers get control of airtime by offering failing television stations cheap and nasty programming … The new models for barter offer quality choice and flexibility.' (*Daily News* 2004a) Still others were wary of what new approaches might do to long-standing arrangements. Brian Lacey, executive vice-president of children's outfit 4Kids Entertainment, was of the opinion that: 'The biggest challenge for content providers is sorting out the financial models that make sense for web casts, 3G and all the other emerging new media. But we have fears about damaging long-term relationships. We need to develop strategies that employ new media to effectively build your brand without undercutting broadcast or satellite.' (*MIPTV Magazine* 2006) One CEO even doubted whether rational calculation was the way forward, preferring instead to back 'individuality, luck and circumstance' (Guider 2007c).

For the most part, though, there is a headlong embrace of the future and the apocalyptic change that it will bring to the international television business. Old specializations, it is felt, are outmoded and of no use in the brave new world. The technological and other changes now afoot in the international television industry render these capacities redundant. As Jayne Pitts, sales director at UK music specialist 3DD, put it: 'We no longer employ sales people in the way that distributors did ten years ago. Now we have people who are able to diversify, understand

and deal with the realities of 3G, VOD, IPTV and all the other new rights opportunities that are coming along.' (*MIPTV Magazine* 2006) Executives must be ready to redefine the business they are in – although, surprisingly, this turns out to have a friendly, familiar feel to it: 'We can adapt as long as we don't see ourselves as being in the TV business, but in the business of entertaining audiences on whatever device they choose.' (*MIPTV Magazine* 2006)

Others, though, see the continuing need for a particular specialist. In the face of technological change, the person of the engineer may be vitally important, because this figure alone is equipped to understand where things are going. As Ashley Highfield from the BBC told the MIPTV *Daily News*: 'In the past companies needed lawyers to understand the licensing contracts, now they need to hire engineers to understand the new technologies and devices.' (*Daily News* 2006d) Another executive at the same market also believed that producers were now beholden to IT and engineering specialists: 'TV producers will have to befriend a nerd! And ask them to explain how important metadata is.' (*Daily News* 2006d)

What kind of content?

If old truths have to be abandoned or modified to make way for new technology, new business arrangements, new specializations and so on, what about the program content necessary as the engine for these new configurations? Some traders are of the opinion that it is (old) content that will support the new technology. As Nikesh Arora, chief marketing officer at T-Mobile, explained: 'What we are effectively doing is dressing mobile applications with content.' (*Daily News* 2004d) Under such an arrangement, the mobile phone becomes a miniaturized travelling form of television – itself an old technology. Some saw the new technology as important but still peripheral to their main business, which remained television broadcasting. Hence one executive told *Variety*: 'People want on-demand programming and niche content to fill these new channels... Our main biz is still television, but there's clearly more focus on serving these niche communities.' (Guider and Foreman 2007) But the mass television audience was itself seen to be contracting with niche groups such as youth going elsewhere.

New kinds of program content were vital in the face of this situation: 'Technology, for example, is making high-quality documentaries cheaper to produce. Feature, full-length documentaries appear to entice the very audience that is defecting from television in droves and that advertisers are desperate to reach audiences aged under 30 (Edmonds 2006). Still others call for new kinds of content for the new configuration. According to Keith Hindle, vice-president of Integrated Marketing and Interactive, Americas, at FremantleMedia Licensing Worldwide, new kinds of content are called for. As he explained: 'It's important to provide bespoke content – repurposing TV content will not work.' (*The Moving Picture* 2006) Above all, the new content must be flexible so that it can be made available at a series of outlets. As *Variety* put it: '[It's] the one thing stations are crying for: content that can be multiplatformed and interactive.' (Guider and Dempsey 2007)

Hybrid content of one kind or another is an obvious response to conflicting demands – a means of serving two masters at the same time. So far as genre is concerned, the reality mode

Figure 3.2: Feature story in MIPTV's *Daily News*.

still has some champions. Chris Sharp, Zone's chief programmer, backed the form because of its perceived authenticity: 'Reality TV captures real-life drama as it actually happens. It's about everyday people having extraordinary experiences.' (*Daily News* 2004c) For others, reality programs and formats were attractive because of their commercial record. As Doug Orr from Hothouse Media put it: 'I think the concept makes sense to MSOs – but they are also impressed that reality TV is such a strong global brand and attracts blue-chip advertisers. (*Daily News* 2004c). Zone, a Polish producer and broadcaster, set up a cable and satellite reality TV network in its home market for equally solid business reasons: 'With Reality TV becoming increasingly popular in numerous territories – especially in English speaking countries like the UK and South Africa, and with a growing programming library to pull from, Zone Vision set its sights on the US.' (*Daily News* 2004c) In turn, industry soothsayers could then imagine various forms of hybrids that built on a reality program base. Peter Bazalgette from Endemol offered one vision of what was coming: 'One of the most interesting trends in the future development of format programming will be the development of a new generation of shows that are partly scripted and partly reality.' (*Daily News* 2006b) Others believed that comedy was the genre that was best equipped to suit the new media environment. Shane Murphy from FremantleMedia put the case as follows: 'We are partnering Channel 4 to provide exclusive content from *The IT Crowd* for mobile and online platforms. My view is that comedy lends itself to adaptation across platforms as it is readily compacted into bite-sized portions. As such the opportunities seem endless in the current climate.' (Fry 2006) Others also favoured comedy, but warned that it must constantly update itself and seek to be different. As Ash Atalla, editor of comedy at Talkback Thames in the United Kingdom, explained: 'Right now there is a taste for a certain style of comedy that is much more naturalistic, where jokes are exchanged for character driven scenarios. The key to any successful sitcom is evolution. *The Simpsons* has all the core elements of a sitcom, but just happens to be animated. This gives it a fresh twist.' (Fry 2006) In the face of these different generic preferences, why not combine the two – cross-breed comedy with reality? Hence Mark Young, CEO of BBC Worldwide, Americas, reported that: 'Comedy is still strong, but it has had to adapt...Ricky Gervais's breakout hit *The Office* sold to 31 territories...The comedies punching through are the ones that combine comedy with narrative elements which echo reality.' (Fry 2006) Lauren Corrao, executive vice-president of Comedy Central, echoed this sentiment: 'It's always been our remit to be productive, which is why we are home to shows like *South Park*. Our own lineup has been influenced by the reality trend such as *Reno 911*, a bitingly satirical spoof of reality series like *Cops*.' (Fry 2006) Nicholas Bonard, vice-president of program sales for MTV Network International, also saw the relevance of comedy/reality hybrids: '*Notorious* has actress Tori Spelling starring in a scripted show that resembles her own life – including a *Charlie's Angels* voiceover appearance from her own father, Aaron Spelling. It's a show that promises to leave audiences wondering where the comedy begins and the reality ends.' (Fry 2006)

Be that as it may, criss-crossing genres such as comedy and reality was only one of several ways of taking out commercial insurance in the face of the future and its underlying uncertainties. Another part of the industry with which many marketeers were eager to combine was advertisers. Hence Ben Silverman spoke of a new partnership between content creators and advertisers: '[It's] only a matter of time before Europe joins the trend to put advertisers at the heart of program creation. We should create "unscripted reality shows" that feature sponsors' products.' (*Daily News* 2004e) The same point was made elsewhere in relation to a specific program: 'We got financing for *The Restaurant* from three brands – American Express, Corrs and Mitsubishi – those advertisers are totally organic to the concept.' (*Daily News* 2004e) Silverman went on to explain some of the other attractions for advertisers: 'Aggressive consumer brands will want to be more vertically involved. They will see it as not just pushing their products, but also of getting a piece of the equity.' (*Daily News* 2004e)

Cross-breeding is also called for in order to somehow wed the parochial and the local to the universal and the global. Comedy is one area where claims of such a marriage have been advanced. Shane Murphy, head of acquisitions at Fremantle International Distribution (FID), explained this as follows: 'There is a delicate balance when it comes to creating comedy that retains its local integrity yet is also internationally accessible. It's important that a program not be too parochial ... Three types of comedy that travel well [are] sketch comedy, ... pure physical

FEATURE: ASIA

61

N AND INDIA

ntent flows into Asia

N SUPERPOWERS — JAPAN, CHINA AND INDIA
UNIMAGINABLE RICHES TO EXPANSION
/ESTERN COMPANIES. BUT, ANDY FRY
S, NOTHING WORTH DOING IS EVER EASY

ITH a population of 3.5 billion — around 60% of the global total — it's no surprise that Asia has long been regarded with fascination by western media players. But it is only recently that this vast and diverse market has started to open its doors to non-Asian content-owners.

Given that Asia comprises around 30 countries, there are numerous reasons for this lack of progress. But if you had to identify four broadly universal themes it would be these. First is cultural protectionism. Given that many Asian countries only ejected the colonialists half a century ago, their governments are understandably cautious about the influences they are willing to let back in. Whether for moral or political reasons, large swathes of western content have been deemed unsuitable for local consumption.

Second, and related to this, has been the desire to protect home-grown industries from cultural imports. Many Asian markets are dynamic film and TV producers in their own right, and are concerned about the negative impact on their talent pool if western acquisitions flood the region.

Third, there have been, and still are, economic barriers. While China and India both have populations in excess of one billion, the reality is that many people in these countries survive on a pittance.

And four, there is a persistent problem with piracy. With much of Asia still unable to legally enforce IP protection, content-owners have had to put up with everything, from ripped-off game-show concepts to DVD piracy to television-signal theft.

Despite the above, there has definitely been a shift in East-West relations. From the Asian perspective, rapid economic growth has brought with it a new-found confidence. Today, Asia wants to be a player on the world stage and it has recognised that it needs to be more open in order to achieve this. Whether it's China's decision to host the 2008 Olympics, Korea's assault on the global mobile market, India's emergence as a game-show production hothouse or Singapore's media hub ambition, the impetus for collaboration is spreading.

> *They asked us why no one ever did anything on China. We said that the road was littered with heroic failures because of official roadblocks and unrealistic financial expectations*

Meanwhile, western companies are learning diplomacy — Asian-style. Having realised that nothing gets done in Asia unless there are demonstrable business benefits to both parties, the emphasis is firmly on joint ventures, shared ownership and locally revisioned productions.

A classic example of this shift in approach was last year's news that Viacom has joined forces with Shanghai Media Group (SMG) in a production and distribution venture called Ha Ha Nick. Under the deal, the two partners will make locally-produced animation and live action for the under-14s. This is then aired on the SMG-owned cable network The Orien-

tal Channel, which has been renamed Ha Ha. The deal gives Viacom a foothold in China, while SMG gets help in building a local talent base.

Sony Pictures Television International (SPTI), which already has a track record producing shows in India, Japan, Indonesia, Thailand and Taiwan, has also been patiently courting China. And after 10 years of trail-ing, it is beginning to break through. Early in 2005, SPTI formed a joint venture with Hua Long Film. Based in Beijing, the new venture, called Huaso, will produce sitcoms, dramas and entertainment for distribution both within and outside China.

It is not just Asian media groups that seek good partners. In January, MTV Networks Asia signed a four-year pact with the Singapore Tourism Board (STB), which will lead to a range of Nickelodeon and MTV events being held in Singapore and televised across the region. Again, what is fundamental to the partnership is MTV's contribution to Singapore in industry. With the ultimate goal being to position

Lion Television's The First Emperor, in HD

Scene from the local version of Fear Factor for Malaysia's ntv7

Figure 3.3: Talking to the trade – *The News*.

comedy such as *Benny Hill*, and … sitcoms in which the subject matter – be it British suburbia, a rural vicarage, etc. – is painted in broad, even stereotyped terms to make it accessible to international audiences, such as *Father Ted* and *The Vicar of Dibley*.' (Fry 2006) At the same time, others saw the need to serve local needs in the face of a possible global standardization. Anatole de Suze of Chum, Canada explained such a move as follows: '[T]he provision of local news is the bedrock for success in the emerging "news universe" … Our competitive edge is telling people what happened in their world today.' (*MITV Magazine* 2006)

A preference for content with global appeal was reiterated by another executive: 'The key is to find subjects that transcend territorial boundaries. On our slate is *Everest*, about tragedy on the world's highest mountain, retelling the *Bounty* story, a drama about Atlantis and a slick thriller set in the global oil business.' (*Daily News* 2006e) David Ellender, MD of Fremantle International Distribution, agreed: 'We need to identify UK programming that will match the success in the international marketplace of our US formats, such as *American Idol*, *Project Runway* and *The Apprentice*. I think many of these … are a big issue for companies operating in genres such as movies, sport, music and docs.' (*MITV Magazine* 2006) Louise Pedersen, managing director of All3Media International, also leaned in the same direction: 'Getting stars to do local interviews ... is important, but so is being alive to structural shifts in the market ... there are also regulatory considerations, such as European content quotas, which make it easier for us to get drama into markets like France. We are having success with *Wild at Heart*, a story about a vet in Africa, sold to TF1 in France and Network Ten in Australia. It's exotic and has family appeal that makes it flexible in schedules.' (*Daily News* 2006e)

National dreaming

If the future has a technological dimension, a business dimension and a content dimension, then it also has a national dimension. Thus China becomes part of the promised land of what is in store. One executive was of the opinion that the 'general growth in the Chinese economy along with upswing in country's advertising sector and increase in CCTV-8 are positive indications for Encore's future in China ... Our ultimate aim is to find a compatible partner and together to sell a package of branded channels to cable operators on an affiliate basis.' (*Daily News* 2004f) Chinese media executives were equally optimistic about the People's Republic's future in television broadcasting: 'Beijing All Media and Culture Group chairman of the board Ma Chaojun said that accession to the WTO and the reform of China's media policies brought unprecedented opportunity.' (*Daily News* 2004f) The market's own publicity voice added to this same chorus: 'The highest level Chinese delegation ever to attend an international broadcasting event in recent times revealed a media industry going from strength to strength.' (*Daily News* 2004g)

In fact, the blue skies of market expansion lay over China and also over several other national territories in Asia. Korea was one of these. Jay Ahn, vice-president of corporate development at Korean Telecom, explained that: 'Korea will be a land of convergence, personalization and digital production and delivery. All genres and types of content will be available and accessible, any time and anywhere.' (*Daily News* 2006f) Elsewhere, the report card on Korea's future prospects in the new media landscape was just as rosy:

> The perception of Korea as the promised land of media convergence is the result of a carefully cultivated strategy launched by the government in the mid-1990s. Last year the territory launched the world's first digital multimedia broadcast service (DMB). This caused a worldwide stir and Korea has become a major test bed for a range of digital services like interactive, multichannel and video-on-demand. DMB is operated by TU Media, a privately owned consortium having 440,000 subscribers and has crystal video and audio images accessed at speeds of up to 150kph. They offer 12 channels including 24-hour news, movies, music and sport (*Daily News* 2006f).

But the boom was by no means confined to the Asian markets. Instead, some of the same developments and prospects could be seen elsewhere. In Northern Europe, for example, Margaret Edmonds, a staff writer with MIP's *Daily News*, could 'discover ... a thriving media sector in tune with the future ... big changes are afoot in the Nordic territories (among) ... stations whose growth has been stunted by their more limited penetration' (Edmonds 2004). She quotes one Nordic spokesperson: 'The larger turnover brought about by consolidation has enabled us to bring down costs', adding that 'not to be outdone, SF's arch-rival Nordisk Film is also revving up its TV production ... Bonnier is clearly eyeing a bigger piece of the TV pie.' (Edmonds 2004) Even one of the very oldest of television and media markets, the United Kingdom, was poised to share in this bonanza: 'Perhaps most importantly, we are running trials to understand audience behaviour and needs in the on-demand world such as iMP (BBC's integrated media player, now on trial) which will drive broadband take-up and usage, and get us to a digital Britain faster.' (Newby 2006)

Perhaps, perhaps, perhaps...

The blue skies market discourse that has been sketched so far is by no means universally accepted. *Variety*'s Elizabeth Guider, for instance, voiced a good deal of caution in her report of one 2007 market, aware of general industry trends that tend not to be noticed in some parts of trade fair literature. As she put it, 'everyone ... was rattled by the shifts and rifts in the biz – and no one seems to know how to monetize any of them'. Instead, 'to hear the futurist-fanatics at NATPE, [we] will be swept away by the digital tide over the next decade' (Guider 2007). These, she suggests' 'wax on about how great user-generated content is ... whereas some producers correctly worry about a return for the content that they plan to use paying little or nothing'. '[The] bottom line for Sands is that these folks with their pumped-up PowerPoint presentations need to pay for the content they stream.' (Guider 2007)

But even on the floor of the marketplace, others from the trade were also more cautious and sceptical. On the subject of news, for example, some believed that older media still had a central place for audiences. Jacques de Suze, senior director of station development at Chum International, Toronto, put it this way: 'Why would people now want to watch TV news? For many reasons. Firstly, Mobile SMS, 3G and the Internet provide only very basic info. People want more than just the headlines and abstract facts. They want storytelling and personal relevance which, in general, they won't get from the new digital platforms.' (*Daily News* 2006b) Similarly, Mark Wood, chief executive of ITV UK, offered an example of older media's continuing viability: 'BBC News24 gets about 25 per cent of the audience, the same as ITV. It's 20 times the audience of the rolling news channels.' Given the recent closure of the ITV 24-hour news channel supplied by ITN, he pointed to 'Channel 4 News at 7.00 pm as a serious hour-long program and has the fastest audience growth among the under 25s in Britain' (*Daily News* 2006b). Both these observers are based in the United Kingdom. However, in case their general view seems parochial and not applicable elsewhere, it is worth adding the words of Yu Guen, president of the Korean Broadcasting Institute, on the same matter: 'DMB will compliment traditional fixed media, but I don't believe it will have a huge impact on the conventional industry in the short term. People will still sit in front of their TV sets for a significant part of the day.' (*Daily News* 2006f)

If the brave new world of the future seems uncertain and troublesome, traders are always able to plunge back into the past for lessons to help them navigate uncertain times. Perhaps there is no change and development in the market, but simply repetition and cyclicality? Maybe what worked in the past will work again in the future? Nick Witkowski, founder of Alchemy, explained such a view as follows: 'At the end of the 1990s, I was selling British drama overseas and it was proving really tough because of the competition from local drama. So with Alchemy I looked back at the kind of titles that had sold well and used that as a basis.' (*Daily News* 2006e) Esther van Messel, CEO of First Hand Films, saw this same pattern at work in another genre: 'Interest in the feature length documentary is cyclical, it slips in and out of the shadows in terms of popularity.' (Edmonds 2006)

Yet we must note the most recurring truth of all. If a genre such as documentary has come back into fashion, then this underlines the fact that audiences want to be amused and engaged. Nick Fraser, BBC's commissioning editor for the Storyville documentary strand, was of the opinion that: 'We are living in a time in which the best documentaries are not just pedantically concerned with issues, but quirkily entertaining films about subjects that the directors and writers are passionate about. If there is anything the feature documentary does it is to defy pigeonholing.' (Edmonds 2006) For Michael Burns, director for Documentary Channel programming, the matter was just as simple: 'In my opinion there is absolutely no difference between feature film movies and feature documentaries. It's a question of what will entertain you most...Distributors cannot book theatres if the film they are trying to book has been on TV.' (Edmonds 2006) It was left to Peter Bazalgette from Endemol, who will be encountered again in the next chapter, to voice the last sentiment in favour of fun and diversion as the core of the business: 'All the "techie" talk, changing business models, new interactive formats, new ways of delivering content and getting people to pay for it – all of this is fine. But there is still a constant principle – which is that people want entertainment. They like to be told stories.' (*MITV Magazine* 2006)

Summary
The television market is engaged in an ongoing conversation with itself about the business and the culture. Talking to itself about itself, its most constant question is 'Where are we going?' Part of the business of being at the market, then, is not only constituted by the practical reasons for being there – selling, buying, making deals, forming new relationships, securing finance, marketing services and goods and so on. It is also dictated by the need to get some grip on the future, to develop a sense of where novel developments and ideas are taking the trade. The confident prophecies and prognostications of seers, gurus and oracles who also happen to be business executives, producers, program devisors and sales executives are very much part of the market culture. The urge is to know the future so that prophecy and oracle are much in demand. In turn, the visionaries who command most attention in forums, panels and guest lectures, as well as in the media more generally, are those with the most successful commercial track records. These are the industry's stars; they are among the trade's most celebrated figures. Therefore, the next chapter investigates these idols of the television trade fairs and conventions as another opportunity to further understand the global television market.

4

STARS

[The professional celebrity is] the crowning result of the star system in a society that makes a fetish of competition ... It does not seem to matter what the man [sic] is the very best at; so long as he has won out in competition over all others, he is celebrated (C. Wright Mills, quoted in Ganson 1994: 29).

Introduction

In contrast to their fame and stardom so far as the public is concerned, celebrity television and film actors and performers who appear at the trade festivals and exhibitions such as NATPE and MIP receive relatively scant attention from executives, sales people and other industry personnel attending these events. These stars and media luminaries are simply part of the promotional package designed to help sell a television product. Little excitement or interest registers among the gathered executives and sales people as these public luminaries move among them. Hence, as already mentioned in Chapter 2, the story is told of how, in 1993, the US documentary cable channel Discovery, for its first foray as a seller, brushed up its profile by dressing its stall as a movie set. Actors were employed to create live action scenarios around a World War II theme to coincide with Discovery's use of Normandy landing documentaries as its flagship programs (Cunningham 2004). Meanwhile, in 2004 television actor John Nettles was brought to Cannes to attend MIPTV for a day. His role was to help promote the UK detective series *Midsomer Murders*, distributed by All3Media. Nettles stars as Inspector Tom Barnaby in the series, and previously had a starring role in the detective series *Bergerac*. With the new series selling to over 160 countries, Nettles' job at Cannes was to meet with international buyers and the media to help promote the series. Neither he nor the actors portraying scenes from the World War II Normandy landing excited any fan adulation or worship among the Cannes delegates.

The fact is that, in the arena of television programming distribution, public celebrities in the shape of actors and other on-screen performers are taken for granted as part of merchandising operations. In the very partisan and subjective arena of a television trade fair, fame and stardom attach to other figures drawn from the business itself. The market is structured not only according to the ordinary run of buyers and sellers, but also by the presence of celebrity or luminary traders. In their personae and in their business trajectories, these figures are seen to embody qualities and achievements that set a standard for the business as a whole. Therefore, as a means of further clarifying the cultural dynamics of the TV marketplace, three figures are investigated as trade celebrities – business personalities whose industry trajectory has conferred a stardom or renown upon them. This celebrity status further explains the particular nature of the industry. To help get a handle on the phenomenon of market fame, I have divided the chapter into two sections. The first furnishes the lens through which the wonder of trade stardom can be viewed. Recent theoretical analyses of celebrity are examined with a view to learning what purchase they provide for the understanding of television trade fame. Second, three case studies are undertaken, with the emphasis falling not on the distinct individuality of the figures in question but rather on the kind of trade type, or persona, that they portray. Ostensibly, each of the trio is different in terms of their star qualities and in the particular facets of the business in which they are incarnated. Collectively, however, they help to point up some of the institutional features of the television trade, most especially how it relates to larger dynamics in the economic, political and social domains.

Seeing stars

Much of an earlier research tradition concerning showbusiness fame has to do with the writings of Richard Dyer and his preoccupation with film stars such as Marilyn Monroe and Judy Garland, and with Richard de Cordova and his investigation of the emergence of the star system in American film (Dyer 1979, 1986; de Cordova 2006). A later interest has, by contrast, been more concerned with broadening the category of the public persona into other parts of the entertainment industry. A major innovation here has been the embrace of the notion of the celebrity. The idea of the celebrity is usefully understood as a structure for 'valorizing meaning and communication' (Marshall 1997: vii). The notion has been preferred to the idea of star as a more inclusive category of investigation. Spearheading this initiative have been Ganson (1994) and Marshall (1997, 2006). It is worth reviewing their insights as a means of framing the discussion that follows.

Ganson, like other writers on the subject of public adulation, sees fame as dualistic, widely understood as both a rise to greatness and as artificial construction. He historicizes celebrityhood, looking briefly at its antecedents in hero worship in the past before identifying the twentieth century as the time of its commodification. This era is marked by two stages in the output of the celebrity text.

The first saw the emergence of celebrityhood, thanks to the onset of mass media and the desire to extend branding to the new entertainment industries. Tensions between the production of greatness, and the consumption of stars (sporting, political but especially Hollywood film stars) began to be explained by being 'discovered' or acquiring 'the lucky break' (Ganson 1994: 15–19). The emerging discourse surrounding stardom included the implicit question of 'How do we know the famous deserve fame?' – which in turn solicited the answer 'Because they have it!' One of the several tasks of the publicity system has been to make sure the public know this. By the 1930s, a new publicity machinery had taken a permanent place in the institution of celebrity. However, a second dimension of celebrityhood soon emerged. A figure such as Marlene Dietrich was seen to be nothing but manufactured glamour. According to Ganson (1994), the 'machine' could not be hidden, so gossip columnists began taking the audience behind the scenes, as it were. According to this new feature of stardom discussion, the audience was privileged to 'see through the publicity-generated, artificial self to the real, deserving, special self.' (1994: 20–39). The second stage of celebrity-making was triggered by various shifts in entertainment and information industries that began in the mid-twentieth century. Film was joined by a second wave of screen media, beginning with television, while the public relations industry related to personality has grown considerably. There has been a significant increase in star-making, but also a major shift in its orientation. This has to do with the development of an ironic, reflexive dimension that takes its place alongside older frames of understanding. Celebrity audiences are now treated to the knowledge of how they, and others, become the 'sucker born every minute' – and thus avoid becoming the sucker themselves: 'The irony is more than defensive, it is proud. From Barnum onwards, publicity includes a fascination with the mechanics of manipulation. In this sense, what is celebrated is not the star but a power elite, the star-makers, able to make and control images, able to direct mass attention through marketing machinery.' (Ganson 1994: 40–54)

Meanwhile, in more recent analysis, Marshall (2006) has emphasized the links between celebrity and power. Power is, of course, a complex notion and it is necessary to see its operation in a variety of overlapping contexts, including those of politics, finance and culture. While the celebrity inhabits all these domains, their relationship to power is a complex one that involves actual impacts as well as more symbolic ones. While celebrities frequently manifest both political and economic power, it is in the cultural realm that their power is most manifest. Simply, celebrities seem to be allowed a larger public standing and a greater freedom of action and authority than are other members of the society. They move in the public realm where they are constantly in the spotlight of attention, whereas others are reduced to being spectators on the margins and in the shadows.

Celebrities function as types – even stereotypes – in the social world. They are seen to offer (mythologized) insights into its functioning, its human membership and its values. Marshall (2006) rightly stresses the manner in which the celebrity connects identity and individuality. The public persona appears to embody uniqueness, either at the level of a whole personality or at the level of particular qualities or traits that help constitute that personality. In either case, the celebrity functions to express an apparent singularity that makes her unique, a heightened and purified version of a special or dominant trait that might be found elsewhere, but never in such an unadorned and pure form. As such, in their presentation of self to the world, celebrities stand as emblematic and representative of the human type. The figure appears to confirm the possibility of individuality and singularity in an era that has little real use for such qualities. Hence, as Dyer (1986) has noted elsewhere, there is always a strong note of utopian desire tied up in the figure of the celebrity. The function of this kind of star or hero is to offer a narrative of identity construction in the modern world. It is the ability of the contemporary celebrity to incarnate the masses in the individual, which discloses their cultural image as potent. Marshall (1997) asserts that 'celebrities represent the disintegration of the distinction between the private and the public' (1997: 20–39). Identity is fashioned in the private sphere and carried into the public. As an elite, celebrities suggest that the self is the locus of individuality, of psychological sovereignty, meaning and value.

These insights of Ganson and Marshall are certainly rich in their connotation and suggestiveness, but they need some degree of anchoring in terms of the particular public personality that is seen to be embodied in a specific individual. This need, in turn, leads us back to the matter of the television markets and the trader celebrities that bestride such a world.

Trade fame

While the modern phenomenon of the star or celebrity emerged in connection with the cinema, nowadays it is widely recognized that this entity has long transcended such a boundary. The machinery of stardom has been applied to more and more domains after its initial application and refinement in the film business nearly a century ago. Celebrities and luminaries have for some time been acclaimed in related fields of entertainment, including those to do with radio, television, popular music and sport. In turn, this second phase of celebritization has been overtaken by a further wave of applications. Marshall (2006) understands what he calls the celebrity culture as lapping a series of other fields, including the literary world, religion, politics, the legal system and academia. The point is a valid one, for the notion of a symbolic elite is no longer confined to film and cinema but instead touches many elements of modern economic and social arrangements where image and symbol are deliberately and extensively cultivated.

In designating particular figures who are part of television trade fairs as celebrities, I am following a line of argument that Street (2006) has developed concerning the connections between politics and showbusiness. He argues that:

> We cannot hope to understand the ways in which political communication works … without acknowledging the activities of a key intermediary … In focusing on politicians, and in thinking of them as 'symbol creators', the focus shifted from commodities and marketing to art and style (Street 2006: 366).

The realm of trade constituted by the television market offers itself for a parallel interrogation. Both the political and the business spheres are, after all, arenas of symbolic power. The television trade fair is concerned with a part of showbusiness, in the shape of the global entertainment industry – albeit the business end of that institution. More importantly, trade in television programming has an expressive as well as an instrumental dimension, and it is important to take stock of the self-presentation performance of traders. This is, of course, about creating an identity that may subsequently be exploited by market strategies on the part of the individual or the company concerned.

Accordingly, this part of the chapter is given over to an examination of three contemporary television traders, less known in the world at large although famous among their peers in the business. Each is analyzed not so much according to their biographical details, but rather in terms of the various performative selves that cluster around their name. As Dyer, Marshall and others have emphasized, the celebrity sign is by no means a coherent ordering of the themes of self, so what follows in each case is an identification of a loose assemblage of particular tropes and metaphors rather than any congruent or logical articulation of these. Collectively, these semantic clusters may add up to nothing more than a set of shifting, ambiguous signs. That said, it is necessary to track the way in which these star themes dovetail, overlap and slide off from each other as a means of grasping the star imagery associated with the television market trade. Star image is always anchored in a 'real' self. It is useful, then, to note selected career details as a preliminary step towards grasping the specificity of a particular celebrity.

Each profile, therefore, begins with a short biographical sketch before examining various elements of imagery associated with the figure's identity.

British 'enfant terrible': Peter Bazalgette

While he would become intimately linked with the format of *Big Brother* in the mind of the British media, if not in the eyes of the viewing public, Peter Bazalgette's principal role in the TV format industry to date has been that of executive producer and public defender rather than as devisor. Although *Big Brother* had already been a big success in both The Netherlands and Germany before its launch in Britain in 1999, nevertheless the British news media seem to irresistibly associate Bazalgette with the program and its apparent excesses. The latter appeared happy to accept this association and eagerly led an enthusiastic countercharge, motivated not only by commercial beliefs but also those of cultural outlook.

Bazalgette was born in Britain in 1954. After secondary school, he took a degree in law from Cambridge University. Burns (1977) has argued that there is a good deal of overlap between the world-view of Oxford and Cambridge and that of the BBC, so it was unsurprising that Bazalgette then joined the public broadcaster. The BBC graduate news training scheme was his first appointment before he went on to become a researcher on the TV lifestyle program *That's Life*. Baz, as he likes to be called, reported on several other programs before leaving the BBC to set up his own corporate video company, Bazal. By this time, television programming production in the United Kingdom was being outsourced to independent companies – and who better to help meet the needs of the public broadcaster than a former employee? Bazal produced a popular BBC2 program, *Food and Drink*, from 1983 to 2000. In 1990, the company was taken over and eventually became part of Endemol UK. Bazalgette remained as creative director and took programming output in the direction of light daytime leisure and lifestyle. However, it was the first UK series of *Big Brother* that really began to give the tall, lean, good-looking Bazalgette a public profile as he basked in the publicity and notoriety of the show. Endemol rewarded him for his frontline role by making him chairman of the UK company. In 2005, he became chief creative officer, ensuring a continuous stream of new program ideas

Figure 4.1: Peter Bazalgette.

from the 30 countries in which The Netherlands-based parent organization operates. Baz also retains the role of Endemol UK chairman.

If this is the 'real' life story of the figure, then the celebrity that is Bazalgette constitutes an intersection of various different personae. The figure acts as catalyst, bringing together a series of other characteristics that form the public persona. These identities can be grouped in terms of (1) public standing; (2) knowledge worker; (3) market populist; and (4) shocking the bourgeoisie.

Public standing
Baz is the British face of Dutch company Endemol. He is well equipped for such a role, coming from an upper middle-class family with his formative years spent at three classic English social institutions in the shape of a private secondary school, one of the oldest and most venerable of British universities and the great public broadcasting organization. His standing is further enhanced by his being a great, great-grandson of Sir Joseph Bazalgette, a civil engineering hero to Victorian England who was responsible for solving London's sewage problem. Peter Bazalgette was president of the Cambridge Union Society, and this turns out to be important not only as part of his background credentials but also as an element of his capacity for public representation in speech and writing on behalf of the television industry and culture.

Nor is Baz's status as modern British businessman based only on these earlier connections (Currie 2005). Even outside of his book, *Billion Dollar Game* (2005), there is the fact of his television industry status. Baz has been recognized by Britain's Royal Television Society and is the recipient of a British Academy of Film and Television Arts fellowship. He delivers addresses at the trade fairs and was a featured speaker at the Zeitgeist Europe meeting in 2006. Articles written by him turn up from time to time in *The Guardian*. He is colourful, and has made a good deal of money from television so that interview profiles appear in quality British newspapers such as *The Independent* and *MoneyWeek*.

Altogether, his is a distinctly British fame that is at once class conscious in its attention and parochial in its anxieties. Despite his French ancestry, Bazalgette can claim to be distinctly national. In this capacity, he is ironically claimed as reversing the action of his great-grandfather by inundating British television viewers with cultural sewage such as *Big Brother* and *The Farm* (James 2002; Smith 2005; Lewis 2006). Known as a British 'bad boy', the UK press has also dubbed him 'the man who has done more to debase television than anyone else' (Smith 2005).

Industry wordsmith
Bazalgette is in the public eye not just because of his work as a television executive but also because he is an author. But his writing is not confined to newspaper pieces. Three books he wrote or co-authored while at the BBC, associated with lifestyle programming, helped prepare him for his self-appointed role as recorder of the exploits of Endemol's John de Mol and the TV format industry (Bazalgette 1987, 1989, 2005; Sanders and Bazalgette 1991). The earlier books were aimed at a middle-class, food- and diet-conscious public. The most substantial was *The Food Revolution*, which appeared in 1991. Interestingly, in keeping with both the libertarian *zeitgeist* of the West in the recent present and the personal inclination of a television producer who would shortly be an articulate proponent for a new, renovative television regime, Bazalgette's *The Food Revolution* is not so much concerned with food but rather with the human body and its relationship with food.

However, it has been *Billion Dollar Game: How Three Men Risked It All and Changed the Face of TV* (Bazalgette 2005) that has brought Baz to the attention of a wider public. Written as a fast-moving story about the emergence of reality television in 1998 and early 1999, the book is a substantial piece of work that would have entailed considerable time spent interviewing and poring over archival materials as well as writing up the story of how *Survivor, Who Wants to Be a Millionaire?* and *Big Brother* were devised and developed. *Billion Dollar Game* was published by Time Warner, and has sold well – not least because of the inside account it offers of the coming together of television, telephony and the internet as represented in these programs.

But although Baz attempts to star each of the devisors of these program formats in his narrative, it is John de Mol who takes most of the limelight. The Dutchman is the looming presence in the book, and Bazalgette is his chronicler – a kind of latter-day Boswell to de Mol's Dr Johnson (Farrer 2005; Mosey 2005).

Figure 4.2: Channel 4 logo for the eighth UK season of *Big Brother*.

Market populism

As though to advance his credentials to comment on popular taste and the television industry's role in catering for it, Baz has mentioned that he was 'a Bolshie teenager'. Now he is a television market populist who champions the right of the majority audience to be entertained rather than being educated and informed (Lewis 2006). Part of the response to such criticisms as the *Evening Mail*'s claim that he was among the 'Ten Worst Britons' for the series *The Farm* is a muted recourse to a free-market calculus. Profits and earnings under such a regime vindicate whatever creative choices were made. In an era of television neo-liberalism, market success is self-vindicating.

There is little democratic instinct at work here in the stance and style of Bazalgette. Rather, what is dramatized is the clash of a new elite with an older one. Returning to a kind of class understanding of British television, Bazalgette rails against a perceived cultural elite who have hitherto, in his view, exercised considerable power that reality television now calls into crisis (Smith 2005). Such an elite is not confined to the television industry. Regulators, for example, are advised to relax rules concerning advertising and product placement. So too, many TV critics and audience members are males aged over 50 and these too are incapable of appreciating a *Big Brother* as soap opera or understanding it as 'entertainment, a pantomime' (Lewis 2006).

Shocking the bourgeoisie

As a former Cambridge debater, Baz is well able to counter the aggressive charges of his opponents. One tactic is to simply ward off verbal blows by sheeting the matter back to the personality of the opponent. On other occasions, however, he comes out verbally swinging against opponents during interviews (Smith 2005). Labelling his critics as cultural elites is one tactic in his repertoire. A variant of this is the clever punning joke, the deliberate mockery of the morals and sensibility of the British middle classes. Hence, for example, he disingenuously defends the Endemol reality program *The Farm*, in which Rebecca Loos became intimate with a pig: 'That was a rather charming incident. A serious exploration of animal husbandry.' (Smith 2005)

His personal manner seems to further emphasize a style that is deliberately shocking. The *Sunday Telegraph* pointed out that, although he was now 52 years of age, Bazalgette still seemed to think of himself as an *enfant terrible*. He claims to like 'to be hated', calls people 'Darling', sips coffee from a mug labelled 'Gorgeous' and wears 'blaringly loud socks' (Smith 2005).

Attuned to living and working in the cross-gendered world of television entertainment, Baz's big break at the BBC came when he was picked by Esther Rantzen in 1977 to be one of her 'boys': 'Everything I did [subsequently] was learned at Esther's knee.' In another moment of apparent self-revelation, he suggests: 'I'm a fishwife at heart. I'm like Les Dawson in a hairnet gossiping over the fence.' (Lewis 2006)

Living the American dream: Mark Burnett

The second trade figure to be examined is similar but different. Like Bazalgette, Mark Burnett was born in the United Kingdom, although there any national resemblance between the two ends. While Bazalgette has remained steadfastly British, a public figure in its television culture, Burnett has overseen a different kind of celebrity project wherein his identity is made over as a mythic American type. If Bazalgette is associated with one key reality format in the shape of *Big Brother*, then Burnett comes to public attention through another, equally significant program, *Survivor*. Like Bazalgette, Burnett is also an author. His name appears on several books that, in part, offer a collective extended insider account of the US television industry (Burnett 2000, 2001, 2005). But, where John de Mol is the hero of *Billion Dollar Game*, Mark Burnett emerges as the star of his own, oft-told story of success in the New World.

Burnett was born in East London in 1960 (Burnett 2000). The area was working class, and Burnett had little opportunity for upward mobility. Instead, he joined the British Army Parachute Regiment and came under fire on tours of duty in Northern Ireland and the Falklands War. Demobilization was followed by a trip to Los Angeles where he picked up a job as a nanny. Several jobs later, by the middle 1990s, Burnett had created his first successful television series. This was the *Eco-Challenge* game, a multi-sport endurance competition that would be staged in natural surroundings in different international locations. Shortly afterwards, he came across the format for the reality program that was to become *Survivor*. As *Billion Dollar Game* (Bazalgette 2005) recounts, the format had been devised in the United Kingdom by Charlie Parsons, who found himself unable to license it in either the United Kingdom or the United States. Instead, in 1999 the format was taken up by Strix Television in Sweden, and the adventure reality series *Castaway Robinson* played quite successfully on Swedish television. Burnett secured a licence option for the format, and sold an American remake to CBS. The first US series of *Survivor* appeared in the summer of 2000 and was an enormous hit. Subsequently, at least eleven series of *Survivor* have been produced by Burnett, while there have been nine series of *Eco-Challenge*. In between, Burnett has become a devisor and producer of his own reality formats, including the business series *The Apprentice* and the boxing series *The Contender* (Burnett 2005). Seeking to become a major presence in US television – cable and syndication – Burnett set up his own production company, Mark Burnett Productions, in Hollywood in 2003, although more recent reports suggest that his interests are struggling (Grego 2005; Frutkin 2007).

In turn, these biographical facts become the scaffolding on which the Burnett star persona is constructed. Like the other two trade figures discussed here, Burnett's trajectory is a success story. After all, the market is not especially interested in stories of failure. However, in Burnett's case, his commercial success in California is a key theme in his celebrityhood – one that is emphasized repeatedly in the autobiographical writing in four books that bear his name. Five

Figure 4.3: The program that gave Burnett his big break.

overlapping themes help make up this particular cult of celebrity. These are: (1) American success story; (2) self makeover; (3) example and exemplar; (4) symbolic elitehood; and (5) reflexivity.

Self-reliance and the attainment of success
Burnett sees his different reality series, most especially *Survivor*, as containing various practical lessons in self-reliance. Competing and winning is ultra important, whether it be in a television reality program or in corporate life. Both his television programs and his books have an inspirational purpose (Murray

Figure 4.4: Mark Burnett.

2001; Wright 2006). According to his various autobiographical writings, Burnett learned to rely on his 'gut instinct' in America. He is a convert to an extreme form of *laissez-faire* individualism, which he promotes as self-reliance. He is evangelical about his insight for survival and success, whether this be in primitive settings or in corporate boardrooms. Despite the apparent purpose of entertainment in the case of the television series and dramatic narrative in the case of his accounts of his own adventures as film producer, both are intended to tutor their audiences in self-reliance and the rewards it can bring (Wright 2006; Franko 2006). Burnett's books function as both fast-moving adventure stories and as motivational business primers. Like a secular pilgrim on the journey of life, he is constantly on the lookout for opportunities for self-discovery and self-motivation in all that befalls him.

The body is the most immediate arena for practising self-reliance and discipline. Such chastisement is quite in order for Burnett, both as former soldier and especially as living embodiment of self-control. He continues to discipline his body and hone the attendant physical skills. As the *Survivor* website puts it, Burnett has trained in scuba diving and skydiving, and has completed a whitewater guide course. This background befits him as television producer to devise reality programs centred on physical endurance in a military context such as *Combat Missions* (2002) and *Eco-Challenge* (2001) that pitted US and Canadian armed forces against each other (http://www.cnn.com).

Adventurer and businessman
Burnett's forte is heroism and adventure. Service in the Falklands, which saw him experience warfare and death and receive a medal on his return to the United Kingdom, testifies to his heroism. Soon after his return, a spirit of adventure drove him to Los Angeles without a job, contacts or work skills. But 'adventure' is a genre with strong colonial roots and ideological baggage. Burnett himself underlines the capitalist inclinations of a program such as *Survivor*, which he associates

Figure 4.5: An allegorical guide for the times.

with the narrative genre of adventure, especially the castaway story (Burnett 2001). In this kind of tale, the adventurer ends up in the wilderness by accident but, drawing on inner qualities of self-reliance, soon gains morally exemplary advantages from circumstances. As Murray puts it: 'Castaway narratives reinforce the dominant encoding, for they often feature self-reliant individuals who undergo self-revelation and, through their ingenuity, resourcefulness and perseverance, convert an inhospitable environment into a place where they can sustain themselves and profit.' (Murray 2001: 49). These wilderness stories have their capitalistic counterpart in Burnett's other reality series, which variously have to do with such business ventures as boxing, becoming a businessman, making a casino profitable and getting ahead in the film business (Lowry 2007; Rice 2007). All feature high-stakes 'adventures' that call for self-reliance and parallel Burnett's own successful transition from being a new arrival in the United States without a job to becoming one of the most influential businessmen in Hollywood.

Reflexivity
This parallelism highlights a further theme of Burnett's celebrityhood that has already been foreshadowed by Ganson (1994). This is the quality of self-reference that saturates a good deal of Burnett's activities. An alleged paralleling between Burnett's shows and elements of his life is heavily underlined in both commentary on websites and elsewhere, and by several of his books (Greco 2005; Franko 2006). But, even more than programs such as *Eco-Challenge* and *Survivor*, there have been the more explicitly reflexive television series, including *Commando Nanny* (2004) (Burnett 2005: 209) and *On the Lot* (Rice 2007). The adventurer producer devised *The Apprentice* with businessman Donald Trump, who took time out from writing his own inspirational tomes such as *The Art of the Deal* to appear in *The Apprentice* and consented to write a laudatory introduction to one of Burnett's own books (Burnett 2005).

Figure 4.6: Burnett's co-devisor and mentor, businessman Donald Trump.

Burnett is most fascinated with his own bravery and self-reliance. As already suggested, he is the hero of his own autobiography. This can continually be inspected for the inspiration embodied in his adventures, coupled with ongoing disclosure of the self-reliance that leads to success in the physical and the corporate world. As he describes them, each of his encounters with the corporate elite is revelatory. They confirm his upward passage to the heavenly gate marked 'success'. More fundamentally, they affirm his very being. A welcome by a Hollywood celebrity from before or behind the camera also proves that – Cinderella like – he has metamorphosed from a working-class London youth into a Hollywood celebrity. As media luminary, Burnett moves in a mythically democratic world where he is immediately accepted and on familiar terms with the famous and the legendary. He writes: 'I was still a Hollywood outsider. I was still the kid from London's blue-collar East End who had struggled to build a career since the first day I arrived in America. But as I shook Sly's hand, suppressing a burst of euphoria, I thought, "I've met Stallone. I've made it!"' (Burnett 2005: 69)

American success

Espousing the doctrine of self-reliance, Burnett becomes a modern-day Horatio Alger hero, moving

Figure 4.7: Surviving in the business jungle.

from a working-class background in London to become a Hollywood television production tycoon. He becomes quintessentially American, not only in terms of his passport but also in terms of the capitalist ideology that he comes to espouse. As he puts it: 'I learned in America that Americans are into results. Americans don't care where you came from, what your family did, what school you graduated from...They care about if you can deliver the results. That's what makes America the country it is.' (Burnett 2005: 214) Fostering American myths of success, Burnett models the process through which the 'true self is discovered, cultural and economic capital acquired, and the American dream achieved'. As Murray has noted, success here is defined in Alger's terms of 'opportunity, social mobility, and material gain' (Murray 2001: 47).

As ideologue for the American dream, Burnett gives motivational, leadership and team-building speeches for major corporations (Wikipedia 2008). This access to the corporate boardroom is one of several signs of attainment. However, the one that Burnett most values is membership of the symbolic elite that is Hollywood showbusiness. His writings are replete with glimpses of capitalist paradise, utopian spells of contentment as he moves among the rich and famous. Hence, completing a business deal with Martha Stewart at her house, Burnett writes that: 'Afterward we all sat down to the most delicious Martha Stewart breakfast. The rest of the weekend was filled with delectable meals, great conversation, hiking in the nearby mountains, and even a boat trip to the mainland in Martha's famous picnic boat, which she piloted herself.' (Burnett 2005: 261)

Businessman celebrity: Simon Fuller

Where Burnett positively basks in the spotlight of success and celebrityhood, and Bazalgette more than tolerates stardom, Simon Fuller mostly eschews fame. He is a business celebrity in the mould of a Howard Hughes, a presence in the media shadows. Personal fame and public recognition are in no way important to the Fuller business project, so even though the name and some of the various business arrangements are known, there is little in the way of a public image or persona. However, *Pop Idol*, which he devised, has achieved wide international success, including triumph in both the United Kingdom and the United States. Neither *Big Brother* nor *Survivor* has attained such simultaneous popularity on both sides of the Atlantic. In other words, there is good reason to make Simon Fuller the subject of this last star profile.

Figure 4.8: Simon Fuller.

Fuller was born in 1960 in Hastings, where his father was headmaster at a grammar school (Hay 2001). While at school, he learned something about the pop music industry through the hiring of bands for school dances. His brother, Kim, was drawn towards a career in the media through becoming a BBC scriptwriter, while Simon had a brief period in publishing after leaving school. There followed a stint as an A&R talent scout for Chrysalis Records. In 1985, Fuller discovered keyboardist Paul Hardcastle and went out on his own, managing Hardcastle. Hardcastle had a big hit with the Vietnam song '19', and Fuller named his company 19 to mark this success. Over the next few years, he added other performers to his stable, including Cathy Dennis and Annie Lennox. But his own industry stardom came in 1996 when he took over the management of the Spice Girls. Over the next eighteen months, he turned this foursome into a worldwide phenomenon with music, a film, television, promotion and marketing (Hay 2001).

By now, Fuller's image as a tough businessman was taking shape, with media rumours that he was charging 50 per cent fees from the Spice Girls. Fuller was dumped as manager, although the group broke up shortly afterwards and two of the foursome, Emma Bunton and Victoria Beckham, subsequently placed their career management back in his hands. Shortly afterwards, he launched the very successful group, S Club 7 and followed this in 2001 by devising *Pop Idol*, in which FremantleMedia became a production partner (Burt and Gautam 2004; Hay 2001). By 2005, Simon Fuller's privately owned 19 Group – which began with 19 Management – comprised at least ten other companies, covering TV, music management, music publishing, recording, artist/writer and producer management, sponsorship and promotion, and was involved in the creation of almost 100 number 1 singles, over 350 hit singles and 80 hit albums. To further bankroll his upcoming activities, Fuller sold 19 to the US group CKX, which – among other properties – manages the name, image and likeness of Elvis Presley. Fuller has a long-term employment agreement with CKX and is on the company's board.

These are the relevant details of the business career. However, unlike the other two trade celebrities already discussed, Fuller contributes little more to the construction of a public persona. There has been a conscious scarcity in the way of newspaper and magazine interviews and profiles, while there are no books of any kind. Nevertheless, there is a Fuller public image whose celebrityhood is constituted by three recurring themes: (1) the name without a face; (2) celebrityhood as business; and (3) ruthless commercial logic.

The name without a face
Even if they are largely an outcome of media representations, most luminaries in film, television, music and other culture industries are seen to be constituted by a core or essence, a kind of

authentic self that is subsequently celebritized. Simon Fuller is, however, a more elusive and shadowy figure. Very few pictures of the entrepreneur turn up in the press or on television. One article suggests that Fuller 'operates in a low key manner without flamboyance or much publicity' (Hay 2001). This certainly seems to be the case, prompting another article to model him as a 'pop Svengali'. His area of operation is behind the scenes rather than at the shop front. As the mastermind who manages stars of music, sport, fashion, and so on, Fuller operates at the business end of the entertainment industry rather than at its more public and glamorous end. Publicity is the elixir of life for the media stars that he controls, but seemingly unimportant to Fuller himself.

Indeed, Fuller is sometimes even mistaken for a more publicized and televisualized Simon, Simon Cowell (Currie 2005). Cowley co-devised *Pop Idol* with Simon Fuller, co-pitched it to both ITV in the United Kingdom and to Fox in the United States, acted as the most ascerbic of judges on both the British *Pop Idol* and on *American Idol* and even, briefly, was in legal dispute with Fuller over a clone format (Burt and Gautam 2004; Hay 2003; Carter 2005). However, Simon Cowell is not Simon Fuller – even if he has extensive business contacts with the latter, broadly resembles him in appearance and even mistakenly passes for him in some media coverage.

Simon Fuller is a name almost without a face, a figure mostly without a public identity. The businessman, aviator and film producer Howard Hughes was among the most famous of this kind of reclusive, solitary celebrity, but Fuller is of the same general type. Indeed, the *Financial Times*, in one of the very few profile articles concerning Fuller, described him as 'a card carrying hermit' (Burt and Gautam 2004). It is easy to see why this seems to be the case. Publicity is unimportant, and therefore mostly shunned and ignored. Fuller lives in Nice in the south of France, and is not readily accessible to the British media. He gives few interviews, and those that he grants are very difficult to arrange and accomplish. One legendary interview took more than a year to set up and then fell through. The *Financial Times* article (Burt and Gautam 2004) reports that it took more than 30 telephone calls, twenty e-mails, two faxes, one failed trip to a *Pop Idol* gig and fifteen months of waiting before another interview took place (Sanghera 2002). In the famous case of Howard Hughes, his reclusivity was due to personal eccentricity. However, in Fuller's case, the reason for this introversion is less colourful. Simply put, he sees himself as a businessman rather than a creative figure in the field of entertainment, whether it be television or music. His business has to do with the publicity and fame of others, and he appears to have little interest in being in the spotlight himself (Mosey 2005).

Celebrityhood as business
The two celebrity traders examined in the first sections of this chapter have connections outside as well as inside television. Bazalgette has a public persona in British cultural life while Burnett is the adventurer and ex-soldier *par excellence*. The Simon Fuller figure goes much further. As the biographical notes above suggest, his springboard to trade stardom has been the pop music industry. *Pop Idol* has been a crossover vehicle between pop music culture and the television industry culture. As part of his business dealings, he also manages sports stars, and has plans

to enter the fashion industry. Fuller sees himself not as a television producer or executive but rather as a businessman whose field happens to be that of celebrityhood. As he puts it: 'My business is creating fame and celebrity, and I'm one of the best in the world. I know it to the finest detail.' (Mosey 2005) Elsewhere, the celebrity manufacturer has elaborated on this distinction between the entertainment industry and its celebrity results in relation to the television talent show: 'Pop Idol wasn't primarily created as a TV show; it was created as a mechanism for me as a manager to find new artists who could become stars while forgoing conventional routes of promotion.' (Hay 2003)

Figure 4.9: *American Idol* – part of the star-making machinery.

Ruthless commercial logic

Where others in the television format trade talk of revenue streams and convergent technologies, Fuller is far more tough-minded and clear-headed about the possible exploitation of his properties. He is accused of producing packaged music with artists that he treats as commodity brands. He has even been reported to be reviving the 1960s pop group cum television program *The Monkees*. This is in line with the actions of a music entrepreneur who was always less interested in creating fine records than in generating commercial opportunities around music, sport and other stars. To that end, Fuller has concluded deals with large corporations in which his star brands cross-market with many of the world's biggest multinationals, including Nestlé, Gillette, Adidas, Coca-Cola and Pepsi (Hay 2003).

Of course, given this highly commercial outlook, Fuller is widely seen as the enemy of creativity and art in the music industry. One writer, for example, has described him as the most destructive force in the business over the last decade (Hay 2003). Others, however, are less persuaded that this is the case, and see Fuller as representing new ways to help keep the industry viable (Mosey 2005). To that end, he claims to be unconcerned about what the Internet and downloading are doing to record labels, concentrating instead on tie-ins, advertising and cross-marketing between large global corporations and music, sport and other kinds of celebrities.

Summary

This chapter has focused on the human subject of the market traders. Just as the trade is manifested at trade fairs and conventions, in discourse and language, in know-how and knowledge, so it is embodied in human agency. Several commentators have recently pointed to the increasing homogeneity of outlook among the personnel of the global television industry as they progressively adopt the same business norms, handle the same commodities, share the same trade outlook, and so on. In turn, this standardization becomes the context in which the phenomenon of the trader celebrity appears. However, rather than treating this type in occupational and sociological terms, I have emphasized the type as a hero of the industry and of its milieu. The approach has been a cultural one, with the intention of achieving a more complete grasp on the phenomenon of the television markets by examining the public persona developed around three market celebrities. Bazalgette, Burnett and Fuller appear to be different in their relationships to the television industry and in terms of the particular star images that they precipitate. Analyzing these different celebrity images enables us to move out into the larger cultural, economic, political and social context in which these figures are embedded, thereby grasping how different forms of power are articulated in their specific form and style. For most of the year, however, the television industry – including its luminaries – pursues its craft and commitment in various home territories. There, those in the industry are at the coalface of production, marketing, packaging, format development and application.

In the chapters that follow, I concentrate on the global reach of the television market into home territories of national industries and cultures.

5

LANGUAGES

Unchallenged as the *lingua franca* of the world, the English language makes its presence known in music, movies, advertising, on the Internet and at academic conferences, proving that global capitalism speaks it quite fluently. 'English' is a category that does ... incorporate an extremely diverse body of dialects and accents that may be close to incomprehensible to one another, carrying in them conflicts and power relations that require an extended discussion ... [While] English is the native tongue of many who are perceived of as marginalized in a global configuration ... still, English and global capitalism are bedfellows in much the same way as Latin and the Catholic Church once were (Pennycook 1994: 11 – 14).

Introduction

In Chapter 3, concerning market discourses to do with television programming, one salient linguistic reality was left to one side. This has to do with the languages operating in the various spaces of the TV market place, whether that space be centralized in a Las Vegas, Cannes or Singapore trade fair, localized in production settings in such territories as Brazil, Canada or Denmark, or embodied in particular producers whose nationalities may be Russian, Chinese or Greek. Despite the fact that there might be linguistic commonalities, such that business deals might be discussed in Arabic, Hindu or Japanese, the fact is that the major 'language of advantage' in television trade-related matters is likely to be English. Indeed, despite the claims of transnationality and globalism frequently offered in its name, the television format trade can be linguistically homogeneous as well as linguistically diverse and heterogeneous. Linguistic commonalities and differences are to be found at different points of the global market. Accordingly, this chapter concentrates on the tongue or tongues through which the trade communicates with itself and with others. The analysis has four parts. First, as one of the many fields in which a specific instance of linguistic globalization is being played out, the market language of the TV format trade is framed in terms of a more theoretical debate concerning the evolution of a global language system. This discussion paves the way for two more empirical investigations. The second part of the chapter has to do with the Anglophonic tendency operating at the centre of the trade. English tends to be the language in which a good deal of the TV format business is conducted. However, business dealings and distribution belong to one kind of order while production and local broadcast may be another. The third part of the chapter highlights this reality by focusing on the linguistic diversity exhibited in the international circulation of a telenovela program originating in Columbia. In the last part of the chapter, I reflect on the linguistic multiplicity of TV format programming.

English, media and modernity

English is a world language – perhaps even the *lingua franca* of the globe (Smith and Forman 2000; Wallraff 2002: Rubdy and Saraceni 2006). In making such a claim, it is necessary to be more precise about what such a proposition actually means (cf. Pelton 1981). Certainly, English is seen to be wedded to worldwide media in a variety of different modes, so its pervasiveness comes as no surprise (Hobley 2002; Charlemagne 2003). Tunstall, for example, has recently suggested that the media are Anglo-American – an assertion that supports this linguistic reality (Tunstall and Machin 1999). Similarly, from a socio-linguistic perspective, Hjarvard (2003b) notes the high degree of interpenetration between the English language and a series of international software industries, including business, science, computing, the music industries, information technology, film, television, advertising, public relations, and new technology generally. In short, on the basis of both this general mediatization of language and the size of its linguistic community across the world, English has been identified as a world language. As Crystal (2003) notes, even until well into the twentieth century, there were several dominant international languages. These included English as well as French and Spanish. Over the past 50 years, however, this relationship has changed. English is, or is becoming, a world language while those others are not. Of the approximate 6.5 billion people on the planet, some two billion speak English either as a first or second language. No other language matches this kind of increase. Even Chinese falls short of this growth. The latter is understood by approximately 1.1 billion, although it consists of eight different spoken languages that are in fact united only by a common writing system (Crystal 2003). Chinese, French, Spanish and several other languages might be described as world regional languages. This category refers to those languages that are used both within a national territory and beyond its frontiers. English also belongs in this category of a world regional language, although no other language is a world language. Two other incidental observations can also be made concerning the apparent ubiquity of English. The first is the fact that there are more native speakers of the Chinese language than there are of the English language (Mar-Molinero 2000; Crystal 2003). Instead, it is the very large number of those who have English as a second language – estimated to be 1.6 billion – that compels its recognition as the *lingua franca* of the planet. Second, it may be that in the present and in the future various linguistic communities other than an English-speaking one will make larger and larger claims on various media. The Internet is currently seeing a rollback of the pervasiveness of English as other linguistic communities get access to this hitherto Western-dominated medium (Crystal 2001). Likewise, the Anglo-American cinema may in the future suffer a 'loss of domain' to other regional cinemas, including those of China, India and Egypt (Cowan 2002; Scott 2005).

The phrase 'loss of domain' is taken from an essay written by Danish researcher Stig Hjarvard concerning the spread of the English language and the role that the media play in that process. In apprising the development of the global media system, Hjarvard (2003a) analyses this process in terms of Anglo-American cultural imperialism. Drawing on the work of such researchers as Phillipson (1993) and Pennycook (1994), he argues that 'the media both are vehicles of Anglo-Saxon culture and contribute to the Anglicization of global culture…[they] are more than a neutral channel…they actively contribute to cementing the paramountcy of English over other languages' (Hjarvard 2003a: 14). Hjarvard is aware that this is a totalizing position, yet he ignores the more powerful arguments in favour of viewing such processes as modernization rather than as Anglicization or Americanization (cf. Tunstall and Machin 1999; Tomlinson 1991; Sinclair, Jacka and Cunningham 1996; Staubhaardt 1991). More interestingly, Hjarvard refers to another Danish linguist, Preisler, who suggests that the media reflect rather than create cultural developments. According to the latter, Denmark is undergoing a general Anglo-Americanization, and this is evident in Danish media as well as elsewhere in Danish society and culture (Hjarvard 2003a: 18).

Two observations might be offered about this line of reasoning. The first is the claim that media are a central engine in this so-called Anglo/Americanization. Clearly the media are important, but it is easy to exaggerate and overestimate this importance. Media practitioners – owners, executives, managers, producers, and so on – may need to inflate the claims of their business for obvious reasons, but media researchers need to be more critical and circumspect. Hence, for example, it may be the case that the massive worldwide relocation of populations that began last century might, in fact, turn out to be more significant for linguistic change than the aforesaid media. Second, 'Anglophonization' (itself an updating of 'Americanization') may be only one way – and not very useful at that – to understand the complex changes associated with the emergence of English as a global language. Crystal (2003), for example, is altogether more cautious and careful in generalizing about the spread of English. Admittedly, English is for this author a first language (although so too is the Welsh language). Even so, Crystal does not subscribe to the linguistic imperialist thesis. Rather, he sees the emergence of a more interesting linguistic situation wherein a community begins to use one variety or language for alternative standards for different purposes (Edwards 1985; Jenkins 2006). To illustrate this tendency, Crystal (2003) refers to the situation of dieglossia as found in 'high' and 'low' varieties of such languages as Greek and German. English, he suggests, is already moving in this direction at the global level. Interestingly, Hjarvard (2003b) also glances at this possibility at one point in his argument when he notes that, with the Internet, websites are increasingly in the 'local' language as well as in 'global' English (2003b: 22). Crystal (2003) goes a little further, noting the coexistence of two languages or varieties in such places as Singapore and the Philippines that serve two different functions: 'Already, in such locations as Singapore, we see two spoken varieties co-existing…one being used for intelligibility (Standard British English) and the other for identity (Singlish).' (2003: 192)

This discussion frames the two empirical case studies that follow. The first concentrates on the business context of the television program format trade, and notes the prevalence of English as the linguistic means of exchange and interaction between business parties. However, it is simplistic and probably mistaken to use this tendency, as Hjarvard does, as evidence of Anglophonization – a steady march towards a common world language. The second case study focuses on the production and the broadcast dimension of TV formats. Here, one finds far less significance attaching to the English language, except as it has to do with territories where English is the first language of the majority of the population (the United Kingdom and its former colonies, including the United States).

Commercial intelligibility and English

What are some of the macro issues to be examined concerning the circumstances of the TV program format development and distribution trade? These can briefly be characterized as having western beginnings, whatever their subsequent regional cultivations. How do we obtain a clearer view of such connections? Although many TV program formats have originated in other regions and countries, such as East Asia and particularly Japan, nevertheless it is the case that most of the formats in international circulation are western in origin. This amorphous region may be said to centrally involve the United States, the United Kingdom and Western Europe, as well as more outlying regions of former white European settlement including Australia, New Zealand and Canada. Put another way, this region can be designated as the Euro-American/Anglo-American bloc. In fact, with the notable exception of Japan, these territories include the richest and most affluent market territories of the world regions so far as the research, development and application of new media technologies and software are concerned (Tunstall and Machin 1999).

If we test this proposition in terms of companies operating out of the region, then the following corroborating detail emerges. In 2004, some 68 companies in North America, 64 in the United Kingdom, 228 in Europe and nineteen in Australia and New Zealand – a total of 378 Western companies identifying themselves as involved in the TV program and multimedia format business – were present at the MIPTV television trade fair at Cannes in France (MIPTV 2004).

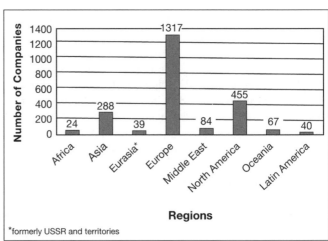

Figure 5.1: Regional TV companies at Cannes, 2004.

*formerly USSR and territories

By contrast, companies representing other regions were in the minority. Asia constituted the second-largest cultural and economic region with some 63 comparable companies operating in the same area of the media software industries also present at the same event. By contrast with the Asian contingent, company delegations from the other continents were much smaller and stood at fourteen from the Middle East, twelve from South America and four from Africa. Figure 5.1 offers a percentage breakdown of this bias.

This overwhelming Anglo-European/Anglo-American presence is not surprising (Alvarado 1996). After all, the great majority of formats are currently devised and developed in the West, although that situation may change. Over the past half-century, US network television has been the key source for classic television game and quiz show formats. From the 1980s onwards, the United States, United Kingdom, Australia and other markets in the same region have also been significant sources of fictional formats, such as sitcoms and soap opera. And within the past decade, the same region – especially the United Kingdom and Western Europe – has originated a very large number of formats in newer genres, including reality, lifestyle, makeovers and DIY (Schmitt, Bisson and Fey 2005).

In all of this, the national powerhouses of format devising and development have continued to be the United States and the United Kingdom. The recent past has also seen these joined by other national marketplaces, including those of The Netherlands, Germany, Sweden, Australia and New Zealand, with such territories as France, Italy, Spain, Belgium, Portugal and other adjoining markets functioning as eager participants in the early research and development (R&D) and broadcast of new formats.

Similarly, in considering this cultural and economic intersection between the West and other parts of the globe, we should remember that the great bulk of TV program format trading occurs in the West. Hence, as already discussed above, the major television trade fair, MIP, occurs twice a year in France and this is part of a busy round of trade events that include screenings and fairs in Los Angeles, Las Vegas, Brighton, Monte Carlo, Budapest, Lucerne in Switzerland and elsewhere in Western Europe. By contrast, the only international television trade event – including the marketing of formats – occurring in the Asia region has been the Singapore-based MIP Asia/Television Asia forum and the recently announced MIP Singaporean Amazia. The first was conceived before the Asian currency crisis of the late 1990s and launched in 2000 in the hope of becoming an Asian version of the fairs in Cannes. However, by 2002 it was clear that the Asian television market was not capable of sustaining it as a marketplace (Grantham 2004). It remains to be seen whether such a marketplace can be replaced by the Amazia event.

A further element that must be considered in this examination of the institutional culture is the fact that the language of the TV program format trade, including that of the TV markets themselves, is English. As already noted, over the past two or three decades English has come to occupy a singular position among world languages. As part and parcel of this situation, one can suggest that television is a medialect of English, and this can clearly be seen in operation with program formats.

Linguistic facets of TV format business

Formats appear to be culturally and linguistically neutral, highly transparent and malleable, so this kind of template can be adapted into another market with consequent adjustments regarding matters of culture, customs, history, religion and language. Still, these are not single, isolated, stand-alone entities, culturally and linguistically innocent. Rather, TV program formats are complexly structured entities embedded and shaped by particular contexts of the sort already outlined. By way of underscoring this point, we can focus on five linguistic facets of the format institution and culture that support a claim about English constituting a growing medialect.

Business language

Consider the fact that, for the most part, formats are written and are presented in English, whether or not they were developed in a territory where English is not a first language. A good example has to do with the format of *Survivor*. Initially, this was devised and developed in the United Kingdom, but its owner found that no company on either side of the Atlantic was willing to license an adaptation. Instead, in 1997 Sweden first licensed the format, with local company Vegelius making the first adaptation of *Survivor* as *Expedition Robinson* (Bazalgette 2005). Although the personnel in the broadcast program spoke Swedish, as did those involved in the business negotiation and adaptation, nevertheless the format continued to exist in English, in which form it was licensed by US network CBS (Bazalgette 2005).

The language of the market floor

We return to the linguistic reality of the trade fairs in TV program formats. Although MIPTV and MIPCOM are held in the French city of Cannes, where French is the language of the city and even the streets surrounding the Palais des Festivals where traders meet, nonetheless English is very much the language spoken on the market floor. Trade stands, programs, signs, and so on are printed in the English language, while French security guards speak to delegates in English. Such an environment makes it clear that this is the *lingua franca* of the international television business, including the format trade. Where public discussions and workshops at the markets and festivals involve non-English speakers, their words are interpreted aloud in the English language. By contrast, there are no concessions made to other national or world regional majority languages, such as Spanish and Chinese. At this level, the TV program format is implicitly driving English as its chosen language of business.

FRAPA and IFLA

Another instance of the English language-bound nature of the format programming business has to do with several trade associated bodies that have already been mentioned. Again, their primary language of communication is English. Agencies in question include the Format Registration and Protection Association (FRAPA) and the International Format Lawyers' Association (IFLA). FRAPA was formed in 2000 at Cannes as an industry body that would include most of the various private and public organizations operating in the development, distribution, production and broadcast of television format programming. Although hosted by the provincial government of Westphalia in Germany, the principal *lingua franca* of the organization is English – a fact highlighted by FRAPA's website, which is in that language.

THE FORMAT RECOGNITION AND PROTECTION ASSOCIATION

Figure 5.2: FRAPA, the trade body for all TV companies involved with TV formats.

Figure 5.3: IFLA, the international network of English-speaking legal format experts.

IFLA is a much more recent organization, being formed in 2005 by a German attorney and a British lawyer. It is much smaller in size than FRAPA, representing as it does a network of lawyers with particular specialist skills and knowledges, whose clients can include members of the larger trade organization. In fact, its aim is not to grow in size and membership but rather to help clients identify legal professionals with expertise in format-related matters in different legal jurisdictions across the world. London-based lawyer Jonathan Coad explained IFLA's origins and skills base as follows:

> I had the idea in a Swiss television festival called the Golden Rose Festival ... it occurred to me that the television industry probably needed a network of specialists in this field. So that if the format devisor in country A found what looked like an infringement in country B, he could tap into a network of specialists and be able to go directly to a lawyer who he knew would be competent both in the field of television, secondly in intellectual property and thirdly would be able to converse and do business in English. Those are the criteria of the IFLA (Alvarado 1996).

An English-language consultancy service

Another instance of the English language-bound nature of the format trade concerns one of the services sold on by a company to an adapter as part of a format licensing arrangement. This involves a consultancy service whereby a producer or other figure, already experienced with the adaptation of the format, spends several weeks with the new producer as they develop this new adaptation of the format. Frequently, licensor and licensee do not share a common language. But again, English becomes the meta-language of communication concerning the various production details and issues. Not surprisingly, a short primer on the devising, development and distribution of TV program formats contains the following advice:

> The second task of the Consultancy Manager is to look at how best to structure the consultancy and to whom by first establishing contacts with key production personnel in the appropriate territory. It is at this stage that relationship and confidence building is so important. [in territories where English is not the first language an interpreter should be appointed by the consultants] (Bodycombe 2002).

Hence, in 2000, Red Sail in Shanghai commissioned a loose adaptation of the British soap opera *Coronation Street* from Granada (Ferguson 2005). As part of this process, a UK producer

Figure 5.4: *Joy Luck Street*, an unlikely Mandarin Chinese remake of *Coronation Street*.

highly experienced with the former production spent almost a year helping to set up the production system of what became *Joy Luck Street*. A team of students and others who spoke both Chinese and English were assembled so that storylines, scripts and other written production documents were translated back and forth to facilitate the communication and the adaptation.

Tutoring the locals

Chapter 7 deals with the international consultancy services that format devising and distribution companies offer to local broadcasting and production companies in the regions. Here, though, we can emphasize the importance that English plays in the production tutoring process. Hence Bob Cousins, a senior producer with FremantleMedia, has been active in the area of format start-up with various genres of format in the company's catalogue. These have included situation comedy and game shows. In the former capacity, he has helped oversee the adaptation of several classic sitcom series in Eastern Europe and Russia. In the case of *The Honeymooners*, *I Love Lucy* and *Man About the House*, as well as several other series, various linguistic templates are in place, including original scripts as well as broadcast episodes of the series. Consequently, Cousins could use this Anglophone base as a means of controlling new scripts being adapted for the different series in such languages as Russian, Polish and Czech. Although he did not read or write any of these languages, nevertheless he was able to use English not only as a means of monitoring what cultural translation was occurring but also as a system for helping to tutor new writers in the requirements of the series. As he put it, talking about the development of the Polish version of *The Honeymooners*:

> I give them what I think of as the early episodes and then they translate those. I then get them to translate them back into English so I can see where they have changed. And then we sit around the table for a couple of days and talk about the cultural changes – why we've done this and that. And then I give them blocks of scripts which I know are going to be tough for them because I want to see how they will respond to them ... What we do is keep coming back to the source. And we find if we cross-reference to other nations or languages for, say, an episode, it gets very diluted (Cousins 2005).

These five examples where the English language provides linguistic machinery that helps the international television format trade to function can be multiplied many times over. What the instances highlight is a more general fact about the Anglophone nature of the global television format business. This is not so much to do with any linguistic takeover of global trade in this particular television commodity, but rather with the fact that English has a central place in the cultural exchange of format markets. These examples confirm it as the business language of the global TV market. Of course, licence discussions and deals do take place in other languages. Sarah Chausey, European sales and acquisition manager for Distraction in Western Europe, noted that those in the London office spoke a total of nine different languages and that this kind of linguistic versatility was important in dealing with clients. In other words, despite the central importance of the English language in international business dealings to do with television finance, programming, intellectual property, and so on, the fact is that another language (or languages) is likely to be in use at any particular local production, marketing and broadcasting situation.

Linguistic politics
Despite the centrality of English as the language of television commerce, the international circulation of television programs must also take significant account of another linguistic reality. This has to do with the existence of different geo-linguistic markets (Sinclair, Jacka and Cunningham 1996). Hence, despite large amounts of imported programming, frequently requiring dubbing or subtitling, 'television programs in vernacular languages continue to anchor a sense of cultural belonging and function as a privileged site for the reproduction of nations' (Waisbord 2004: 373). Billig (1995) suggests that language, including that used in television programs, is a form of banal nationalism in and through which nations are reproduced. Waisbord amplifies this by suggesting that 'television regularly keeps nationhood alive by "flagging" spoken languages and drawing and sustaining linguistic boundaries.' (2004: 375)

At this point, it is useful to recall Crystal's perception of an emerging linguistic versatility in nation after nation, each of which uses different alternative standards for different purposes. Internet websites alert us to the frequent existence of twin linguistic worlds of 'global English' on the one hand and a 'local' language on the other. English is used for 'intelligibility', while another – perhaps local – language or lingo is used for 'identity' purposes. In Chapter 7, the overwhelming significance of the local adaptation of television program formats is pinpointed in the encounter between a producer consultant sent by a licensing company to oversee and guide the indigenization of a program format to suit local viewing conditions, including audience cultural expectations and understandings and a nationally based production team, the members of which are active participants in this process. The often-fractious relationship between English and local, national or regional languages and accents is played out daily in quite specific domestic detail and intensity (cf. Jenkins 2006).

Here, however, a more macro view of such contestations can be traced in another way that serves the same purpose of underlining the complex linguistic situation that is the present subject (Edwards 1985; Garcia Canclini 1995). In fact, although English enjoys a pre-eminent position in the world of global television format program trading, it is by no means the case that this tongue constitutes a global medialect that displaces all other languages or is likely to do so in the foreseeable future. After all, when TV formats are localized for a particular territory, they are inevitably adapted to take cognizance of local linguistic realities. Although Granada Television in the United Kingdom and Red Sail in the People's Republic of China used English in their communication about the Chinese adaptation of *Coronation Street* into *Joy Luck Street*, nevertheless the latter was a Chinese-language serial produced in Beijing with writers, production crew, actors and others all using the Mandarin Chinese language.

An even more salient example of television format programming's linguistic multiplicity that prompts further qualification of any thesis of universal Anglophonic imperialism is the recent international circulation of the telenovela *Yo soy Betty, la fea* ('I am Betty, the ugly'). This series originated in Latin America and has had a good deal of international circulation as both canned programming and format programming. A brief overview of its distribution history highlights the multiplicity of linguistic realities at work in the international world of television production and broadcasting.

First, the linguistic story of *Yo soy Betty, la fea* in both its canned and format forms. The program began life as a Spanish-language Colombian telenovela. It concerns an unattractive, intelligent and ambitious young woman who works among the 'beautiful people' of the fashion industry. The series was devised by an experienced local television writer, Fernando Gaitßn, and began on RTN Television in Columbia in late 1999 (Sutter 2001). The telenovela proved to be very popular with audiences, and this helped with regional sales for other Spanish-language markets. However, as Sinclair (2000) has suggested, the Spanish spoken in different national territories in Central and South America is by no means undifferentiated. For instance, Mexican Spanish has come to dominate cultural importation in other markets in the region so that programs in another accent such as that of Columbia may be intelligible but are not readily acceptable. The particular national variety and dialect have a good deal of bearing on the exportability of TV programming into other Spanish-language markets in the region. Thus the Spanish of the Columbian version of *Yo Soy Betty, la fea* was acceptable to many markets in the region with the notable exception of Mexico. By late 2000, the original telenovela had been sold into such South American markets as Chile, Ecuador, Venezuela, Bolivia and Argentina. Several Central American television markets also bought the program. *Yo Soy Betty, la fea* repeated its rating success in many of these markets, including Ecuador and Venezuela (Sutter 2001). In the United States, the telenovela

Figure 5.5: Publicity image for the Spanish-language Columbian telenovela original of *Yo soy Betty, la fea*.

also developed a strong Spanish-speaking community of online fans. These, it has been claimed, helped persuade the US Spanish-language network Telemundo to air the Colombian series. *Yo soy Betty, la fea* was broadcast by the Telemundo network from late 2000 and achieved good ratings (Hernandez 2001; Sutter 2001).

This screening highlighted the way in which a particular linguistic programming challenge was being resolved. The question was whether the Columbian telenovela could offer Spanish-speaking audiences in other parts of the world sufficient familiarity and identification to make it worthwhile to broadcast the series, even if local Spanish was appreciably different to that spoken in Columbia. The indicators were that it was. The following year, the original telenovela began broadcasting in Spain on Antena 3. *Yo soy Betty, la fea* was also screened in the Philippines and Brazil. In both cases, it was hoped that native speakers of Taglish and Brazilian Portuguese respectively would be able to understand enough of the Columbian Spanish for them to be come keen viewers. Dubbed versions of the original have also screened in Hungary, Bulgaria, Italy and Japan. Table 5.1 summarizes the international distribution of the original telenovela, whether with a Columbian Spanish soundtrack or with a dubbed soundtrack (Wikipedia 2006).

That *Yo soy Betty, la fea* had sold well not only into Spanish-speaking territories but into other linguistic markets as well suggested that if the telenovela were made available as a format package then its international licensing potential might further be enhanced. After all, the linguistic mobility of format programming is not impeded by linguistic frontiers. The first officially franchised version of *Yo soy Betty, la fea* appeared on Indian television in 2003. *Jassi Jaissi Koi Nahin* (There's No One Like Jassi) was produced by Sony Entertainment Television (SET) in the Hindi language and was reasonably successful, running until 2006 (Jasper 2003). In 2004, the United States-based Spanish production company Ventanarosa acquired the US format rights and, in a joint-venture agreement with Reveille Productions and ABC Television, produced an American version as an English-language comedy-drama series entitled *Ugly Betty* (Kissell 2006). The program rated well in its first season, and this in turn allowed it to further circulate as both canned programming and as format programming. The US adaptation has been sold as canned programming to almost all the English-language broadcasters elsewhere, including CityTV in Canada, Channel 4 in the United Kingdom, RTE Two in Ireland, the Seven Network in Australia and TVB Pearl in Hong Kong (de la Fuente 2005).

Table 5.1: National broadcasts of Columbian original version of Yo soy Betty, la fea.

Region	National television market
Latin America	Argentina, Bolivia, Chile, Ecuador, Venezuela, Brazil, Central America, Honduras, Guatemala, El Salvador
North America	United States
Elsewhere	Bulgaria, Hungary, Italy, Japan, Philippines, Spain, Turkey

When it is broadcast in any of these markets, *Ugly Betty* is, to all intents and purposes, an American series. The story is set in New York and its characters speak American English. Hence, although the program is linguistically accessible to audiences in places such as Ireland and Hong Kong, nevertheless, *Ugly Betty* registers as foreign and imported principally because of the subtle but definite differences between American English on the one hand and Irish English or Hong Kong English on the other (Crystal 2003).

Format adaptations have the capacity to achieve cultural fit in many different language markets. In 2005, Sony Pictures Television International (SPTI) acquired the Russian remake rights to *Yo soy Betty, la fea* and a Russian-language remake of the original Spanish-language version, *Ne Rodis 'Krasivoy'* (Don't Be Born Beautiful), became highly successful (Clarke 2005). As Nordenstreng and Varis (1974) pointed out almost four decades ago, Russia exports a good deal of programming to various territories that it controls or used to control, so there are opportunities for *Ne Rodis 'Krasivoy'* to be sublicensed for rebroadcast in some of these neighbouring markets. A Turkish version, *Sensiz Olmuyor* (Won't Work Without You) began the following year, although this format version has proved less successful than those released elsewhere. This was not, however, the case with the 2005 German adaptation *Verliebt in Berlin* (Love in Berlin), which has achieved very high ratings (Clarke 2005). Yet another franchising occurred with the production of a Mexican version of the format that appeared in early 2006. Entitled *La fea mes bella* (The Prettiest Ugly Woman), this version was broadcast on Televisa in Mexico as well as on the Spanish-language Univision in the United States (de Pablos 2006). Most recently, Dutch, Spanish and Greek versions of the format have also gone to air (Wikipedia 2006). Table 5.2 provides a breakdown of the different linguistic adaptations of the format.

Table 5.2: National/linguistic remakes.

Territory	Language	Title
Germany	German	*Verliebt in Berlin*
Greece	Greek	*Maria, i Asximi*
India	Hindi	*Jassi Jaissi Koi Nahin Jassi*
Israel*	Hebrew	*Esti Ha'mechoeret*
Mexico*	Spanish	*La fea mßs bella*
Netherlands	Dutch	*Lotte*
Russia	Russian	*Ne Rodis'Krasivoy*
Spain	Spanish	*Yo soy Bea*
Turkey	Turkish	*Sensiz Olmuyor*
United States	English	*Ugly Betty*

* Unlicensed

Further compounding this impression of linguistic complexity, this Babel of tongues so far as television distribution is concerned, is a series of other paradoxes associated with the *Yo soy Betty, la fea/Ugly Betty* property in both its canned programming and format programming forms. Hence the American remake of the Columbian original could air in Italy, France and Sweden only after it had been dubbed into the national languages of these territories. Elsewhere in the world, this English-language American version of the format has found less favour as a programming vehicle for linguistic redubbing. Underlying the need for a perceived cultural proximity, the Mexican Spanish-language remake of the original was preferred for dubbing into Portuguese for its broadcast in Brazil as *A Feia mais Bela* (Straubhaar 1991). A similar tendency appeared to be at work in parts of Western Europe. There, dubbed versions of the German-language adaptation have appeared in Hungary, France, Belgium, Switzerland and Slovakia. Even more intriguing so far as both culture and language are concerned has been the situation in Turkey, where a 'Turkified' remake of the format has proved to be less popular than the original Columbian version dubbed into Turkish and broadcast some years earlier (de Pablos 2006). The dubbing of adapted versions of the original format is summarized in Table 5.3.

Stepping back from the details covered in this part of the chapter, we can note the complex linguistic situation in the Americas, Europe and parts of Asia that is highlighted by the accumulated outline of the circulation of the program in both its canned and format forms. *Yo soy Betty, la fea/Ugly Betty*'s further possible circulation in other regions including East Asia,

Table 5.3: National-export broadcasts of remakes.

Home market	Export market	Dubbed
Germany	Belgium	Yes
Germany	France	Yes
Germany	Hungary	Yes
Germany	Slovakia	No
Germany	Switzerland	No
Mexico	Brazil	Yes
Mexico	United States	No
United States	Australia	No
United States	Canada	No
United States	France	Yes
United States	Hong Kong	No
United States	Ireland	No
United States	Italy	Yes
United States	Sweden	Yes
United States	United Kingdom	No

Southeast Asia, South Asia, the Middle East and Africa seems likely to only add to the picture of linguistic complexity. Certainly, one can suggest that while English might indeed be the globally favoured form for conducting business in the area of TV formats, for helping to oversee and manage elements of distribution and even production so far as reversioning is concerned, nevertheless this language (or family of languages) has no particular preeminence when it comes to the international linguistic accessioning of the program. Any account of Anglophonic media dominance drawn from the centralized activities of the TV format trade must also have regard for the veritable linguistic kaleidoscope in which global television program distribution occurs.

Summary

This chapter has examined the linguistic dimensions of global television program distribution. The hub of such an operation has a systematic preference for English as the language for business communication. This pull towards homogeneity and cultural convergence is countered by a linguistic impulse in the direction of cultural specificity and identification, a tendency towards heterogeneity and difference – whether at the local, national-regional, national or even world-regional levels. However, it is not a matter of preferring one inclination over the other but rather one of recognizing that the two work together, complementing, contradicting, meshing, grating and buffeting each other. In focusing on the languages of the TV format trade, this chapter is a *locus classicus* of this push–pull tendency. What we find in the languages at work across this area of the media demonstrates that both orientations are at work alongside each other. English is the 'language of advantage' so far as the business of marketing and circulation is concerned. While it is not invariably the language favoured in making the terms of business intelligible to different parties involved in an exchange, it is the language that is most often preferred for this exchange. This generalization is not necessarily true when it comes to format adaptation and broadcast. While English may be the sole world language, it is not the language spoken by the bulk of the world's population. As the case study of *Ugly Betty* makes clear, the linguistic reality is that many tongues come into play, and English is only one of these. Audiences worldwide call on many vernaculars in their identification with this or that version of the program. The chapters that follow offer a more dispersed sense of the international television market.

Accordingly, the next chapter examines the TV trade's own sense of the planet. It asks what maps the industry carries in its head concerning the different regions and territories of the world.

6

GEOGRAPHIES

The best telenovelas I've come across are from Colombia with the best example being *Ugly Betty (Yo Soy Betty, La Fea)*, which is an Ugly Duckling story. It's now being redone in the States. It's going home so to speak – having played on Telemondo in the Spanish version ... *Ugly Betty* works because it's not a glitzy show and the girl playing Betty in the original series ... starts to transform ... and the female audience begins to identify with her. It works in any cultural territory (Spenser 2006).

Introduction

Television geography is the abiding concern of this study. It is also the overt subject of this chapter. The global market is by no means a level playing field; instead, power in business relations is skewed towards some companies and away from others. Trade is intensive in some regions and much less so in others. Some vendors are highly influential while others struggle to close a deal on one property. Those who license formats play an important economic and cultural role as gatekeepers in the global format distribution business. Their world-view of companies and broadcasters in different territories and regions forms a powerful mould, helping to shape the spatial outlook of television so far as audio-visual commodity vending is concerned. Accordingly, this chapter has to do with the world-view of the global format business held by international programming franchisers. It seeks to recover the industry's sense of its own geography. What are the prized markets with regard to licensing? Where do the business's most important and valuable formats originate? Where do they end up? Apart from attending markets and festivals, how do format traders attempt to cover the world so far as their own commercial activities are concerned? And how significant are older ties having to do with culture, religion and language in shaping commercial itineraries, travel priorities, destinations, layovers and trade visits?

Answers to these and other questions are provided in this chapter. The first section has to do with the world of national markets, where a series of summary overviews of particular territories in the main arena of the global TV program format trade is provided. The section furnishes a broad map of the global market. The second part of the chapter concentrates on the world of television business. It is concerned with the perception of different regional and national territories from the point of view of the format traders. How do sellers negotiate sales and trade? What do these tell us about the cultural gatekeeping involved in the TV format trade? How do these contribute to the cultivation of local and national taste? The chapter ends with a case study that tracks the international distribution of one program. The various linguistic incarnations of *Yo soy Betty, la fea* were discussed in the previous chapter. Tracking its circulation in this chapter further illuminates the geographical and cultural shapings of the world with regard to trade in one particular program. The chapter therefore maps the commercial corridors of television program franchising across the world, looking at the routes and passages that lead from the centres of trade to the outskirts of local production, broadcast and reception sites.

National market clusters

The formalization and maturation of the television format trade have only occurred over the past dozen or so years; nevertheless, two useful regional studies have already appeared. The first of these is the 274-page report *The Global Trade in Television Formats*, produced by the London-based *Screen Digest* for FRAPA in 2005. It forms a valuable source of information and judgement concerning the international market for this form of television programming (Schmitt, Bisson and Fey 2005). A total of thirteen national markets are discussed, although two (the United States and Australia) lie outside the geographic region being investigated. Otherwise, the markets are all located in Western Europe. With the partial exception of Japan, the centre of format development and trade lies in Western Europe and the United States, so this investigation is an important first step towards obtaining a total global perspective of the trade. The second analysis is concerned with Asia and the Pacific. A dozen different territories in East Asia, Southeast Asia and Oceania were analyzed (Moran and Keane 2004). However, the Indian market is the only territory analyzed in South Asia, thereby omitting Pakistan, Sri Lanka and Bangladesh.

The continental-market clusters represented by these two studies are among the world's richest market concentrations of format devising, franchising and licensing. An overview of national television format import and export based on these sources sheds a good deal of light on the global market as a whole. Both analyses survey the regions on a country-by-country basis, so the summaries that follow repeat this order.

Europe

Where does Europe begin and end? This general problem is raised by the European survey (Schmitt, Bisson and Fey 2005). What we find is not an exhaustive inquiry into Western, Central and Eastern Europe, but rather a selective and sometimes incongruous survey of national markets that invite different sub-regional designations. Five different clusters comprise one or more national markets in the FRAPA-backed survey as follows.

The Anglophone mediascape

The *Screen Digest* report includes profiles of the United Kingdom, the United States and Australia without explanation or justification. However, as Chapter 9 discusses in more detail,

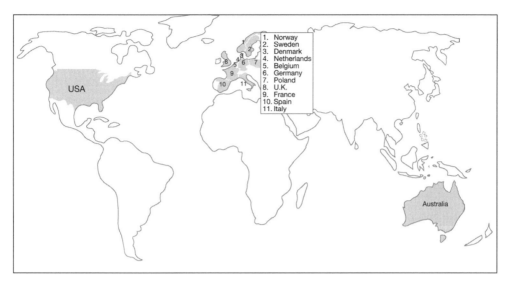

Map 6.1: Europe-centred format survey.

the United Kingdom is also part of what Tunstall calls the 'Anglo-American media connection' that includes other markets such as Australia, English-speaking Canada, Ireland and English-speaking Hong Kong (Tunstall and Machin 1999). The three markets surveyed answer to three different levels of this cluster so far as economic and cultural power is concerned.

Until around 1980, three commercial networks enjoyed a monopoly in the US television market. However, changes due to new technologies, business lobbying and government outlook have led to a very crowded television marketplace, with up to 850 different stations on air. From the 1950s, the United States has supplied an unending stream of formats to international markets, most especially in the area of game shows. It is equally significant that one of the most valuable format catalogues, the Goodson-Todman game show catalogue, is now part of UK FremantleMedia's library. While format programming has had a decisive impact on the US market since 1999, nevertheless it remains a market dominated by canned high-budget drama, which continues to have enormous export potential. The networks have a particular leaning towards US-originated formats as against imported ones, despite the outstanding success of *Survivor* and *Who Wants to Be a Millionaire?* Game shows remain important – although reality, dating and makeover have all improved in popularity. The United Kingdom and The Netherlands are the chief format sources, although US devising continues apace. The BBC distributes the most hours of format programming, and FremantleMedia is the largest originator of formats in the United States.

British broadcasting is the world's largest devisor and distributor of contemporary TV format franchises. Programs such as *Who Wants to Be a Millionaire?*, *The Weakest Link* and *Pop Idol* were all originated by UK companies. Despite the public service charter of British television, there is a considerable history of format import and remaking, especially from the United States. Despite the important place that it fills in world format trade, UK broadcasting remains disposed towards its home territory. It spends less compared with Germany, The Netherlands and France in producing imported formats. It also shows a distinct preference for format-based programming that has been devised in the United Kingdom. Finally, the report notes that game show formats constitute the largest number of format-based programming appearing on UK television.

Chapter 9 offers a case study of formats relating to the Australian television production sector. Some of the general features of the format landscape are worth noting. Australia has had a mix of public and private service since television began. This is now supplemented by cable and community TV services. There has been a tradition of adapting overseas programs for local television – hence the public service broadcaster the ABC borrowed heavily from the BBC while independent producers went to the United States for formats. FremantleMedia's catalogue includes formats first developed in 'major minor' markets. Nowadays, the main genres of format imports are game shows, reality programs and makeovers, and the predictable national sources are the United Kingdom, the United States and The Netherlands.

Northwestern television markets

Another convenient grouping of national television markets is located on the upper edge of the continent. The Netherlands, Germany and Flemish television in Belgium might be said to have had common cultural, religious and linguistic heritages. Historically, Dutch television exhibits two tendencies. Like many other markets in Western Europe, The Netherlands only introduced commercial television in the late 1980s. Hitherto, there had been a long-defined use of public channels by sanctioned religious and political groups. By then, Dutch television had also built up a thriving cottage industry in international format program trade. Endemol, IDtv and Eyeworks are the most important companies in this trade. Game shows, reality programs and drama serials are the main genres of format programming. Most formats have originated locally, although UK-headquartered FremantleMedia now surpasses Endemol in the number of hours of adaptations produced in Dutch studios.

Germany forms the largest and most valuable television market in Europe. A public service duopoly existed until the 1980s, followed by the onset of private commercial television. Cable and satellite channels soon followed. Format licensing took off in the 1990s in such genres as drama, game shows, sitcoms, reality and makeover shows (Heinkeilein 2004). Germany is Europe's most valuable market for formats, although few German-devised formats are exported. There has been a long involvement with independent television production. The United Kingdom is the market's most favoured format source, with reality programs, game shows and drama among the genres perpetuated through format import. FremantleMedia is the dominant format importer and producer, followed by Endemol and Granada International.

Meanwhile, Belgium is one of Europe's smaller television markets. It is included here because of Flemish-language broadcasting in the north. With its links to The Netherlands, Flemish Belgium is the scene of a good deal of traffic in format program production. There has been a doubling in format franchising adaptation in the last five years. Several independent production companies, including Eyeworks, De Televisiefabriek, Kanakna, Woestijnvis and Endemol Belgium, have emerged to handle this demand.

Nordic television markets

This cluster consists of Denmark, Norway and Sweden. Danish public service channels enjoyed a monopoly until the late 1980s, when commercial television arrived via UK-originated satellite broadcasting. Still, public service channels continue to dominate audience ratings. Game shows, reality shows, dating programs and makeover shows have been the most favoured genres of formats, mostly originating in the United Kingdom, The Netherlands and – less frequently – the United States. Endemol's dominance is slipping, although it has a 33 per cent stake in local production company Metronome, whose main rivals are Stryx and Nordisk Film.

Norway also follows the pattern of public service television monopoly. Again, a commercial service was introduced via satellite but the public sector soon reasserted dominance. Format licensing arrived in a big way in the early 1990s, and reality has been a dominant genre. The United Kingdom, the United States and The Netherlands have again been major suppliers of program franchises, while Endemol, Stryx and FremantleMedia have been the leading licensors. In turn, Metronome is the leading production house.

Sweden is the dominant television market in the Nordic region. It ranks with the United Kingdom, The Netherlands and the United States in terms of being the only markets where locally originated formats are more important than imported ones in terms of hours broadcast. Until 1989, Sweden had a monopoly of two public service channels. This was broken by a satellite commercial service, followed by the introduction of terrestrial commercial stations in the 1990s. Public service broadcasting began to farm out some of its productions to the independent sector and format licensing fuelled this development. Meter (with Endemol holding a 35 per cent stake), Stryx and Zodiac are the largest companies in this sector.

The Latin audio-visual space

Named after the designation of Mattelart, Delacourt and Mattelart (1984), this supranational set of markets applied to Europe comprises three territories that exhibit broad linguistic, geographic, cultural and religious commonalities. The markets are those of Spain, France and Italy. Rather like Germany, these comprise relatively large populations and exhibit a good deal of affluence. Collectively, these elements ensure that they are very valuable territories so far as the importation of formats is concerned. They are, however, weak in terms of format exports.

Spanish television first operated under direct state control. After 1975, the system changed to a controlled diversity that catered to the different cultural and linguistic nations constituting Iberia. The early 1990s ushered in commercial television, satellite and cable services. Franchised program production also began then. Formats have been drawn from the United States,

Germany, Italy, The Netherlands, the United Kingdom and even Spain itself. Game shows, reality programs and variety have been the most popular format genres, while Endemol has dominated the market.

By the late 1980s, French television had seen a massive shift from a public service monopoly to the introduction of commercial advertising, commercial stations and the privatization of an existing station. Adaptations of imported game show formats began to appear. After Germany, France is Europe's most important format market so far as production value is concerned. Game show formats originating in the United States and United Kingdom are especially popular. Endemol France, FremantleMedia and several smaller local groups divide the local import production market between them.

Meanwhile, Italy's RAI enjoyed a television broadcasting monopoly until the mid-1970s, when a great multiplicity of local broadcasters came on the air. Entrepreneur Silvio Berlusconi developed three commercial networks and became a dominant media figure in both Italy and Europe (Murdock 2004). Today, RAI and Berlusconi's Mediaset share the television audience between them. The United States was a leading supplier of game shows in the 1980s. Nowadays, the leader is the United Kingdom, followed by The Netherlands and the United States. Italy is now the third most important format market in Europe, having developed more rapidly than any other territory except Sweden. It was therefore no surprise that in 2007 Berlusconi acquired a large stake in Endemol.

A Central European television market
Poland is the only national television market considered in this cluster. The early 1990s saw a revamping of the state service under the banner of public service, and the 1992 introduction of commercial television. The former attracts most viewers despite the fact that there are now six terrestrial channels as well as satellite and pay services. Licensed format remaking began with heavy emphasis on game shows, with prizes of cash and consumer goods. Reality shows, dating programs and scripted sitcoms make up most of the rest of the format slate. Despite the country's large population, Polish television is less valuable as a format market than any of the other national markets analyzed. Production budgets are relatively low. The United Kingdom, United States and Sweden are the favourite format sources, and the three largest format companies are FremantleMedia, Sony Pictures and Stryx. Because FremantleMedia produces, licenses and distributes, its revenues from this impoverished market are reasonably significant.

Asia
Like Europe, Asia might be regarded as a cultural continent, although a second glance suggests that there are several sub-regional and supra-national formations only. Hence the national market profiles that follow are variously linked as well as being separate. There is an East Asian cluster of television markets where a good deal of 'cultural proximity', including various flows of television program formats, exists (Straubhaar 1991, 2007). This grouping answers to the older name of the Far East. Hence a Sinological footprint includes Japan, the People's Republic of China (PRC), Taiwan, Hong Kong, South Korea and Singapore. A second sub-regional

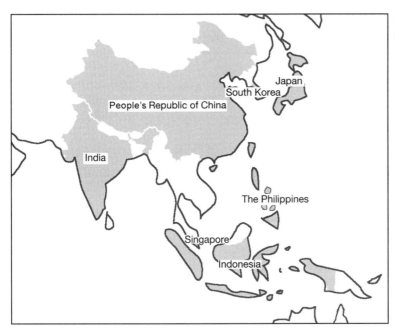

Map 6.2: Asia-centred format survey.

market is located in South Asia, although only Indian television is profiled. Finally, two other national television markets in the geographic region are examined: the Philippines and Indonesia. The two are distinct from these clusters and from each other.

The East Asian Chinese cluster

Japan has sufficient population and wealth to be one of a dozen giants of world television (Alvarado 1994; Iwabuchi 2002, 2004; Mules 2004). It has the second largest television market in the world. Once colonized by US television imports, Japan now has a service that is 95 per cent locally produced. Over half a century, a considerable audio-visual export trade has been added in such culturally neutral areas as technology, animation and advertising. Japan exports as well as imports formats in both television and cinema, noticeably to the United States and United Kingdom, from which they are redistributed in other territories. Its most successful television formats include *Funniest Home Videos* and *Iron Chef*. Japan may be (for the moment at least) a minor player in global format trade, but it is a sub-regional giant, dominating neighbouring television systems in South Korea, Taiwan and Hong Kong.

Meanwhile, close at hand in the People's Republic of China (PRC), television has a huge audience, a very large number of stations and networks, and is centrally administered (Keane 2004; Hong 2004). Thus, like other cultural invasions, foreign material is accommodated, transformed to its own needs or thrown out. Since 2000, stations – especially in Hunan – have followed the practices of other Asian countries by both buying in global formats and copying without authorization, largely from Taiwan and Hong Kong. Among formats licensed into China have been *Happy Family Plan* from Japan, *Coronation Street* from the United Kingdom and *Sesame Street* from the United States. On the other hand, *Into Shangrila* was an unauthorized copy of *Survivor*. Most formats are copied illegally, but there is no mechanism to prosecute piracy. Another factor has to do with the very large numbers of stations who compete by copying each other. Most copying happens between channels in other cities and throughout the countryside, where barter is the principal means of getting programs produced. This may slow as the protection of the few high-rating hits becomes financially important (Keane 2004).

Offshore and to the south lies the former island state of Hong Kong. As an entrepôt port, the city is an Asian nexus for global TV as well as the PRC's offshore arm. Satellite and cable channels have not made serious inroads into the market, which is dominated by two very profitable free-to-air stations (Fung 2004). The latter have been in a strong position both to initiate local production and to adapt imported formats. A lot of TV has been dubbed or subtitled into Cantonese for local and mainland consumption. Formats come from the West and Japan, and can even be initiated in co-production with PRC and Taiwan interests. They are almost universally licensed, although many unauthorized spinoffs and derivatives occur. Since reunification, almost all TV has been produced or adapted with a view to global export, with Hong Kong now also the hotbed of media and toy piracy. In the future, global formats may trial there with an eye for the huge market in Mainland China.

A small North Asia market, Taiwan has been politically colonized by Japan followed by the United States, with the PRC currently in the wings. As a television market, it is highly saturated thanks to four commercial networks, a public TV service, 68 cable channels and 128 satellite channels (Liu and Chen 2004). With fierce competition, the channels have tended to follow American practice and then each other. However, US influence is waning in the sector, with the market becoming more disposed towards its own region. A good deal of Japanese programming is finding its way there, directly or through South Korea and Hong Kong. Exhibiting a tendency towards program contra-flow (Thussu 2008), Taiwan has been especially quick to adapt Japanese 'Idol-dramas', which come from the *manga* comics. These have been produced in the local Amoy dialect and are then changed for export to Mainland China. They also turn up in Hong Kong and elsewhere (Liu and Chen 2004).

The South Korean television market exhibits a familiar pattern (Lee 2004). It consists of a mix of long-established terrestrial stations and newer cable and satellite channels. Like Taiwan and Hong Kong, South Korea's TV has been dominated by that of the United States and Japan. Now, however, US programs only dominate programming on the newer services, which attract a fringe audience. Instead, the majority of the population watches locally produced programs on the terrestrial stations (Lee 2004). Japan makes its presence felt here in the form of a great deal of unauthorized adaptation of Japanese formats (Iwabuchi 2002, 2004). Among the genres in question have been dramas, variety shows and game shows. There is also a degree of cloning of US programs, again without any payment of licence fees. Nevertheless, format licence fees are sometimes paid and the government is cracking down on this unauthorized traffic, thereby hoping to encourage local devising as well as local production (Lee 2004).

The island nation-state of Singapore is the last part of a Chinese diasporic formation. In fact, the four million population of this entrepôt port boasts a mixture of ethnicities, with four languages being officially recognized. Juggling these ethnicities is often a difficult affair, and this is especially the case with television programming. There are nine free-to-air television stations owned by two companies with cable, satellite and pay TV also operating (Lim 2004). However, 90 per cent tune into four mass entertainment channels (Lim 2004). Locally devised drama is the mainstay of the popular audience, but formatted programs are also a significant source of local production. US game shows are frequently produced in all languages, although – more controversially – the UK version of *Who Wants to Be a Millionaire?* was restricted to a Mandarin Chinese version, later followed by an English version (Lim 2004).

India and the South Asian region

With a population of a billion people, India is a television giant in the supra-national cultural continent. The majority of its population is not wealthy, so the industry is not significant in global television trade. Still, piggy-backing on the success of the Bollywood film industry, the relatively new television industry supports an immense and complex domestic TV industry that exports to Pakistan, Bangladesh, Nepal, Sri Lanka and the Maldives (Thomas and Kumar 2004; Sonha and Asthana 2004). Monopoly state broadcasting ended in 1991. That year, the cable network StarTV, owned by News Ltd, began unregulated local broadcasting with four channels in English and one in Hindi. Currently, there are over 100 stations with new ones opening every year. Many different languages are in use (Sonha and Asthana 2004). StarTV and Star Plus broadcast in English and Hindi. SunTV adopts Tamil, which it transmits to Tamil Nadu, Sri Lanka and Singapore. Meanwhile, Asianet can be broadcast in Malayalam to Kerala and expatriate Keralans in the Middle East. Gemini and Eenadu channels in Telugu transmit to Andra Prodesh. In addition, international companies in India, such as CNN, StarTV, SonyET and Discovery, source programs from within for local and international broadcast (Thomas and Kumar 2004). Bollywood has had a long history of pirating film stories, and this has helped set the tone of such activity in television. Nonetheless, because of the presence of the international companies mentioned and others, there have been a number of cases of authorized format remakes, including those to do with *Who Wants to Be a Millionaire?, Charlie's Angels, Family Feud* and *Mastermind* (Spenser 2006). However, like the situation in the PRC, these authorized remakes are very much the exception rather than the rule. There are many ripoffs of formats from elsewhere, and there are even unlicensed copies of these formats on other cable and local channels.

An anomalous national market?

Just as Australia and New Zealand are linguistically and ethnically out of place at the bottom of East Asia and might better belong in the mid-Atlantic, so The Philippines might be culturally rehoused in Latin America. It neither imports nor exports canned or format television programs to its near geographic neighbours, but rather looks instead to Latin America, the United States and to the West generally (Santos 2004). The market boasts over 70 stations, with free-to-air channels having an 80 per cent dominance in Manila and being even more popular elsewhere. Taglish is the local language, although one in twenty of the population speaks Spanish and more recognize it (Mattelart, Delacourt and Mattelart 1984). About 75 per cent of all programming is local in origin, although frequently based on adaptations and clones (Santos 2004). Still, programming is also drawn from elsewhere. Telenovelas from Latin America are very popular, so that – as will be seen later in this chapter – this market was one of the first outside Latin America to import and screen *Yo soy Betty, la fea*. It also imports and dubs cartoons and children's programs from the United States and Japan. *Who Wants to Be a Millionaire?* is one of the few format programs imported into the Philippines for which a straightforward franchising agreement was put in place. For the most part, however, there is a great deal of piracy of formats from elsewhere, including the United States and Mexico. In many instances, the pirated adaptation has turned out to be very successful, both in terms of popularity and in terms of building the local production industry. Audiences, of course, tend to believe that such programs are home grown, and in a real sense they are.

Television on the edge of the Muslim diaspora
Indonesia is not as culturally isolated in Southeast Asia as the Philippines. It is, after all, the most eastern part of the global Muslim diaspora, and its population speaks a form of the Bahasa language that it shares with Malaysia (Kitley 2004). Previously under the control of a military government, television is now commercial and unrestricted with the very great majority of people still wedded to free-to-air channels. Again, about three-quarters of programming is local, with imported formats frequently providing the basis of production (Kitley 2004). However, there is more of a history of format licensing than there is elsewhere. Australian companies were very active in the area of game shows in the past (Cunningham and Jacka 1996). More recently, formats have been imported from the United Kingdom, Japan, The Netherlands and elsewhere, with the market again broadcasting a local, authorized version of *Who Wants to Be a Millionaire?* (Kitley 2004).

The world of television business
However, national television markets are usually not encountered by industry sales and production personnel or critical researchers on the one-off basis presented in the previous section of this chapter. Instead, territories are linked together into larger physical configurations. This occurs for two principal reasons. One of these has to do with realities of history and geography. National television markets are drawn into larger cultural clusters because of long-standing social ties. These include physical proximity, language, history, culture, ethnicity, religion and politics (Sinclair, Jacka and Cunningham 1996; Straubhaar 2007). These groupings are more than the sum of their different national parts. Instead, there can be supra-national ties as well as larger world-regional groupings. There can and will be hierarchies of cultural and economic power in which one or two national markets will dominate others for reasons of population size and relative levels of wealth (Tunstall 2008). Further determining flows of cultural product, there are particular urban locations that, adapting Curtin's notion of media capitals, might be thought of as television capitals (Curtin 2003, 2004). These are sites that see the accumulation of relevant resources and know-how, that witness the clustering together of dense precincts of broadcasters, distribution companies, production offices and so on, that favour the development of technological innovation and cultural initiatives. Most especially,

these variants of media capital dominate their own hinterlands within and outside national territories so that the cultural capital they already possess tends to multiply itself.

The other broad reality shaping the television business world has to do with the exigencies of business. Although most companies operating in the domain of television program distribution are transnational, this does not mean that they do not have a home base in a particular territory, be it Los Angeles, London, Amsterdam or Mexico City. In turn, these and others set about rearranging the world so far as their business operations are concerned. Agents, local offices or some kind of joint venture arrangement can function as a means of looking after one or more national markets. Trade fairs serve particular regions as well as aiming to cater for a global clientele. Sales executives may be competent in particular second and third languages, which will make some territories more accessible than others. And, of course, underlying these practical arrangements are those deeper ethnic and cultural ties touched on already.

A company's sense of sales geography is based on the relative value of different markets so far as its accounts are concerned. The question then arises of how best to handle these different national and regional territories. In some instances, a sales executive may visit on a regular basis. In other instances, it may be most convenient to appoint an agent, though the latter may then have to juggle several portfolios on behalf of a number of different companies. The third alternative is to open an office that facilitates serving a national market and even perhaps covering a group of such markets. How, then, do companies decide on one of these options? In particular, why and how is the decision taken to set up an office in a foreign location?

Locating regional offices
Of course, certain of the larger regions are perceived as difficult from the point of view of those trading in television programming, most especially that to do with format franchising. Latin America and Asia are two such territories frequently mentioned by executives. Thus, when FremantleMedia came into existence in 2000, it found that one of its originating companies, Grundy World Wide, had established a Latin American office in Santiago in Chile as early as 1993 (Moran 1997). The intention was to serve the markets of Central and South America. Several factors lay behind this decision: a short history of local production in that market; perceived financial stability of the country's economy; and the avoidance of larger markets such as Brazil and Mexico, where the newcomer would have to compete against giants such as Globo and Televisea (Sinclair 1996). This story was repeated in Southeast Asia, where the company opened a permanent regional office in Singapore (Skinner 1995; Moran 1998). The same considerations came into play. There was perceived to be financial and political stability there, and the island state promised access and opportunities not so readily available in larger markets such as Japan and the People's Republic of China (Skinner 1995). Singapore also offered a convenient springboard to other markets in the region, including near-neighbours such as Indonesia, Thailand and Malaysia, as well as to others in South Asia.

Besides serving as distribution and production offices for the different territories, regional offices can also be allocated other responsibilities. They can, for example, function as production offices for the mounting of supra-national versions of particular format programs. This was the case in 1997 when Grundy produced a regional Latin American version of *Man O Man* (Moran 1997). This version drew inspiration from an Italian summer version made in conjunction with RAI. It was produced during the southern region's summer season and broadcast in three of the countries in the Mercosur group – Argentina, Uruguay and Paraguay. Meanwhile, a regional office in another place could serve another function. In 1997, for example, the Chilean office undertook work for Dutch company Endemol. At the time, the latter lacked a facility in the region so that the undertaking was a straightforward business arrangement. (Shortly afterwards, Endemol would enter into a joint venture arrangement with several Latin American companies, most especially with Brazil's Globo, to overcome this market handicap).

Regional and sub-regional clusterings

Perceptions having to do with business priorities on the one hand and deep-rooted cultural and territorial imaginings on the other run through such business decisions. Supra-national affinities are in play here. This is highlighted if we look at the territorial 'beat' of Sara Chausey, a senior marketing executive with Distraction, a company with twin headquarters in Montreal and London. Based at the latter location, she specializes in television program format distribution (Chausey 2006). Her territorial responsibilities include the United Kingdom, Germany and Western Europe. In turn, this executive officer manages a junior executive who takes care of Scandinavia, Russia, TIF and the Iberian markets. Paris hosts an office exclusively devoted to France. The Montreal office covers French-speaking America, Latin America and Canada, while an office in Los Angeles is oriented to the giant US market. Poland, Slovakia, Hungary and the Czech Republic are the province of a Warsaw office. There is an agent in Asia while a Sydney office facilitates coverage of Australia and New Zealand.

Particular geographical patterns are to be expected on the part of television companies. For example, licensors take up options that will cover, say, Scandinavia, or perhaps France, Italy and Spain. But other lines of cultural connection across national boundaries are a little more unexpected. Sara Chausey described one such set of linkages:

> Poland and Russia, from a continental perspective, look to Italy. Poland and Italy – because they have a lot in common. They are both Catholic countries. The people are a bit similar in that they are very warm, they are very family oriented. They are a bit socially conservative (Chausey 2006).

As well as the larger geolinguistic cultural regions, it is also worth identifying sub-regional or supra-national cultural clusters. These usually comprise two, three or more adjoining television markets which are sometimes aggregated or treated as one for purposes of licensing, finance, distribution and marketing. Australia and New Zealand constitute one such obvious grouping, as do the Scandinavian markets. Meanwhile, Latin America – itself a large cultural continent when it comes to television as well as much else in the way of symbolic goods and services – comprises four sub-regional clusters (Sinclair 2000). One is associated with an Andean sensibility and consists of the territories of Columbia, Ecuador, Bolivia and Peru. Brazil is a second distinctive market, with its own language and a very large viewing population. A third cluster is focused on the southern cone or Mercator nations, and comprises Paraguay, Uruguay, Argentina and Chile. Again, a different cultural outlook is at work there: '[They] like to think of themselves as European but they have Latin sensibilities.' (Spenser 2006)

Finally, there is Central America, a region made up of a group of small territories dominated by Mexico. Mexico constitutes a kind of Hollywood of the Spanish-speaking television world (Sinclair 2000, 2004). Not only do its television networks and production companies have important holdings in the smaller markets of Central America, but Mexico also functions as a cultural gateway or media capital whereby finished programs or formats being broadcast in the US market are picked up and moved into the Latin American mediascape. As one distribution executive put it: 'Central America is very dependent on what Mexico wants, partly because that's the alliance and ownership of TV stations, but also because if a format is successful in the USA then the Latins will pick it up.' (Spenser 2006)

The commercial traveller
Often, however, national and regional offices are not operated by a single company. Instead, operations will be handled from centres such as Los Angeles, London and Amsterdam. This was the case with ECM (European Communications Management), which allocated the South American beat to a management executive based in London. It could afford to do this because the latter had extensive experience in business and culture working in Buenos Aires, Sao Paulo and Mexico City (Spenser 2006). This executive emphasized the routine of salesmanship involved in licensing. For, although companies might first hear and see a program format in Las Vegas or Cannes, it is in their home offices in these territories that deals are closed. As the same distribution executive put it:

> We would sell formats on month-long trips, moving from producer to producer and country to country. It worked better that way. [For] some markets you needed to actually be there in front of people. Sometimes they come to you but nothing beats going to their own office and saying, 'What are you after? I've got this and this, would it be of interest?' When you turn up in a country, its easier to get meetings than if you phone or email them (Spenser 2006).

The marketplace or the home office
Having an office in a particular region and having pitching meetings with executives in their own offices is the necessary complement to get-togethers at the trade fairs. Sara Chausey – who, like Graham Spenser, has undertaken a lot of travel as part of her work as marketing executive – explained how these two activities complemented each other:

> To go from Turkey to Amsterdam in one week – it's certainly not something you can do from week to week. Although I do try to get to these territories as often as possible. So, MIP – from a very practical perspective – is about seeing clients from far-flung territories around the world in one place to follow up. And – as you know – having a face-to-face

conversation with a client is much more valuable than having a telephone conversation (Chausey 2006).

It goes without saying that company executives will only attend market fairs at which broadcasters and others from territories that are part of their beat will be in attendance. Thus, as already explained, the format distributor Distraction has major offices in Montreal and London. Sales personnel from the first will attend NATPE while executives from the latter office are on hand at the European fairs, especially MIPTV and MIPCOM.

On the other hand, there are regional television markets that serve particular territories to which executives from other regions are not attracted. There is, for example, a Russian television market held each year in November. Very few television executives from the West attend. One factor is the problem of border entry, as visas are often difficult to arrange. Few foreign television executives speak the language, and this compounds the problem. For the most part, then, the principal attendees are companies located in Russia or in its satellite territories.

Other regional markets can also remain relatively untouched by the larger western companies. This was the case with the Middle East markets in the early years of the new millennium. At the time, Endemol had an enormous international success with the *Big Brother* format, which achieved worldwide franchising on a scale never before seen (Bazalgette 2005). A group of Middle Eastern cable operators saw various early versions on different satellite broadcasts and contracted with Endemol for the series. However, these operators did this as a response to market excitement about the program, and without paying enough attention to the cultural, religious and ethnic dispositions of national audiences in their own region. Graham Spenser described the developing situation as follows:

> A friend of mine sold it [*Big Brother*] to a Middle Eastern broadcasting company who … outraged [the audience]. Even after they [the franchising company] tried to be as 'cultural' as possible by respecting the religious issues, having Islamic and Hindu … There was no question of boys sleeping with girls but even so the result was that just the interaction in that hothouse atmosphere was somehow culturally wrong. And the station was forced to pull it due to massive viewer outrage … [It was] less so in Lebanon, whose French influence made it more open. But in Saudi Arabia, there was anger (Spenser 2006).

As will be seen in the next chapter, a franchisor will usually provide a consulting service to facilitate the translation of a format program into a form comprehensive and acceptable to national audiences. Clearly, whatever effort was provided by a visiting producer or envoy was not successful in this instance. The case illustrates the kind of uninformed business decisions that can be taken by ill-informed elements of the international market.

The world of *Ugly Betty*
So far this chapter has examined various determining effects on the flow of format programming based on broad social factors on the one hand and specific business decisions on the other. It is

Figure 6.1: Publicity still for the original Spanish-language version of Yo soy Betty, la fea, produced in Columbia.

Figure 6.2: Principal character in the Columbian original.

useful to complement and highlight these with a specific case study of the worldwide distribution of one particular program. The example in question is that of Yo soy Betty, la fea/Ugly Betty, the linguistic circumstances of which have already been investigated. Here, we analyze the program's geographical itineraries. What is discovered is a series of originating centres from which program exports ripple out to other territories, with at least some of these patterns familiar from past investigations of the circulation of canned programs (Alvarado 1994; Cunningham and Jacka 1996; Steemers 2006b). The advent of global trade in format programming complicates and enriches this network, overlaying it with new structures famously described by Tracey as a 'patchwork quilt' (Sinclair, Jacka and Cunningham 1996).

Broadly, the movement of Yo say Betty, la fea – whether in canned or format form – finds its way into six different regional groupings of national markets in different parts of the world. These are dealt with here first in terms of the canned program, and second the various format remakes. The territorial galaxies of the first are: (1) an original Betty la fea grouping with Columbia as its hub; and (2) a complementary, international-spillover cluster. Meanwhile, the four other groupings to do with the movement of the format program are: (1) a constellation having to do with an Anglo-American remake; (2) a German-based adaptation grouping; (3) a further set of remakings that is partly European but spills over into Asia and the Americas; and finally; (4) a more anomalous set of markets that have seen both ripoffs and spinoffs of the original program.

The canned program flow
The first grouping associated with the property occurred around the original production of the broadcast serial Yo soy Betty, la fea (I am Betty, the Ugly). The serial had its debut on RCN Television on 25 October and turned out to be the

Map 6.3: Broadcast-version exports in the Americas.

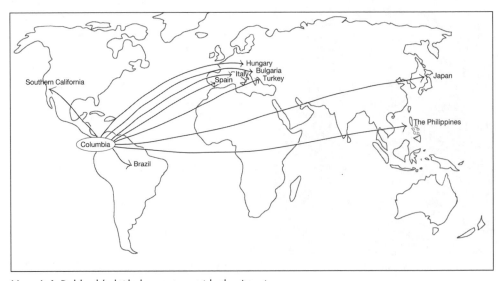

Map 6.4: Dubbed/subtitled exports outside the Americas.

highest-rated telenovela of 2000, with a peak viewership of 3.3 million and a 72 per cent market share (Sutter 2001). The Columbian audience popularity soon led to its sale to other Latin markets. These included Chile, Ecuador, Venezuela, Bolivia and Argentina. *Yo soy Betty, la fea* rated very well in many of these national markets. In Ecuador, for example, it gained a 58.9 per cent share while in Venezuela the figure reached 41.5 per cent (Sutter 2001; Wikipedia 2006). The canned program also developed a strong community of online fans. Late in 2000, US Spanish-language network Telemundo aired the Colombian show, achieving strong ratings for eleven months. *Yo soy Betty, la fea* was also sold to several Central American television markets.

In addition to its penetration of this Latin American regional market, the canned program also achieved international spillover to other territories across the waters. *Yo soy Betty, la fea* was dubbed or subtitled in these other markets. In some instances, this was probably based on a perceived cultural proximity for audiences, whereas in others the licensing was undoubtedly motivated by price. In 2001, the Columbian original appeared in the Philippines on the GMA network, and in Spain on Antena 3. The following year, it was shown in Brazil as *Betty, a Feia*, and on cable channel Telemundo in the United States. By then, the program had reached the international television markets in the United States and in Europe. *Yo soy Betty, la fea* won the Mejor Telenovela (Best Soap Opera) at the TP de Oro awards in Spain that year (Hernandez 2001). By 2003, the original version had moved beyond the Iberian footprint. Dubbed versions were broadcast in Hungary and Bulgaria in 2003 and in Turkey, Italy and Japan in 2004. Meanwhile, other flows of the program were appearing thanks to the international franchising of the format (Clarke 2005).

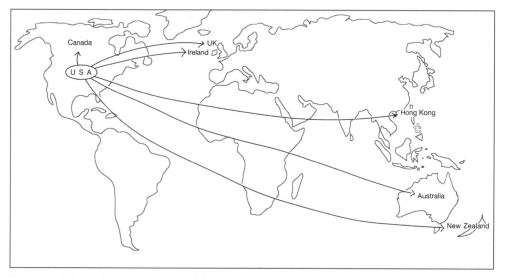

Map 6.5: US remake exports to English-language markets.

The format program flow

Telenovelas made their first impact in Europe and outside Spanish and Portuguese language territories in the 1990s, although this was without definite and lasting impact (Thussu 2007). However, *Yo soy Betty, la fea*'s commercial success, together with the further expansion of international trade in television format program licensing, ensured that the program was likely to gain extensive international distribution in format form. This has been the case, and a further four regional configurations based on adaptations and remakes can be identified.

Another overall flow cluster, and the first associated with *Yo soy Betty, la fea*'s franchising, had to do with the program's remake in English and its circulation in the English-language television territories. This flow was discussed in Chapter 5, and will be returned to in Chapter 9. The export path traced by the English-language version follows historical cultural contours

Figure 6.3: Marketing image for the US English-language version, *Ugly Betty*.

associated with the British Empire (Tunstall and Machin 1999). The primary move involved the US production of an English-language version, *Ugly Betty*, after the Hollywood television company Ventanarosa, headed by Mexican actress turned producer Salma Hayek, acquired the licensing rights to the telenovela's format. In turn, JVA with Reveille Productions and ABC Television Studio (formerly Touchstone Television) handled the production of the series, with the ABC network putting it to air in 2006 (de Pablos 2006). Claiming the largest viewing audience

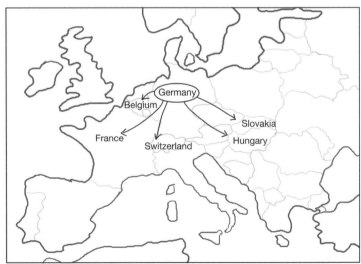

Map 6.6: Dubbed exports of German remake.

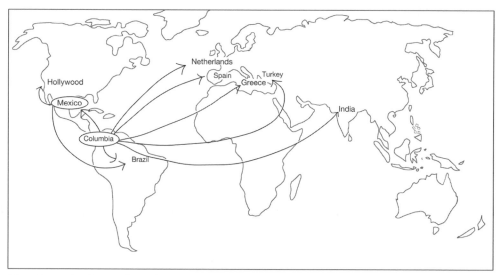

Map 6.7: Other licensed remakes.

of any new series of the fall season, *Ugly Betty* seemed to benefit from months of internet buzz generated by fans of a Mexican version. The series was reconfigured as an hour-long weekly 'dramedy', as opposed to the five-nights-a-week telenovela format in other countries. A team from Colombia's RCN served as consultants. In turn, the US version was sold to CityTV in Canada, Channel 4 in the United Kingdom, RTE Two in Ireland, the Seven Network in Australia and TVB Pearl in Hong Kong.

Figure 6.4: Publicity still for German remake of *Yo Soy Betty, la fea.*

A German-based franchising of the format had an even greater geographical footprint. In 2005, German TV network SAT 1 began airing a local version produced by FremantleMedia/ Grundy UFA TV Productions (Kissell 2006). The telenovela *Verliebt in Berlin* turned out to be a big success and attracted five million viewers daily (Wikipedia 2006). As well as its 364 episodes, the German remake spawned an astonishing nineteen specials as well as a TV movie. The main narrative – Ugly Lisa's relationship with David, her boss at the fashion house – was resolved at the end of the first season. The series continued with new protagonists. The following year, 2006, saw a dubbed version of the German remake exported to other parts of Europe. Hungary's TV2 ran the dubbed *Verliebt in Berlin* remake of the original as *Lisa Csak Egy Van*, while on Switzerland's Television Suisse Romande it became *Le destin de Lisa*. Other European television companies to broadcast dubbed versions of the German (remake) original included France's TF1, Belgium's RTL-TVI, and Slovakia's TV JOJ (Wikipedia 2006).

Aside from the US and German adaptations, the format version of the program has also been customized and remade in seven other territories in Europe and elsewhere (Jasper 2003; de la Fuente 2005). FremantleMedia has been especially associated with several of the European remakes. A Dutch version, *Lotte*, began in early 2006. It was produced by Blue Circle (a FremantleMedia company) and was broadcast on John De Mol's Tien TV (formerly Talpa TV). Later that same year, another licensed remake, *Yo soy Bea* (I am Bea), began on Spanish television. Again, the remake was produced by FremantleMedia International and put to air by Telecinco. Screening weekdays in the early evening, *Yo son Bea* became the country's top-rating daytime program. Another European franchiser came on board early in 2007 when Greece's Mega Channel began broadcasting *Maria, i Asximi* (Maria, the Ugly).

Meanwhile, several other licensed remakes saw the format moving further afield (de la Fuente 2005). Turkey, standing on the edge of Europe and the Middle East, had already seen a dubbed version in 2004. The following year, a format adaptation, *Sensiz Olmuyor* (Won't Work Without You) was produced and screened on Show TV and on Kanal D, but without a great deal of success. On the other hand, Sony Pictures Television International had a big success in Russia with its remake of the Columbian original, beginning in 2005. The program's title, *Ne Rodis' Krasivoy* (Don't Be Born Beautiful) was based on a Russian proverb, and the series followed the original storylines very closely. However, many of its predecessor's feminist and gay references were toned down for the Russian market. Sony was also responsible for an Indian makeover of the program in 2003. There, it was adapted as *Jassi Jaisi Koi Nahin* (There's No One Like Jassi). However, after four years on air, ratings had fallen so production ceased.

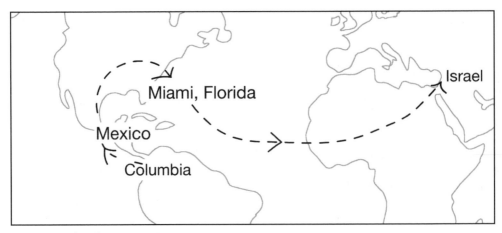

Map 6.8: Other derivative programs.

An even more intriguing loop in the format's circulation had to do with its remaking in Mexico (de Pablos 2006). As already noted, Mexico is the Hollywood of the Spanish-language market and is well placed to ensure high production values and good distribution (Sinclair 2000; Barbera 2004). Early in 2006, *La fea mes bella* began. The adaptation was produced by Televisa SA de CV, and was put to air by Televisa in Mexico and the Spanish-language Univision in the United States. Ratings success in both countries led to the series being renewed several times. Meanwhile, the Mexican version's production quality also led to its dubbing in Portuguese for broadcast in Brazil. Its title there was *A Feia mais Bela*. With this Brazilian dubbing of a Mexican remake of a Columbian original, the telenovela had finally reached the neighbouring market of the largest television territory in Latin America.

The final cluster has to do with unauthorized remakes and spinoffs. *El Amor No Es Cono Lo Pintan* (Love is Not as They Paint It) was a TV Azteca production and appeared on Mexican television in 2005 (Wikipedia 2006; de la Fuente 2005). Concerning the intelligent and ugly Alicia who works in a PR firm, it was very similar to *Yo soy Betty, la fea*, but there appeared to be no connection to the Columbian production. A seemingly unendorsed Israeli version began in 2003 on Keshet Broadcasting (Channel 2). Produced by Darset Productions Ltd, *Esti Ha' mechoeret* (Ugly Esti) proved popular enough for a spinoff, *Elvis, Rosetal, VeHalsha Hamistorit* (Elvis, Rosenthal and the Mystery Woman) to appear in 2005. Back in Columbia, RCN Television produced and aired *Eco moda*, a much less successful 26-episode sequel to *Yo soy Betty, la fea*. Finally, TeleFutura, a US (Miami, Florida) Spanish-language broadcast television network owned by Univision, was responsible for an animated *Yo soy Betty, la fea* spinoff. *Betty Toons* focused on Betty's childhood, and was the first Spanish-language adult cartoon series.

Summary

This chapter has continued the engagement with spaces of television market concentration and dispersal. It has mapped geographical routes between the axle, spokes and rim of trade in audio-visual properties. The flow of global TV, especially program franchising, has been traced in three ways. First, the manner in which trade organizations in the market think about and organize the various territories of the world on both a large and a small scale was scrutinized. Second, I have profiled a series of markets in Western Europe and East Asia. These highlight the variations and differences in territories across the two regions and emphasize the extent to which national industries are players as well as spectators in the global trade. Finally, the chapter investigated the cross-border flow of the telenovela *Yo soy Betty, la fea/Ugly Betty*. In its canned version, the program was mostly restricted to sales in Latin America, whereas its international distributive potential expanded considerably when it became a format. A format is not, however, a magic bullet. Its adaptation and remaking to suit a particular domestic market are a complicated matter. The services of a travelling consultant producer who accompanies a format as part of the licensed package are especially important in this negotiation. The next chapter addresses this subject.

7

Envoys

I do not always stick to the author's words, nor even to his thoughts. I keep the effect he wanted to produce in mind, and then I arrange the material after the fashion of our time. Different times do not just require different words, but also different thoughts, and ambassadors usually dress in the fashion of the country they are sent to, for fear of appearing ridiculous in the eyes of the people they try to please (Perrot d'Ablancount, quoted in Heylen 1994: 6).

Introduction

The export of canned television programs has its basis in a series of different recording technologies, including kinescoping, filming, videotaping and digital archiving (O'Dell 2004; Fong 2004; Griffiths 2003). With the second mode of the format television program, its export is more intimately dependent on human agency. Franchising involves a set of services or licensed knowledges which facilitate the program being adapted in another territory for broadcast to local or national audiences. This chapter is concerned with the production figure who journeys to licensing companies in different territories to assist them in developing their own adaptations of particular program formats. Specific production know-how, valuable industrial knowledge, is on the move to all corners of the world in the person of the travelling producer (Wright 2005). One can usefully think of the process of interaction between this consultant and local production teams as that of transproduction (Chalaby 2005). The term represents an amalgamation of the notion of translation and production. Translation should be thought of in physical as well as figurative terms. Knowledge is transported from one place to another by one who visits and then leaves. A source text is transposed as another text that is accessible and intelligible in another culture, perhaps even in another language (Garcia Canclini 1995). Production, the making of television programs, is a central part of this process, reminding us that a complex set of cultural, business and social considerations and practices comes into play in the process of adaptation. What is at stake is not only the putting together of a (new) program based on a program format predecessor but, simultaneously, a translation of one or more earlier texts into one that is more culturally intelligible to audiences in the new territory. The production ambassador representing the format licensing company is a key gatekeeper in this process and is the subject of this chapter (Moran forthcoming; Waisbord and Jalfin forthcoming).

Understanding adaptation

Consultant producers are saddled with the task of adapting a new production of a program format under the terms of a franchising agreement. There is no single, agreed-upon name for the process that brings the new version of the format into being (van Leeuwen 2006). It may, variously and loosely, be called adaptation. What is more important is to get a tighter grasp on the process of transformation involved in the exchange between an earlier and a later version of a television format program. An increasing number of incidental studies of the outcomes of such transformations are now appearing (Schroeder 1992; Moran 1998; Banerjee 2002; Clausen 2004; Frau-Meigs 2006; Hetsroni 2005; Ranganathan and Lobo 2008; Wang and Yeh 2005). On the other hand, only a handful of writers have attempted to understand this process of transformation in more general terms (cf. Mangiron and O'Hagan 2006; Ranganathan and Lobo 2008).

Localizing the global

Two different approaches or models of the process of cultural translation can be identified as background to understanding the work of the visiting program translator. The first is represented by a categorical model of adaptation. Here, the process of change is divided into separate stages in the process. Each stage is distinct and separate, although each has some features in common with the stages immediately before and after. The second model of cultural translation is more analogic and fluid. It stresses the continuity in the process of exchange and might be called a relational model of adaptation.

Categorical models

At least two different authors have proposed examples of a kind of transformation that is helpful in understanding the general context of program format adaptation. Paul Lee (1991), focusing on cultural traffic from foreign places to Hong Kong, has suggested a four-part schema which is theoretically ambitious even if its stages are quite homely and domestic in their designation. Meanwhile, in his work on cultural transmission of literary texts, Yuri Lotman (1990) has developed a semiotic model of exchange that involves five different stages of interaction between cultures. Table 7.1 sets out the different phases of the two schemes and allows a brief exploration of Lee and Lotman's constructs.

After examining developments in cinema, television and popular music imported from elsewhere into Hong Kong, Lee (1991) suggests a typology of what he calls absorption and indigenization of foreign culture. He suggests four different metaphors as a means of indicating elements of this process. The first stage is that of the parrot pattern. Just as this bird can copy a human voice without understanding any part of an utterance, so a preliminary move in the incorporation and localization of foreign cultural form and content may happen with little or no understanding of its

Table 7.1: Categorical stages of cultural translation

Schema author makeover stages	Lee categories	Lotman categories
Minimal	1. Parrot	1. Strangeness
	2. Amoeba	2. Indigenization
	3. Coral	3. National-internationalism
	4. Butterfly	4. (In-between)
Maximum		5. Commendation

meaning. In the case of Hong Kong, Lee suggests that there are few examples of the kind of total transfer of foreign material that is implied in this first stage of absorption and indigenization. The amoeba pattern constitutes a second, less minimal adaptation. It is 'one which keeps the content but changes the form, just like an amoeba which appears different in form but remains the same in substance all the time' (1991: 64). As example, Lee cites a magazine-type television program imported from the United States, which is minimally refashioned for local audiences by having a Chinese host who links the program's unconverted segments together.

The third stage is the coral pattern. It is a practice of indigenization 'which keeps the form but changes the content, just like the coral which maintains the coral shape after it has died although its substance has already changed' (1991: 55). Here, the degree of indigenization appears to be greater than was the case in the amoeba stage and may in fact be sufficient to persuade some audiences that the cultural artefact is of local origin, an apparently indigenous production. The fourth and final stage is the butterfly pattern. The absorption and indigenization of imported form and content are almost complete, and audiences are hard put to distinguish the product from truly indigenous production. Lee argues that 'this pattern usually takes a longer time to take shape and the change is likened to the emergence of a butterfly. A butterfly evolves slowly from the pupa to a full-fledged stage where one can no longer tell its original form or content.' (1991: 66)

Lotman also identifies a series of distinct stages, although his descriptions are less homely. He distinguishes five stages. The first involves a retention of 'strangeness'. The imported texts or formats 'hold a high position in the scale of values, and are considered to be true, beautiful, of divine origin' (1990: 146). There is little attempt to alter or transform any of the elements of the predecessor. In turn, the second stage is one of 'indigenization'. The 'imported texts and the home culture are said to restructure each other' (1990: 147). In this phase, 'translations, imitations and adaptations multiply' and 'the codes imported along with the texts become part of the meta lingual structure' (1990: 147). Commenting on this stage in terms of Australian cinema, O'Regan (1996) has claimed a particular synthesis between the local and the imported: '[It] gives rise to a relatively strict division of labour: the Australian is the content, the flavour, the accent and the social text, while the international provides the underlying form, values, narrative resolutions, etc.' (1996: 218)

The third stage might be called one of national-internationalism. There is a mutual accommodation between the 'imported' text and the 'home' culture, wherein the two reorganize each other. 'Translations, imitations and adaptations multiply. At the same time the codes imported along with the texts become part of the meta lingual structure.' (Lotman 1990: 146–47). This new system is not seen as one dominated by imported codes but rather as an adjusted internationalism. O'Regan (1996) comments that impressions are crucial in this phase. The stage 're-evaluates the culture's product in a situation of assumed international comparison' (1996: 220). The fourth stage is least articulated and developed by Lotman. O'Regan therefore offers his own characterization of it as an 'in between stage' (1996: 220). It seems to be an intensification of the previous stage. As Lotman (1990) puts it, 'the imported texts are entirely dissolved in the receiving culture; the culture itself changes to a state of activity and begins rapidly to produce new texts; these new texts are based on cultural codes which in the distant past were stimulated by invasions from outside, but which now have been wholly transformed through the many asymmetrical transformations into a new and original structural model' (1990: 147). O'Regan also detects an overlap with the second stage (1990: 221). Finally, the fifth stage is one wherein exemplary texts are produced by the receiving culture. The process is one of commendation. The latter culture 'becomes … a transmitting culture and issues forth a flood of texts directed to other, peripheral areas' (Lotman 1990: 146)

Both the Lee and Lotman typologies are, up to a point at least, clear and relatively easy to apply. This is not, however, to deny the blurring that occurs between any of the categories and their neighbours. In addition, both Lee and Lotman indicate that the different types may be in operation simultaneously and that, in practice, the stages are not sequential or progressive. They hint that the process of absorption and indigenization may be more dialectic than this kind of model is capable of suggesting. Accordingly, in anticipation of the analysis of the interaction between a travelling consultant and a local production team, the second part of this survey of cultural indigenization theory turns to a different kind of explanatory model.

A relational model of cultural translation
In his two essays, 'Discourse in the Novel' (1981) and 'The Problem of Speech Genres' (1986), Mikhail Bakhtin is concerned with dialogic processes that operate in the domains of communication and culture. Implicitly arguing against communication as a simple act of meaning transfer, he stresses the notion of the utterance as the way in which speech obtains a concrete reality belonging to an actual subject. In turn, dialogue emerges out of those utterances as a second speaker listens and then responds to the first (1984: 276). However, Bakhtin stresses that even an initial utterance that may appear to initiate a particular dialogue is already a part of other dialogues, both immediate and remote, which are saturated with meanings and will, in any case, be responded to in the present and in the future (1984: 279). In other words, dialogue is a complex, multidimensional environment without discernible or predictable boundaries and limits. As Miller (2000), commenting on Bakhtin, has suggested, 'as the message and its speaker become enmeshed in a web of meanings beyond their immediate apprehension, so too does the respondent' (2000: 12). Or, as Bakhtin himself puts it, the utterance:

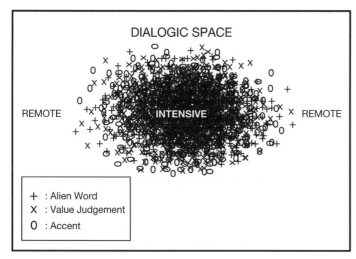

Figure 7.1: Relational model of cultural translation.

enters a dialogically agitated and tension-filled environment of alien words, value judgements and accents, weaves in and out of interrelationships, merges with some, recoils from others, intersects with yet a third group: and all this may crucially shape discourse (1986: 80).

This proposition is very resonant for the matter in hand, the process whereby a television format is actioned at the local level in an operation through which it becomes a television program that has an enduring, material existence. The process of acclimatization is a complex one that involves many elements negotiated between a visiting consultant and a local production team. Some parts of such a process seem to lend themselves to understanding under the categorical model of program translation while others are more usefully seen in the light of this relational model of cultural adaptation. In effect, both are useful tools in coming to grips with the activity of the localization of a television format. The visiting consultant is a pivotal figure in this process.

An ambassador to foreign courts

As a first step, it is important to recall the system or network that is put into place and maintained through the practice of local adaptation of format programming. Format programming is developed and distributed from a global television metropolis that is principally the American-European rim. In turn, this centre compels and facilitates a periphery constituted by those local television broadcasting and production groups that license these formats as a means of ensuring that they are producing and scheduling that which is deemed to be modern, topical, fashionable and innovative (Waisbord 2004; van Leeuwen 2006; Mangiron and O'Hagan 2006). Thus a worldwide network of television programming suppliers and supplied is organized and maintained by means of the mechanism of the format. To deepen one's understanding of the global ramifications of format distribution, it is necessary to analyze activities of the travelling producer and his or her dealings with regional production companies.

It is worth outlining as a first step the circumstances under which the production of a licensed adaptation takes place. A complex, coherent body of knowledge is made available to the would-be production company in another territory as part of a standard franchising arrangement. While part of this involves such elements as written material (synopses, notes, scripts, 'bible', etc.) and software (electronic files of graphics, music, off-air recordings and so on), another part has to do with human expertise. This consultative service frequently comes in the form of a visiting producer sent to help oversee the initial production of a format program in that territory. While this process is motivated by the licensor's desire to protect the integrity of its property, including the avoidance of known cultural and technical pitfalls, the operation is an interactive one involving ongoing negotiation with the local producer and production team. Of course, this kind of interaction is by no means necessarily confined to two individual figures, but may occur across a larger number of personnel representing licensor and licensee respectively.

Several figures may fulfil these roles. With the Indian version of *Who Wants to Be a Millionaire?*, licensed from Celador in the United Kingdom, which went to air on Star TV as *Kaun Banega Crorepat*, there was more interaction between more figures in the original setting up of the adaptation (Spenser 2006). Celador put a great deal of work into this, not least to ensure the success of the program and to maintain the value of the brand and the franchise. Three staff from the London office were sent out to India to train a local production team. In turn, four Indians then went to the United Kingdom for further training.

Even more important than how many production personnel fill the role of consultant producer is the matter of production responsibility. Who makes the final decision between visitor and local? This is hard to answer conclusively. After all, a visiting producer has the knowledge and expertise that is attached to a format, whereas a local producer has an expertise arising from the specific production situation and the local culture as a whole. That latter team will inevitably be beholden to the licensing company in order to ensure that the adaptation will repeat the popular success of a predecessor production.

Hence the travelling producer, on behalf of the licensing company, must inevitably be seen as a crucial gatekeeper even if a good deal of mutual respect develops over time between the international and the local companies. Stephen Freedman, who has been a travelling producer consultant on game shows for King World, their franchise owner, explained this interaction as follows:

> In Australia and New Zealand, Grundy sublicensed *Wheel of Fortune* from us. Recently, when they changed the host, they cleared it with us. It's really just like a handshake and so long as the integrity of the format is unchanged and there's no legal problem as far as changing the game or the premise or format we have no problem with that. In many cases, the cultural side of it dictates minor changes and we have to agree that they know what they are doing in their own culture (Freedman 1996).

Complicating the matter even further is the situation where several different adaptations of a format have already taken place. Usually, different – even somewhat disparate – knowledges may be tapped in a new adaptation. This was the case with the first production of the Australian *Big Brother* in 2001. As Tim Clukas, senior executive with the commissioning network, put it:

> Early on in the piece we had a production manager from the UK to help. But Endemol didn't like it because the UK Channel 4 version was the one they had no control over. She left at Christmas time and never came back, but in that time she helped us understand how the Brits had made it so successful for an English-speaking audience (Clukas 2002).

The local production company is not usually in a position to choose between different versions of a format and different sets of production experiences. Instead, its activities are likely to be directed and controlled by the visiting producer, even if the latter depends on a team of local workers to carry out tasks necessary to ensure the effective adaptation of a format. The travelling producer is effectively the team leader, the gatekeeper who shapes and moulds the effort of local producers and technicians

Standardization and de-localization

Taken together, what the quotes in the previous section suggest is that there is often a good deal of difference – even struggle – and disagreement as to the permitted degree of variation from an earlier version of the program that will be sanctioned or not sanctioned by the licensing company. One might suggest a range of translation possibilities so far as an adaptation is concerned. At one pole, there is the literal translation, the adaptation that remains very close in form and style to an earlier prescribed version, one that is (to the extent to which it is possible) equivalent to that earlier version even to the point of (approximate) substitutability. Clearly, Endemol had this kind of adaptation or translation in mind when it came to the production of an Australian version of *Big Brother*. It preferred that the Dutch version of the program should serve as the urtext rather than drawing on the UK version and its attendant experiences.

This kind of standardization finds echoes elsewhere in entertainment industries, as well as more broadly in society (Robertson 1997; Ritzer 1998). Burston, for example, has analyzed the situation of popular musical theatre that is based on the licensing of local adaptations of stage formats in such cities as London, Toronto and New York (Burston 2000) He finds that with musical shows such as *The Lion King* and *The Hunchback of Notre Dame*, licence owners have insisted that each adaptation should closely follow a prescribed pattern. There is no opportunity for local imagination or input to come into play. Instead, the clear intention is to standardize each new version of the stage show and ensure that it is equivalent to a source production.

It is rare to find rigid insistence on prototypes and unwillingness to localize adaptations in the field of stage musicals; such insistence is equally uncommon in the arena of television format adaptation. Nevertheless, two recent examples in the area of game shows – Celador's *Who Wants to Be a Millionaire?* and the BBC's *The Weakest Link* – have made few, if any, concessions to local sensibilities and culture, no matter where they have been adapted. Instead, the stipulation has been that there be no variation from a set body of elements when it comes to remakes in particular territories. Graham Spenser, a London-based producer, called attention to this literal tendency in adaptations of the former program:

> In Asia, *Who Wants to Be a Millionaire?* as a format is the same. In every single one of the 120 or so countries, it's absolutely the same, and that was rigorously insisted on both contractually and by the executive producers who went out with it. Because it was a workable format and they believed it was indigenous to people, not to cultures and races (Spenser 2006).

Similarly, another experienced consultant-producer, Bob Cousins from FremantleMedia, who has worked in many different markets around the world helping to develop local adaptations of international formats, noted a parallel standardization with adaptations of the latter format:

> A fairly recent phenomenon ... has been a stipulation that absolutely nothing is changed. If you watch *The Weakest Link* from around the world, they are absolutely identical. Under the format of the BBC they go to great lengths to insist that everything is exactly as the episode produced in the UK is and the only place where they have had much variation on that is the USA. I suspect that is because the US producers have a lot more financial clout when faced with a situation of 'Either we change this or we change the show'. I can't see anybody standing up to that. In the show 'bible' it's specified down to the two-tone colours of the backdrops (Cousins 2006).

These instances of adaptation, where a particular model is standardized and no allowance is made for local sensibility or sensitivity, are the exception rather than the rule. In fact, this course of action may be a strategy where matters of legal protection of the franchise property override local cultural considerations. The thinking appears to be that format owners are in a better legal position to challenge perceived infringement if their own adaptations adhere closely to the same formula (Cousins 2006; Spenser 2006).

Figure 7.2: Australian look-alike remake of the BBC's *The Weakest Link.*

Towards localization

In any case, moving along a spectrum of repetition-within-difference so far as adaptation of format programming is concerned, there is the possibility of a more poetic translation, the remaking that varies the form and style of a source so that it bears a looser resemblance to the latter. The words of translator Perrot d'Ablancount quoted at the beginning of this chapter come to mind. Within a pattern of sameness, then, this kind of adaptation is different to the extent that it is no longer really substitutable for its predecessor, no longer a literal translation. One could suggest that this kind of program translation might still be faithful to the spirit of a predecessor, even while it has taken on board cultural sensitivities having to do with the place of its redeployment.

The latter formulation might be regarded as imprecise and disputable. Still, the model of two polar types of translation allows the mapping of particular format adaptations. Hence one can recognize that Stephen Freedman in the statement quoted above is talking about the second type of adaptation when he refers to the locally enculturated version of *Wheel of Fortune* produced in Australia by Grundy compared with a US-based source version. This more flexible, looser type of adaptation is by far the more common in international television program format licensing arrangements. The simple reason for this pragmatism lies in the fact that licensor and licensee take a large commercial gamble if they assume that a format can be transproduced in other territories without taking local cultural experience and outlook into account. On the other hand, the literal translation and successive successes of the game show *Who Wants to Be a Millionaire?* across many territories in the world seemed to suggest that the model of retaining a very high correspondence between an earlier UK original version and subsequent translations elsewhere would succeed. As Cousins notes above, the BBC then gravitated to this pole with remakes of *The Weakest Link*, refusing as it did to localize the format according to particular territories' culture and peoples. By and large, this strategy was not especially successful and many different national versions lasted only one or two seasons. Graham Spenser drew an important cultural lesson from this history for the consequences of refusing to localize format adaptations in Asia. Indeed this format, with its domineering female quiz compere, presented an insoluble dilemma for such adaptations. On the one hand, both the format owner and its Asian licensees wanted to retain intact the central ingredient of the dominant woman compere. On the other hand, such a figure had no cultural resonance in that part of the world. As he put it:

There are other formats which need acclimatization to make them work, and yet others which are fashionable, and everyone wants them, but cannot work. For instance, *The Weakest Link*. It was big on the BBC so the Asian nations all wanted it. But the dominant woman was a problem in Asia, and the encouragement of the contestants to out each other down and vote each other off, cause each other to lose face, is an issue for the Asian nations. So after one season, it was usually taken off. You cannot change the loss of face element in *The Weakest Link*. You do away with that sort of dominatrix and subservience that is its central structure (Spenser 2006).

Indigenization

The more general consequence not only of this particular adaptation, but of the practice generally, is the need to approach such translation as a kind of cooperative undertaking that requires the valued contribution of both the licensing company and its ambassador consultant, and the licensee company and the human and non-human resources it provides. While it is not necessarily an equitable relationship, it is the case that both parties bring different knowledges and expertise to the business of the program indigenization. The format company has extensive specialist insight about the format while the local production company has cultural knowledge of the region. Variation is almost constantly necessary because, as Freedman notes above, the latter body knows what it is doing when it decides to modify elements of a universal format to suit the needs of a local audience. Again, though, within the international television industry there is a recognition that this toleration of variation cannot become a blank cheque. As Graham Spenser pointed out: 'Too much cultural tinkering ends up with a very bland show which, because of that will fail.' (Spenser 2006) At the same time, there needs to be a flexibility on the part of the licensing company towards a necessary cultural acclimatization of the program format so that it is compatible and accessible to local tastes and outlook. Referring to the production of different national versions of game shows, another adaptation specialist, Bob Cousins of FremantleMedia, explained:

> As a guy who goes around the world doing start-up game shows, my view and our company's view is that shows need to look like they come from that country, and ... there's also sensitivities of a cultural nature, mainly in colour. The show that you see in Sweden, if you take the same show to South Africa the colours have to be very different. If you look at episodes of *Family Feud* in Mexico and Venezuela, the number of hues is huge, the number and intensity. If you looked at *Sale of the Century* from Mexico, the number of colours is huge compared with a European production. We take the view that people in their own country know what they like best, that's why we have local production teams (Cousins 2006).

Writing about the process of translation in relation to linguistic texts, Lefevre (1993) has suggested that three levels of negotiation can be distinguished (1993: 14). These have to do with the domain of linguistic codes, the sphere of inter-textual codes and the realm of larger cultural codes. This is a suggestive typology that will be used to frame the remainder of discussion while recognizing that the concern is with the adaptation of television programs rather than with the translation of literary texts from one language to another (Bagumet and Schiller 1990; Venuti 1995). All the same, the tripartite division is suggestive in ordering the remarks of those practitioners involved in the process of format adaptation. Hence Cousins' thoughts about screen colours in different game show adaptations in different parts of the world might be seen as an instance of the negotiation of textual codes that operate at a level analogous to that of linguistic codes in relation to literary translation. Similarly, Grundy's action noted by Freedman in changing a game show compere or in altering another on-screen detail might also be viewed as part of transformations in the textual code. What, then, of the negotiation of the other two codes in the process of TV format program adaptation?

Figure 7.3: Imagining the British *Coronation Street* as the Chinese *Joy Luck Street*

Globalizing the Local

If textual elements are relatively straightforward to handle in the remaking of a source format as an adaptation, whether by omission, inclusion, substitution or permutation, the manipulation of inter-textual elements is another matter entirely. These are more varied in scope so that their orchestration can set in train other necessary changes. One domain of inter-textual codes affecting the acclimatization of a TV format has to do with the national conditions of television production. When a format is adapted into a local culture, it is tacitly assumed that the conditions of production in the new territory replicate, or can be made to replicate, the institutional framework of production in which the format was first devised, developed and produced. One scholar usefully refers to this phenomenon as cultural proximity (Straubhaar 1997, 2003, 2007). This perceived fit may or may not prove to be the case. In the latter instance, it is common to find that a visiting producer has been forced to make decisive intervention in the production regime of an adaptation. When Grundy World Wide, for example, was producing a Spanish version of *Sale of the Century* by videotaping in a television studio in Madrid, the visiting producer sent from Australia found it impossible to make the five episodes a day that were customary in Australia and elsewhere in the English-speaking world (Kolle 1995; Mason 1998). Daytime temperatures at that time of the year under lights in the studios in Madrid were as high as 50 degrees Celsius. In such hot conditions, cameras simply ceased to function. Initially Bill Mason, the visiting producer, was forced to make the program according to local practice, one episode at a time. However, as executive producer in charge of the production, he realized that temperatures cooled considerably at night. This enabled him to introduce a new production culture in line with the one with which he was familiar. Production was rescheduled to late at night, and this enabled five episodes to be completed at a time.

This point about the visiting producer being a bearer of production expertise, not only concerning a particular format but also with regard to more general institutional conditions and arrangements, is worth emphasizing. A format inevitably has the imprint on it of a whole production milieu, a particular way of doing television and of thinking about television, so that this is the ideational baggage the visiting producer carries with him or her. Increasingly, that production culture shouldered by the visitor is an international one which bespeaks a global television industry (Waisbord 2004; Clausen 2004; Fung 2008). Not surprisingly, this point about having to readjust local production conditions to help facilitate the remaking of a formatted program was raised repeatedly in interviews. Such an emphasis serves to underline the point that the licensing of a format from elsewhere may trigger a cross-cultural exchange that begins with the readjustment of ways of working in television, whether by camera operator, editor, writer or others. Bob Cousins talked about visiting Uzbekistan to set up a production adaptation of *Family Feud* and discovering in the process that he needed to teach a camera operator how to frame master shots and other shots. Bill Mason made the same point about having to explain the basics to production personnel in a new system when he remarked:

> If we take *Sale of the Century* to a new country, we are probably going to train people in that country in a new system of making TV. In the past they have made one or two episodes a day so the first leap is to make five in a day. It's important to have a role model so the set designers, electricians, camera operators, all the technical people have got a model to work from (Mason 1998).

This kind of interchange is hardly surprising. After all, a format franchising involves more than just details that enable a new programming version to look like a predecessor in another territory. Instead, the format (including the consultative services of the visiting producer) represents a comprehensive and complex body of knowledge so that a significant readjustment in local production culture becomes necessary. Norms, routines and practices that are perhaps indigenous to a local television production culture have to be readjusted to a different regime that is more international (Storper 2002). In effect, in its own small and particular way, local television culture is being embedded in a more global system.

Figure 7.4: *The Honeymooners* – the US original.

Figure 7.5: The Polish remake of *The Honeymooners.*

Localizing the global

If a visiting producer is the gatekeeper for a more cosmopolitan production culture, then the local television production team might be said to act as the gatekeeper on behalf of the national television industry. Elements of the local production milieu exert a kind of countervailing pressure, causing an adaptation to become richer and more generative, and to move away from the model provided by an earlier production. The adaptive history of the Australian drama serial *The Restless Years* is one of many examples that support such a suggestion. The Australian original was produced from 1978 to 1983 and became the basis for successive format adaptations in both The Netherlands and Germany (O'Donnell 1999; Moran 1998). The Dutch *Goede Tijden, Slechte Tijden* began on air in 1990 while the German *Gute Zeiten, Schlechte Zeiten* commenced in 1992. After initially following the original Australian scripts, the two adaptations soon began to develop new stories, characters and situations. Both serials are still on air at the time of writing. The example underlines the fruitful influence that a local production culture can have on an adaptation.

Indeed, this positive local impact on an international format seems especially marked with the genre of drama and the drama serial. It appears to be the case that, with this genre, a greater range of elements come into play than is the case with some other program types such as game shows (Moran 1997; Buonanno forthcoming). Various local factors can intervene to introduce new inflections into program adaptations generally and drama translations particularly. One Australian writer explained this process of variation as follows:

> The show in Holland based on *The Restless Years*, for a long time they tried to hold it to just translating the original scripts. But they found that they couldn't after a period of time. Sometimes quite different characters rise to prominence. In Australia there may be a character who seems dominant due to casting. But you may not find such a strong

actor in another culture ... other characters, who were minor here, become more dynamic because of the casting, which changes the emphasis too. In the German version of *Sons and Daughters* the twins are much more dynamic and Pat the Rat is just a minor character. Here it became the 'Pat the Rat' show, but I don't think the German version will (Kolle 1995).

Local details

Production is not a one-way street so far as the registration of place or placelessness is concerned. Frequently, a push in one direction finds itself countered by a pull in another. This is the case with the particular mode or genre of a format and the localizing disposition it might entail. Are there significant considerations that come into play depending on the generic type to which a format adaptation belongs? The answer appears to be 'yes'. In the previous section, I suggested that there is greater latitude for cultural variation with drama series than there is with game shows. This point was echoed by producer Graham Spenser, who believes that game shows and single-issue talk programs are more international than other genres of format programming. These types appear to travel well across national cultures. With talk shows, though, it was a matter of 'How far do you let the audience go with the subject?' On the other hand, a dating show was 'culturally difficult' in different parts of the world. Even with a game show, a good deal of preparation was essential to ensure a necessary accommodation between format and local culture. Adaptation is a dynamic process. Various cultural screenings come into play – some of them are to do with the exigencies of production itself while others relate to the larger, more everyday context in which the production adaptation itself is anchored. Spenser put it like this:

As far as the cultural differences are concerned, it is important to realize that the questions are totally different from one culture to another. They are not just translated. Historical facts vary from country to country. So you have to quickly start to make a

Figure 7.6: Russian adaptation of the US sitcom *I Love Lucy*.

questions databank which is accurate for that country and have it verified and checked again. We use two or three sources to make sure we have the facts right. Then you audition the contestants using those questions because we want a new standard and some idea of what it will be. The writers will need some trial and error to find a level at which some questions are answered correctly but some not. The aim of the show is to get all the audience to get 50 per cent of the questions correct, so that the involvement factor is high (Spenser 2006).

However, this kind of filtering represents only one chain of decisions that must be made in between many others. This travelling producer, highly experienced in the area of game show adaptation, went on to mention a series of further cultural factors that also have to be addressed in the remaking of a franchised program:

Finding the right level of contestants is the next step. The computer people have usually never seen this stuff before and we have to hold their hands, and also the electronics. The sets and hostess dresses are often chosen by the network, which has some favourite ideas and colours, but they have to agree with the skin tones (Spenser 2006).

Cultural universes

Even beyond this need to develop local audience resonance and significance in a format adaptation, there is the matter of a more general cultural overlap or disparity. After all, irrespective of the genre involved, a format program will carry particular situations, figures, subject-matter and issues, and the extent to which these will be recognizable and acceptable within particular cultural settings may vary considerably. Hence Graeme Spenser saw no reason why *Survivor* would not work in Asia and the Middle East, even though no broadcaster in these regions had acquired the licence. After all, he pointed out, *Who Wants to Be a Millionaire?* did enormously well in India. Frequently, though, regional or local culture will deem specific subjects and situations taboo and will not entertain them on local television screens. One case in point was the Middle Eastern version of *Big Brother* that has already been touched on in the previous chapter. This adaptation was broadcast to several national territories in the region. In Lebanon, according to Spenser (2006), the local French influence allowed for a more tolerant reception but in Saudi Arabia there was great anger and outcry.

Similarly, in the early 1990s Grundy Television had developed a telenovela for Chilean television based on a successful Australian format. This was the Australian company's first venture into what was for it a foreign genre. Unlike *Big Brother*, the would-be adaptation did not go to air because its apparent cultural incompatibility with social mores operating in the territory had registered during an earlier phase of audience testing. As one of the storyliners put it:

The Chilean drama fell through because they did a focus group on it and the audience reacted with great shock at the hint of romance between brother and sister, the basic *Sons and Daughters* story. The twins that had been separated [at birth] meet as adults and fall in love. The focus group felt that the audience in Chile [would] tend to react as the government thought they should react, being a very Catholic country. And the channel withdrew it (Kolle 1995).

Macro settings

These two cases of the Middle Eastern version of *Big Brother* and a would-be Chilean version of *Sons and Daughters* constitute relatively external, although highly significant, matters to do with the production culture. On the other hand, there are always larger social matters in play, which may or may not be recognized by those involved in a production. These more general issues frequently have a direct bearing on the very heart of a production, and whether or not it is compatible with more significant mores of the society. This was also the case in Chile with the *Sons and Daughters* telenovela already mentioned, where other cultural differences made it impossible to transfer a significant detail from the Australian original. As the writer recalled:

> Another problem was one of the twins whisking the girl off on her wedding day, a la *The Graduate*. But it fell apart because in Chile … they get married legally a day or two before the big ceremony. And so he couldn't bundle her off in her wedding gown. Chile is surprisingly European but the attitude of men to women is still very chauvinist and it affected the Pat the Rat character (Kolle 1995).

Yet another element that needs to be recognized has to do with the larger historical situation that sets particular cultural elements in play. Attempting to explain the success of the Polish adaptation of the 1950s US television sitcom *The Honeymooners*, Bob Cousins tended to emphasize a set of temporal elements. On the one hand, he detected a kind of universally appealing situation that made the format timeless and eternally appealing to the female part of the general Polish audience. As he put it:

> Women in Poland, they are very patient and sensible and the strength behind [men]. If you look at *The Honeymooners*, she is common sense, when he's blowing his top she says 'Oh, come on Ralph, don't be so silly'. I think there's a lot of that in the Polish female. They do actually have a lot more power than the men would wish and they are the strength behind the patriarch there. As is Alice (Cousins 2001).

At the same time, though, there were perhaps other elements in the program that gave it more contemporary resonance with the larger historical situation in which Polish society found itself:

> There's something in the Polish psyche that says 'Yeah, but I wouldn't do that'. At this time Poland was only ten years out of communist rule and the society was changing a great deal. And the story of a man always wanting to better himself has relevance. People are bettering themselves and moving up from mundane existences in jobs that were created to keep them employed. There's a huge entrepreneurial spirit there now, people set up all sorts of businesses from small beginnings and they like it (Cousins 2001).

Figure 7.7: Culturally offensive? The original dominant woman compere of the BBC show *The Weakest Link*.

Finally, to complete this account, it must be recognized that the success or otherwise of a format adaptation lies not so much in the efforts, sensitivities and actions of those involved in the translation process – whether as visiting producers or as local production teams. These are all important, but the most significant ingredient of all is the national television public. It is the local audience that forms the most relevant yardstick so far as deciding about the degree of successful localization a format has undergone. I will conclude by quoting the case offered by one visiting producer where the localization of a format seemed to be so complete as to persuade one of the members of the home audience that a particular program was not an adaptation based on an overseas format import, but rather a fully homegrown production. The producer described this encounter as follows:

Figure 7.8: Publicity shot for Polish stars of *The Honeymooners* remake.

I was talking to a continuity girl and I said, 'Have you watched *The Honeymooners*?' And she said 'Of course, it's very funny. I watch it every week. Why are you interested?' So I said that the company licensed out the scripts and she said 'No, no, this is a Polish show'. This is the greatest accolade when they believe one of our shows is 'local' (Bob Cousins).

Summary

This chapter has concentrated on the process whereby TV program formats are adapted for broadcast to local audiences in different regions and territories. As I have already suggested, TV program formats are simultaneously global and local. As global commodities, they have a universally unrestricted circulation that is unhindered by language, custom, religion or history. At the same time, they find form only in and through individual productions. These adaptations are translations. They carry formats across space and time to all parts of the world. The travelling producer has been identified as a key figure in this business of format remaking. However, apart from such consultative services, there are other mechanisms that also support and orchestrate activities in outlying television markets. The wares of merchants have always attracted the attention of pirates as well as the interests of respectable traders. Hence the next chapter examines modern-day versions of alleged piracy so far as TV format programming is concerned and looks at the steps that licence owners take to protect their goods.

8

PIRACY

If nature has made any one thing less susceptible than all others of exclusive property, it is the action of the thinking power called an idea, which an individual may exclusively possess as long as he keeps it to himself; but the moment it is divulged, it forces itself into the possession of everyone, and the receiver cannot dispose himself of it... Its peculiar character, too, is that no one possesses the less, because every other possesses the whole of it. He who receives an idea from me, receives instruction himself without lessening mine; as he who lights his taper at mine, receives light without darkening me (Thomas Jefferson 1789, quoted in Vaidhyanathan 2001: 23–24).

Introduction

The development of a mature international TV format industry represents a massive financial restructuring of broadcasting in many parts of the world. The program genres currently undergoing the most widespread use in the new mode – reality, makeover, talent contests and game shows – have proved very lucrative for their format owners, especially when television interfaces with new telecommunications and computer technologies. Even more important than the financial value of this form of cultural commodification is the further transnationalization of production, broadcasting and marketing. Hitherto, this sector of television industries has lain under the control of mostly national agencies and organizations. However, international trade has been beyond the reach of these state instrumentalities. Additionally, there are no such regulatory bodies in existence at the international level. Such a situation is both a curse and a blessing so far as television program format owners are concerned. The lack of an overseeing authority is a misfortune because appropriation of one kind or another of format ideas is common, and there is no supervisory agency that can police such practice. On the other hand, the larger, more powerful television organizations find that they can further strengthen their market position by creating a cultural shortage to do with their formats. Since the early 1980s especially, there has been an implicit aim across the industry to enhance scarcity by linking formats to that domain of law collectively known as intellectual property. The particular methods of enhancing monopoly and exclusivity pursued by format owners are by no means novel. These measures include restricting use, juggling prices, confining licences to a chosen few, using law and the courts against others, threatening and scaring competitors, and making exaggerated claims about legal sanction and support.

This chapter develops a critical perspective concerning the use of law and other measures in the TV format industry as a further, and ever more important, component of that trade. Discussion is divided into two major sections. The first has to do with a series of ideas that are frequently galvanized to support notions of exclusivity and ownership of cultural concepts, especially those to do with TV program formats. Demonizing appropriation as piracy is one such weapon against competitors. But even more useful are particular historical developments concerning creativity, especially the invention of notions of originality and genius. In the nineteenth and twentieth centuries, capitalist forces obtained legal sanction to understand creative ideas as a form of non-physical but very real exclusive possession. The steady, widening march of intellectual property thinking has ensured that over the last quarter of a century there has been a concerted effort to gain legal protection for TV program formats. Intellectual property itself is an evolving arsenal of legal weapons that are increasingly used to press claims of exclusivity and ownership. Meanwhile, the second part of the chapter analyzes a train of legal cases that have facilitated the expanding insinuation of TV formats as intellectual property. These have particularly involved claims to copyright protection for formats themselves. Until recently, TV program formats have not been afforded this kind of legal protection. Nevertheless, there has been a steady stream of recent legal claims alleging infringement. Mostly these have not been upheld, so that generic variation of TV programs by competitors has implicitly been sanctioned by the courts. Paradoxically, though, courts are at the same time increasingly of the view that TV formats are protected by copyright law.

Piracy as rhetoric

Piracy is a dramatic metaphor conjuring up vivid images of physical and violent theft in the past or even in the present, occurring on the high seas and on land by bold buccaneers. The contemporary appropriation of the term to describe elements of interaction within the TV format industry (as well as in many other domains of cultural practice) deliberately demonizes activities of borrowing and adaptation. Although these practices have had a long historical legitimacy in art and entertainment, nevertheless discourses of piracy orchestrated by representatives of TV format owners, film and television producers and others now seek to scapegoat those who appropriate cultural ideas to create their own works. The claim is made that much intellectual labour, including human sweat, money and time, has gone into the devising, development and production of the work appropriated. These claims are frequently made, but usually without any supporting evidence to back such assertions. Instead, the claim continues that to copy, imitate or borrow from a work is to deny the owner or devisor the monetary rewards appropriate to this labour.

Such discourses having to do with theft are central to the manner in which media corporations use law 'to lock down culture and control creativity' (Lessig 2004: 53–82). These aim at consolidating and enhancing their cultural and economic power, even if that threatens to radically reduce the range of cultural possibilities and practices. The discourse of piracy is implicitly anti-democratic in that it seeks to impede and restrict the circulation of ideas in the public sphere (Vaidhyanathan 2001: 10–18). All the same, for well over a century argument has been mounted in legal jurisdictions having to do with robbery, criminal appropriation and so on of entitlement accruing to immaterial cultural entities. What this rhetoric sets out to do is to inscribe cultural ideas as a domain of possession, a form of ownership or property proprietary rights. Such a project is implicitly recognized in the use of the term 'intellectual property', which deliberately expands the notion of ownable holdings and possessions to include not only material goods but also more intangible, abstract and cerebral wares. This concept of the ownability of ideas is directly founded on a set of notions that comes down from the Romantic thinkers in Europe in the late eighteenth and early nineteenth centuries. It is necessary to note a different theory of creativity, which it challenged and in part marginalized, before examining the Romantic aesthetic and its subsequent capitalist appropriation to support notions of immaterial possession in the domain of culture.

Ideas and creativity

Ideas are outcomes of the mind, the human faculty for reasoning and thinking. The common name applied to the outcome of such effort is the term 'idea'. The creative function of the brain gives rise to cultural notions, perspectives, techniques, practices, products of intellectual effort, ways of understanding, accomplishments, imaginings, procedures, and so on. Collectively, these products are referred to as ideas.

Where, though, do ideas come from? What might be said to stimulate the creative faculty? One answer to this conundrum might be that ideas are generated from other ideas, insights, imaginings, thinking, and so on. Such a notion of the sources of creativity emphasizes the role of tradition and convention. This approach, which might be thought of as a more classical model, promotes the continuity of creative imaginings. The implicit assumption is that ideas are fertile and fecund, capable of generating many intellectual offspring, whether singly or in combination. A major stress falls on the role of adaptation and rearrangement of existing notions and concepts in the generation of new ideas. Creativity has to do not so much with originality and authenticity of imagining but rather with the use, criticism, supplementation and consideration of previous works. Exceptional thinking is still necessary, but the seeds of new ideas are mostly to be found in existing ones – although much effort is required to produce the new strain. New ideas represent not so much a break with and a rejection of the past but its continuation and variation – although not necessarily in expected and predictable forms.

According to this view, ideas come from other ideas. They are, however, more than and other than a simple repeat of earlier ideas. Creativity is the recognition of the potential applicability of certain ideas to new situations, surroundings and demands, while also recognizing the need to vary such ideas because of new, changed circumstances. It is the repetition of some elements drawn from one or more sources together with those variations that will enable these to fruitfully meet the present situation. Creativity is thus the manipulation of ideas – repeating, varying and altering them as necessary. Originality means adding to the storehouse of creative ideas, maintaining what is most valuable and fruitful but also adding new elements that will, in turn, further increase their value, relevance and usefulness.

This view of creativity is that displayed by Jefferson in the quote at the beginning of this chapter. Jefferson is concerned with the non-exclusivity of creative ideas. They can be sold as property only if their owner refuses to divulge them to others. However, once ideas are disclosed, they become accessible to all. Being available in the public sphere, they are shared equally by all: everyone is able to use them, including passing them on yet again to others. Creative ideas are inexhaustible. They can enlighten those who first come in contact with them as well as those who have encountered them only very recently. They are beyond ownership and private possession. Instead, creative ideas promote a democratic outlook, for they generate equality among those who share such thoughts.

Repetition and variation are central elements in this way of understanding creative ideas. This aesthetic has been elaborated in a classic essay regarding Hollywood cinema. Examining the latter as both a culture and an industry, Bellour (2008) has noted the variety of levels and instances in which repetition is a key ingredient of this particular institution. Similarity is a crucial feature in the orchestration of film style, in film storytelling, film production, marketing and film consumption. At the same time, the tendency towards repetition has always been tempered by the need for alterity, the principle of variation within repetition. Sequences will vary within familiar formulae, difference and variety will inevitably be introduced, novelty has a sanctioned place within similarity. Seriality is the principal motor of both the culture and the industry.

The tendency towards genre also highlights this inclination. Every cultural text contains something more than what is available in its manifestation. Industrially, such a text contains a kind of tutor code about itself with a series of implicit instructions on how to go about producing such a text. Aesthetically, this is the tendency towards seriality or genre. Genre is the notion of a class or species wherein the constituents both resemble and differ from one another. On the basis of similarity or the repetition of particular features, each instance can loosely be bracketed together as belonging to the class or species while their individual features, differing one from another, mean that the instances are not simply a repeat of one single instance.

Originality and genius

This view of what constitutes creativity was challenged and in part displaced by the advent of Romanticism in Europe towards the end of the eighteenth century. This artistic outlook broke with the more conventional theory of aesthetic creation outlined in the previous section and laid particular stress on the figure of the creator. It furnished a very powerful set of notions regarding human thinking. According to such a set of beliefs, the imaginings that come to thinkers in fields as diverse as art and science are original and autonomous. As ideas, they are authentic and very often revolutionary, owing little or nothing to anything that has gone before. Romanticism infuses creation with a mystic point of origin that is beyond rational understanding.

The progenitor of creativity, whether physical or ideational, is seen to be a unique figure who is identified as a genius. For such a gifted individual, creation is self-generated. Inspiration occurs as a flash of sudden insight, almost divine because it is so inward. The muse tells the poet to look in his heart and write. 'Eureka' is the cry of the scientist as he suddenly realizes how to solve a problem.

Representing a rupture with older forms of imagining creativity, Romanticism lays particular stress on the role of the individual. The novelty and brilliance of an idea as it is embodied in a work of art, a treatise or a scientific statement entitle the Romantic thinker to be perceived as one without peer, a gifted and exceptional being. Genius is the label given such a figure and the name comes to guarantee the quality and novelty of that which is imagined. Even when it has designated such a figure, Romantic ideology still finds itself highly dependent on Platonic thought and metaphysics when it comes to understanding the sources of a notion such as genius, not to mention the ideas spawned by such a figure. Be that as it may, this theory of art has provided a powerful model for understanding creativity in an aesthetic framework that has proved highly amenable to subsequent commercial and legal outlooks.

Intellectual property

Although ideas of legal copyright date back to the seventeenth century in England (Patterson 1968), nevertheless the advent of Romanticism was particularly significant in the invention of the concept of the author (Vaidhyanathan 2001). Authorship was equated with ownership. Such a move implied that possession accrued to those who 'owned' the signature or proper name attached to a work without regard to the contributions or interests of those others in whose lives it figured. This enables and legitimates practices of cultural authority that attempt to freeze the play of difference (and difference) in the public sphere.

There has been a very significant growth of the scope and duration of authorial rights since the mid-eighteenth century, and an even more massive expansion of legal protections in the recent past (Moore 1997; Laughlin 1998; Combe 1998). This has been synonymous with and encouraged a heavy cultural and commercial investment in authorship and ownership. It has also given rise to the notion of a distinct field of legal rights having to do with creative commercial ideas. Copyright is only one element in this ensemble. Intellectual property is assumed to be that knowledge or expression to which ownership is attached.

There is, in fact, no such thing as a single intellectual property law. Rather, intellectual property is 'a matrix of commercial legal protections now known as intellectual property' (Vaidhyanathan 2001). These might be regarded as a storehouse of different legal weaponries capable of being assembled and used to defend cultural monopoly. The weaponry is not all of a kind, but varies in terms of availability, accessibility, cost, perceived effectiveness and capacity to link with other legal measures. The last element is especially important, for it is frequently the combinatory capacity that enables different legal measures to support and strengthen the effectiveness of each other.

Table 8.1: Possible legal protections for TV formats.

Area of law	Specific measure
Intellectual property	Copyright law, trade mark legislation, patent law, trade secrets
Contract law	Contract law
Unfair commercial law	Confidentiality, passing off

Among the legal instruments bent to the purpose have been copyright law, trademark legislation, patent law, unfair competition law and trade secrets law (Penhaligon 2002). These different kinds of legislation have had distinct historical and philosophical backgrounds, although they are variously yoked together as part of an ongoing attempt to assert exclusive ownership of ideas for commercial purposes (Mann 1998). Each of these areas of law is itself composed of more than one element. Vaidhyanathan (2001), for example, points this out in relation to copyright:

> Copyright is more than one right. It is a 'bundle' of rights that includes the exclusive right to make copies, authorize others to make copies, create derivative works such as translations and displays in other media, sell the work, perform the work publicly, and petition a court for relief in case others infringe on any of these rights (Vaidhyanathan 2004: 20–21).

This same general point might be made in relation to the other areas brought together under the collective name of intellectual property. IP, as it is commonly known, is the result of concerted legislation to assemble a formidable set of instruments, procedures, tactics and other aids to intimidate creative practice in the domain of signification (Greenberg 1992). Table 8.1 maps this network of commercial legal protections pursued under the generic name of intellectual property.

Copyright disputes

Format distribution displays classic business symptoms of mutuality and rivalry between firms. Institutions such as market events, symposia, co-venture arrangements and trade associations encourage cooperation, common interest and fellowship. Sometimes major companies even sub-license their television format programs to other companies who are rivals in particular territories but can act as agents elsewhere. Disagreements and disputes are also common among companies operating in the television program format distribution business. Claims of format theft, plagiarism and unlawful appropriation frequently animate legal negotiations and sometimes give rise to court proceedings and civil action. The interconnectivity of global television industries means that, on the one hand, producers everywhere have the opportunity to quickly learn and appropriate significant elements of new successful program ideas. On the other hand, this same interconnectivity has dramatically increased the ability to monitor alleged copyright violations and the speed with which these are litigated. As one analyst has put it:

Like large content producers in other industries, television companies have become increasingly interested in detecting and prosecuting violators. Having extensive operations in the most important television markets, large producers have better chances to find transgressors (Waisbord 2004: 367).

In short, legal communications and outcomes can be seen as constituting another institution belonging to the TV program format trade wherein a kind of forced negotiation of trade matters occurs (Sanghera 2002; McConnell 2003). Formats are widely seen as forming a part of intellectual property. The format industry, like many other parts of digital industries of communications and culture, sees many examples of appropriation and copying. In very large markets such as the PRC and India, local and regional television channels regularly feature unlicensed clones and derivatives of other TV programs and films, which may themselves be adaptations of models taken from overseas (Thomas and Kumar 2004; Keane 2004). For the time being at least, these borrowings are mostly neither tracked nor subjected to legal challenge. The implicit motto so far as Western format owners is concerned seems to be 'out of sight, out of mind'. Instead, as Waisbord (2004) suggests, big legal guns are more frequently trained on alleged violations by fellow companies in the most lucrative markets.

What follows is an outline of a series of recent legal cases that mark the creep of intellectual property claims regarding TV program formats. Copyright holds pride of place among legal disputes concerning TV formats. In legal terms, copyright controls the right to make copies of a given work (Moore 1997: 4-6). This section therefore reviews a series of cases that raise two different but related matters. First, what precisely is a copy? Is it a twin, an attempt to duplicate an original, a faithful imitation that might be mistaken for a forebear? Or is it an adaptation, a reworking, a modified reflection that repeats but varies what has gone before? There appears to be only one case concerning copyright and TV formats wherein the offspring exhibited a very high degree of resemblance to its predecessor. The second matter raised concerns about the issue of whether a copyright always exists in a TV format (Buneau 2000, 2001; Burnett 2001). Are there some works which are deemed not to attract such protection?

Opportunity Knocks

Copyright in such cultural domains as literature and music is a central plank of intellectual property law, so it is not surprising that TV format owners have repeatedly attempted to use such law in legal disputes. One of the first attempts to advance such a claim occurred in the *Opportunity Knocks* case (Lane and Bridge 1990a, 1990b; Lane 1992). In 1988, Hughie Green – originator, compere and producer of the UK version of the program – discovered that a version of his hit quiz show was being produced and broadcast in New Zealand. In 1989, he took legal action in the New Zealand courts against the New Zealand Broadcasting Corporation. Green claimed damages for a breach of copyright in the program's scripts and the 'dramatic format of the program broadcast in the UK'. The claim also included commercial injury due to passing off. The judge dismissed the latter claim on the basis that Green had no commercial reputation in New Zealand so the passing off charge could not be sustained. The 'dramatic format' Green alleged comprised the characteristic elements of *Opportunity Knocks*

Figure 8.1: Hughie Green, owner/producer/compere of *Opportunity Knocks*, who pursued legal action to the UK Privy Council.

including the employment of a 'clapometer' which was said to gauge the reaction of the studio audience to the different contestants, the usual manner of introducing contestants, and the use of stock phrases such as 'It's make-your-mind-up time!' In other words, the New Zealand version of *Opportunity Knocks* was an almost complete imitation of the UK version, with the exception of not using Hughie Green as compere and not featuring contestants from the United Kingdom.

This appropriation of the program was certainly a case of blatant plagiarism. However, plagiarism is an ethical or moral matter rather than a legal one. The New Zealand judge therefore directed his attention to the plaint of copyright infringement. He found no evidence that the show had been reduced to written scripts. The scripts that had been produced by way of evidence were post-production records of what had been broadcast rather than scripts that had guided production. In any case, these transcriptions had occurred in the United Kingdom in relation to the UK series of the program. The claim of a copyright in the 'dramatic format' was not accepted and the action was lost. However, Green decided to appeal the judgment.

The New Zealand Court of Appeal, whilst accepting the existence of scripts, upheld the decision on the basis that they did no more than express a general idea or concept and were not subject to copyright protection. This was an aesthetic decision that has the possibility of being repeated in relation to the formats of much 'live' television. Green had one last legal fling by appealing to the Privy Council in London. Again, the earlier decision was upheld 'on the basis that it is stretching the original use of the word "format" a long way to use it metaphorically to describe the features of a television series such as a talent, quiz or game show which is presented in a particular way, with repeated but unconnected use of set phrases and with the aid of particular accessories' (Lane and Bridge 1990b). The Privy Council also had difficulty with the concept that a number of allegedly distinctive features of a television series can be isolated from the changing material presented in each separate performance and identified as an 'original dramatic work'. It was therefore held that copyright had not been established (Penhaligon 2002: 44).

Big Break
While Green's appeals to both the New Zealand Court of Appeal and the Privy Council in London were unsuccessful, another claim concerning copyright infringement of a TV format mounted almost a decade later proved more so. The case in question had to do with the TV snooker sports program *Big Break*. It was brought by Roger Medcalf against Terry Mardell and others, and came before the High Court in the United Kingdom in 1998 (Penhaligon 2002).

The program had been broadcast by the BBC since 1991 and the legal claim was for an account of profits. The plaintiff was one of the three devisors of the format. Like the *Opportunity Knocks* case, the High Court was required to consider whether a TV game show format was capable of copyright protection and, if so, which version(s) of the format attracts such protection, in circumstances where an original format is developed over time. But, unlike the earlier case, Medcalf's action was successful. The court found that each version of the format was a literary work in which copyright subsisted. In addition, the conduct of the three original creators amounted to a partnership so that copyrights in the relevant versions of the format were assets belonging to this partnership. The other two appealed this decision but the latter was subsequently upheld. The significance of the case lay in the fact that the UK High Court appeared to accept that a TV format might be afforded copyright protection, at least for those which were adequately developed.

Survivor and Big Brother

The *Opportunity Knocks* case was unique in that no generic variation was in dispute. The New Zealand version of the program was a deliberate copycat version of the UK version. In the cases that follow, the possible variation from a format forebear was much looser, with some elements being repeated while others were varied or changed. At the centre of this string of court cases in Europe and the United States was the reality series *Survive*. The latter was developed by Charlie Parsons who, with partners Bob Geldof and Lord Waheed Alli, formed Planet 24 Productions. *Survive* had failed to find a producer licensee in either the United Kingdom or the United States before a Swedish broadcaster had licensed the format as *Castaway Robinson* in 1999. It proved to be an important breakthrough, and the following year the format was remade for CBS in the United States under the title *Survivor* (Bazalgette 2005). This reality filmed series was set on a tropical desert island and pitted two teams of fictionally shipwrecked young men and women against each other with the group voting off a succession of contestants until only a sole winner was left.

Parsons had offered the format to Endemol, which declined it. However, in 1999 Endemol previewed the reality series *Big Brother* on Dutch television (Bazalgette 2005). In this reality show, a group of 10 young people were brought together in a house that was under constant camera

and microphone surveillance. The television audience engaged in telephone voting so that finally a single winner was left in the household. Parsons applied to the Amsterdam District Court, alleging that the format of *Big Brother* infringed the format of *Survive* with at least 11 fundamental ingredients being repeated in the Endemol format (BBC News 2002; Bazalgette 2005).

The case was heard by the court in mid-2000. At this level of the Dutch legal system, evidence is not submitted and the matter is heard in front

Figure 8.2: John de Mol, devisor of *Big Brother*.

of the members of the court on their own. The court ruled that *Big Brother* did not infringe on Parson's ideas and therefore did not uphold the claim. However, Parsons could not be deterred announcing that he was motivated by principle rather than greed: 'This isn't about money – it's about the principle. If I ever won any compensation I would be quite happy to give the money to charity,' he said (BBC News 2000).

Two years later, the matter reached the Amsterdam Court of Appeal. Again, the claim was that the *Big Brother* format was an adaptation of the *Survive* format and that the use of this format by Endemol was a violation of Parsons' copyright (BBC News 2002; Bazalgette 2005). Again, the principle of generic variation was upheld (Van Manen 2003). Counsel for Endemol was able to point to over 12 significant ways in which the Dutch format differed from *Survive*. In other words, the former format was at best a relative rather than a twin. Even more importantly, the Appeal Court ruled that, although the separate elements of the format were non-copyrightable, the combination of several elements could be protected by copyright (Van Manen 2003).

Survive and I'm a Celebrity...

Parsons and his partners were undaunted and shortly resumed legal proceedings against another generic offspring of *Survive*. In September 2002, Bob Geldof announced that he was undertaking legal proceedings in the United Kingdom against Granada Television and London Weekend Television, the makers of *I'm a Celebrity... Get Me Out of Here* (BBC News 2002; Gibson 2003). The company Geldof owned in conjunction with Parsons and Alli, Castaway Television Productions, alleged that the format of *Celebrity* infringed its copyright in the *Survive* format (Lamont 2003). Granada denied that its reality series infringed the latter's copyright.

Meanwhile, *Castaway* had encouraged its partner in the US remake of *Survive*, the CBS television network, to take a parallel legal action against the ABC television network which was producing a US version of *I'm a Celebrity... Get Me Out of Here* under licence from Granada.

Figure 8.3: Owners/devisors of the *Survive* format – Geldof, Alli and Parsons – who took several legal actions against suspected copies.

CBS applied to the New York District Court in an attempt to have the court halt the production of *Celebrity*. It claimed that, because of a number of common features, the *Celebrity* format was a deliberate imitation of the *Survive* format.

After two days of hearings, Judge Loretta Preska rejected this argument and ruled that the program was not a direct copy of the *Survive* format. Significantly, the judge pointed out the connection between the two formats in generic terms:

> The judge said that *I'm a Celebrity*... borrowed no more heavily from *Survivor* than previous US shows with similar concepts, such as *The Honeymooners* and *I Love Lucy* or *Bewitched* and *I Dream of Jeannie*... programme-making was 'a continual evolutionary process involving borrowing frequently from what has gone before' and that both shows borrowed heavily from earlier formats (Lamont 2003).

Further copyright troubles

This string of legal cases concerning TV formats and copyright have been among the most important so far as the creep of intellectual property commercial and legal protection has been concerned. However, in recent years the flurry of copyright claims has by no means abated, with many of the leading players either accusing or being accused of infringement. In 2004, for example, a string of further court cases alleged that generic variations of particular TV formats infringed copyright in other formats (Idato 2004). In US courts, NBC alleged that rival network Fox's *The Next Great Champ* had infringed its boxing reality format *The Contender*. ABC also accused Fox of copying its British import, *Wife Swap*, as *Trading Spouses*. The latter's producer True Entertainment (a subsidiary of the Dutch format specialist Endemol) defended the complaint, claiming that its format had more to do with a National Geographic format, *Worlds Apart*. Additionally, ABC and Fox were in a further legal wrangle concerning other imported formats. *Supernanny* and *Nanny 911* were formats that featured nannies who tangled with misbehaving children. The former had gone to ABC from Channel 4 in the United Kingdom, while the latter had come to Fox from Granada.

Legal action alleging copyright infringement was also being pursued at this time across the Atlantic. In the United Kingdom, 19 TV, owned by Simon Fuller – which claimed copyright ownership to both *Pop Idol* and *American Idol* – sued Simon Cowell together with co-production companies FremantleMedia and Syco, alleging that the latter's *The X Factor* infringed its format copyright (McTernan 2005). In France, two television networks were in dispute over television formats featuring motoring tests. Under its general series *Test the Nation*, Dutch company EyeWorks had already produced *The National Traffic Test* for VRT in Belgium and SBS6 in Holland. It had produced a French version for broadcaster M6. Meanwhile, rival network France2 had commissioned Wai TV to produce another driving test program, *The Big Exam – Fit to Drive?* The dispute between the two broadcasters went to the French broadcasting regulator who resolved that only one program should go to air and decided in favour of the latter (EyeWorks 2004). The same year saw a television format dispute come before the German courts. Action was pursued by the French owners of a live children's TV format, *L'ecole des* fans. The claim, which was refused, was that the latter's format copyright was infringed by a comparable German program, *Kinderquatsch mit Michel* (Idato 2004).

Finally, far away in Australia, another case of alleged TV format copyright infringement also reached the courts early the following year (*Nine Network v Ninox*, see Federal Court of Australia 2005). The action in question took place in the Federal Court of Australia. It had to do with a legal plaint taken by the Nine Network against a New Zealand company, Ninox Television Limited. Ninox had devised and produced a reality series entitled *Dream House* that entailed a competition to renovate a house. The series had been successful so that Ninox had offered the format to the Nine Network in Australia. The latter took an option on the series but decided not to renew this, or sign a contract to produce an Australian version of the program. Instead, it produced its own program concerning the renovation of residential property, *The Block*. Ninox believed that it had a copyright in the format of *Dream House* and that this had been infringed by *The Block*. However, Nine took action in the court, claiming that there was no copyright infringement. It also alleged under the *Trade Practices Act* that Ninox had engaged in misleading and deceptive practice in alleging such an infringement. The court found in favour of Nine's plaint.

Breaching commercial law
Copyright is not always invoked in format disputes as grounds for legal damages. Action concerning the unauthorized appropriation of a TV format may be pursued on grounds other than copyright infringement, or it may be pursued on the joint grounds of intellectual property law and commercial law protection. The fact that the Nine Network of Australia alleged damage to its commercial reputation as part of the grounds for action against Ninox in the case just outlined is one example. It was also noted above that Simon Fuller's 19 TV sued Simon Cowell, FremantleMedia and Syco for breach of contract, arguing that many of *The X Factor*'s production team had also worked on *Pop Idol* when, in fact they were forbidden from working on rival programs (Carter 2005; McTernan 2005).

Commercial law offers protection having to do with such matters as passing off and confidentiality. As was noted above, the *Opportunity Knocks* case had also involved a claim connected with passing off, although this was not allowed. Confidentiality is taken to suggest commercial contract so that its apparent violation might be seen as a breach of implied contract. Two cases are reviewed here with the second case also highlighting the court's acceptance of a copyright protection on a TV format.

Father's Day and The Cosby Show
The first case occurred in the United States and concerned the situation comedy, *The Cosby Show*, which starred popular African American comedian Bill Cosby (Moran and Malbon 2006). The matter began in 1980 when Hwesu Murray, following preliminary discussions with an NBC official, submitted short written proposals for five new shows to the network (Levine 1989). One of these was a situation comedy, *Father's Day*, which concerned a black middle-class family where the father was a lawyer. At NBC's request, Murray expanded several of these proposals. The

proposal for *Father's Day* subsequently grew to two pages and included the casting suggestion that actor Bill Cosby play the lead role. Late that year, NBC returned the material and indicated that it was not interested in the proposal. In 1984, NBC aired *The Cosby Show*, a situation comedy about an upper middle-class family where the father is a doctor and the wife a lawyer. The series starred Bill Cosby. Murray took legal action against NBC and the packaging company that produced the series for the network. The grounds included infringement of the format of *Father's Day* and breach of implied contract. In 1987, the defendants moved successfully in a district court in New York to have the complaint dismissed on the grounds that Murray's 'ideas' (format) lacked sufficient novelty to sustain a misappropriation action. An appeal in the following year upheld this decision. There are various anomalies in the case, most especially in the court's decision, that have been discussed elsewhere (Moran 1998). For the purpose of this chapter, though, it is worth noting two features of the case. The first is the fact that, since the US *Copyright Act* of 1976, the US Copyright Office has recognized television program formats as copyrightable. Nevertheless, the court in this case decided that the format for *Father's Day* was not sufficiently novel as to attract legal protection. The second detail is the fact that the format existed only as a series of verbal ideas communicated by Murray to NBC and as a two-page written outline. Van Manen (1994) makes the general point that the more concrete a format is, the more chance it has of attracting copyright protection (1994: 69–71). The third feature is a set of specific facts associated with the case. The original format for *Father's Day* existed only as a written outline and not in the form of a finished program, which might have been tendered as evidence. In addition, the circumstance that the alleged offence occurred in the same country where the original had been developed meant that legal action also occurred there.

Rock Follies

In 1973, three UK television actresses and singers formed a rock group (*Medcalf v Markel* 1988). By 1975, they had the idea of a television series based in part on their experiences. Together with their manager, who would compose songs for the series, they entered into discussion with Thames Television for the part-fact, part-fiction series which was to be called *Rock Follies*. The idea was communicated orally, and Thames agreed that if the series went ahead as a production then the three actresses would be given first option on the central roles. However, when Thames did decide to go ahead with the series, the first actress was already playing in a musical from which she could not obtain a release. Thames went ahead with the project and cast three other actresses in the lead roles. The original trio sued for breach of contract. They also alleged breach of confidence. In the event, the court found in their favour. They were awarded damages with respect to both a breach of implied contract and a breach of confidence. Finally, it is worth noting in passing that matters of copyright protection did not arise directly; nevertheless, the court did note that there was an obligation of confidence because 'the content of the idea was clearly identifiable, original, of potential commercial attractiveness and capable of reaching fruition' (*Medcalf v Markel* 1988).

Summary

The legal infrastructure of intellectual property facilitates the reproduction and repetition of TV formatted programs under a regime of authorship and ownership. There has been a very significant growth of the scope and duration of intellectual property rights, including their use in TV format program disputes. Owners and devisors have had ongoing recourse to the law in an attempt to freeze the play of signification by legitimating authorship. Although only a handful of cases have been examined in this chapter, it is still important to note the wide geographic range of the legal jurisdictions involved. The setting for the legal resolution of disputes is increasingly global, as the flow of TV program formats moves outwards across the planet. Of course, the ultimate destination of such movement is the remaking of formats, in particular national television markets. The next chapter examines one such destination for this flow.

9

OUTPOSTS

[T]he 'old' Commonwealth countries, especially Australia and Canada, have been crucial markets for US media. Throughout the twentieth century, both were crucial markets and early importers of US media innovations. In 1925, Australia, Britain, and Canada accounted for 48 per cent of Hollywood movie export earnings. Subsequently, these three ABC countries were key innovators of commercial television (mixed with public systems). By 1990, these three countries offered an English-speaking market of 100 million different-but-not-too-different customers. All these countries also played a modest offshore production role for Hollywood (Tunstall and Machin 1999: 266–67).

Introduction

In charting new flows in television, I have traced a one-way path. The worldwide movement of the television format commodity is outward, diverging to often-remote places scattered across the globe. If television industries everywhere are increasingly drawn into a globalized system, then this order of dispersal is marked by quite specific conditions. Even as finance, commercial outlook, business language and trade milieu are progressively homogenized, so program output appears to be steadily diversifying so far as culture and language are concerned. I have concentrated on the latter end of this trail in the past four chapters. The present chapter continues this emphasis by examining the effects on the provinces of trading initiatives and commercial undertakings entered into at the world's television centres. If the latter are the hubs of commodity exchange in television programming, then local production and broadcasting sites and locations in particular national territories make up the rim of such structures. These national television territories are at the end of corridors that lead out from these often-distant locations. Curtain (2003, 2004) has coined the term 'media capital' to designate important global centres of finance, skill, accumulated knowledge, production history, and so on. Likewise, television territories where these qualities are thin on the ground might be labelled media outposts.

What goes on at these latter sites is shaped by the arrangements entered into at the global fairs and exhibitions. Previous chapters have already sketched some of these core–periphery connections. Chapter 2 suggested some of the territories from which television licensing customers at the television bazaars of Los Angeles, Las Vegas, Brighton, Cannes and Hong Kong hail. Chapter 5 stressed the bilingual system operating in the global television business where local languages come into their own in terms of the national indigenization of formats from elsewhere. Chapters 6 and 7 elaborated on this subject by tracing the movement of television commodities along various trade corridors towards specific national destinations and on the role played by skilled, experienced television practitioners working at different outpost production sites in rendering such wares more familiar and accessible to local audiences. The present chapter completes this journey by looking at the program-remake provinces – the final destination of television program format flows.

Rather than treat the subject of the local television production and broadcast homelands in general, schematic fashion, I will use one national example as a case study. The object is to trace the web of transnational relationships between Australian television and the global television industry, especially as this has to do with television program format trade. Without in any way reducing and ignoring the diversity and complexity of factors likely to operate in different television outposts, this case study throws light on the variety of elements operating in peripheral territories when it comes to producing television program formats licensed through deals entered into at the festivals. Accordingly, the chapter is divided into five parts. The first considers general features of the Australian television market. This mediascape is by no means unique among world television markets. At the same time, it is not immediately representative of other markets. In what follows, I link Australian television to a larger cultural continent, one of a handful of such global regions. Therefore, the second part of the chapter examines recent theoretical formulations of the notion of world geolinguistic regions in television. The quote from Tunstall and Machin at the beginning of this chapter anticipates the argument that follows concerning Australia's specific place within an Anglo-American media connection. Broad features of this mediascape are considered in the third part of the chapter as a means of identifying the international family to which Australian television belongs. This relationship is a dynamic one. Part four signals earlier recognitions of Australia's complex relationship with US and UK television. Finally, the last section detects a shift in orientation towards a more Anglo-European media connection, at least so far as television program format exchange is concerned.

Australian television

Confirming its status as a major minor when it came to broadcasting, Australian television began in the mid-1950s as part of a second wave of television services inaugurated in various parts of the world. The first wave had been confined to the major industrial world powers including the United States, the United Kingdom, Germany and Japan. Scientists and engineers in these countries had helped launch the new medium in the 1930s and 1940s. Australia had sufficient wealth and population to be part of the second wave of territories initiating television in the 1950s. (In turn, a third and even a fourth wave would see television starting in territories that were less affluent than the first- and second-wave territories and often with smaller populations).

Australian television was inaugurated as a mixed or dual system, following an earlier pattern of radio broadcasting and its recent confirmation as government policy in such areas as banking, shipping and aviation. The service was to be offered as a partnership between private and public interests. A commercial service would be provided by private, independent operators while the public service operator, the Australian Broadcasting Corporation (ABC), would supply the public television service. This system has served a small but affluent population thinly distributed over the largest island continent in the world over the past 50 years. If dispersal was one reality of Australian television, another lay in the fact that the viewing population was and is marked by a high degree of linguistic, cultural and geographical homogeneity. Television broadcasting was initially limited to specific areas surrounding the state capital cities. Gradually, however, a landline television transmission system was linked together. Australian television became nationally networked in 1987. The mid-1990s saw the modification of the dual system of television with the introduction of both community and pay television services (Moran 2004).

Four sources have supplied the programming needs of this system. Programming from the United States and the United Kingdom, most especially high-quality television drama, has been a staple for the 50 years of broadcasting. This content helped fill the television schedule, provided material that attracted a mass audience and cross-subsidized the production of local program content. The state has also made a contribution to the cost of the latter, most especially in the areas of drama and children's programming, on the basis of enhancing cultural identity, guaranteeing the provision of content that otherwise might not get produced, and helping to sustain a local television production industry. The last source has been the provision of what might be called world television. This refers to the limited amount of ethnic and high-quality foreign-language programming imported from Europe, Asia and elsewhere and screened by SBS TV, the second public service channel.

While this pattern has generally been true for Australian television, it has not been a static one. In particular, Australian television has followed a classic economic tendency of 'import substitution' whereby, after an initial flood of US programs, locally produced popular television programs soon appeared which displaced imported programs in the schedule. In fact, from around 1980 to about 1995, Australian television drama producers enjoyed good sales of canned drama serials to the United Kingdom, Western Europe and elsewhere as broadcasters in those regions struggled to fill schedules in their greatly expanded broadcasting systems (Cunningham and Jacka 1996a). After 1995, however, sales fell off because libraries were exhausted and local production had fallen. Networks began looking for cheaper forms of content and new income streams. Media globalization was afoot, although for Australia – like other broadcasting systems – the emerging television order was best understood at the regional rather than the local or the global level.

Cultural continents

The notion of a cultural continent or region suggests that this is a crucial level between that of the nation and the total international order. Specific nations can rise and fall, but what remains is the complex set of cultural factors that help provide the bedrock for imagining community and belonging (Anderson 1991). The engagement with cultural regions on the part of media researchers is by no means a new phenomenon. In 1974, for example, Nordenstreng and Varis, in their classic UNESCO study of the worldwide distribution of television programming, noted that not all content was universally imported. Instead, cultural factors including language, religion and political ideology frequently mediated the global flow of programming. Blocks or networks of television territories were apparent so there was more trade between some territories than between others. A decade later, Mattelart, Delacourt and Mattelart (1985) returned to this insight and proceeded to elaborate it in relation to a perceived 'Latin' television region. Their argument was that there existed a Romance or Latin cultural formation which included television territories in Central and South America as well as those of Spain, Portugal, France and Italy in Europe. These were linguistically and culturally distinct and could, in effect, constitute a television market that was linguistically and culturally removed from Hollywood (Mattelart et al. 1985).

By the 1990s, the perceived pattern of cross-border television at national and global-regional levels became even more fragmented and complicated. Arguments about international patterns proceeded to go further than before. In their classic account of developing structures in global television, Sinclair, Jacka and Cunningham (1996) asserted that Tunstall's 1977 claim that the media were American was no longer true. A 'one-way flow' of television traffic could not be identified. Instead, a more complex picture was emerging wherein a host of significant new and old players constituted 'a patchwork tapestry' (Sinclair, Cunningham and Jacka 1996: 13). Larger cultural continents were a highly significant element that mediated between national television industries and a world television system. The variables that comprised such networks involved politics, language, history, religion, ethnicity and geography. Frequently, though, these are summarized as geolinguistic regions.

The thinking of other researchers has moved along similar lines. Like Sinclair, Straubhaar is a critical researcher engaged with Latin American television. He has been especially concerned with the operation of cable stations in Brazil, Argentina and elsewhere in the area. On the basis of multi-level activity by cable operators in the continent, Straubhaar formulated the notion of cultural proximity, an ethos at work in cultural regions that helps orchestrate programming decision-making in cable television operations (Straubhaar 1991, 1997). At the same time, European transnational satellite television was under investigation by Chalaby (2003, 2005a, 2005b). A recent collection of studies having to do with contemporary satellite television in different parts of the world (which included both Sinclair and Straubhaar as contributors) emphasizes the necessity of investigating such a subject at the geolinguistic regional level rather than that of the national (Chalaby 2003, 2005a).

Meanwhile, two recent studies by Tunstall (1997, 2008) constitute a major qualification of his 1977 thesis that the media are American. His 1997 study of the Anglo-American media connection, carried out in conjunction with David Machin, was a belated recognition that Hollywood and US media no longer dominated global communication. Britain is recognized as an important player and the study affords more interest and space to the Anglophone media region (Tunstall and Machin 1999). The emerging importance of the European mediascape is signalled, while the foreign takeover of US media companies by firms such as Sony is noted. Meanwhile, in his most recent analysis, Tunstall returns to several of the same issues analyzed in his earlier studies concerning internationally dominant media markets (Tunstall 2008). His argument now is that US media are in a slow decline so far as this supremacy is concerned. A series of supra-national and national media players are emerging in their place. Early in the study, Tunstall stresses the importance of population size in the determination of these complexes and emphasizes the growing significance of Brazil, Mexico, Russia, India and China alongside the Anglo-American media complex. At the same time, he reserves judgement so far as the total displacement of US media is concerned. For the present, he wants to reassert the continuing importance of national media entities in the current world media order (Tunstall 2008).

This part of the chapter, then, can be summed up by noting the necessity of attending to larger cultural formations beyond that of the national television market in any full consideration of cultural patterns and developments. A broadcasting territory cannot be thought of and analyzed *sui generis*. Rather, it is necessary to locate it within a larger, regional mediascape. Where does Australian television belong in terms of this notion of geolinguistic continents? Has its place changed over time or has it remained the same? How does format flows affect these alignments?

Australian television and Asian mediascapes

As already noted, Sinclair, Cunningham and Jacka (1996) have suggested that there are six distinguishing features of world cultural continents or regions. These have to do with commonalities of language, history, religion, ethnicity, culture and geography (1996). Often, however, regions so identified may lack one or more of these commonalities, suggesting that some cultural continents are incommensurate with others. Geography and language are often preferred over other features as a significant means of identifying a shared zone, although even then there may be difficulties. Thus Chalaby's recent collection concerning the subject of transnational satellite television includes a focus on large nation-states such as India and the People's Republic of China, as well as Western Europe among the regions studied (2005a). While the first two withstand the geolinguistic test of relative homogeneity, Western Europe presents an anomalous case of a region that has commonalities of culture, religion and geography but is linguistically diverse (Chalaby 2003, 2005a).

The Australian television market is literally at the other end of the world from trade fairs and exhibitions held in Las Vegas, Brighton and Cannes, and in another hemisphere to the new Amazia market planned for Hong Kong. Geographically, Australian broadcasting (along with that of New Zealand) might be thought of as possibly part of an Asia mediascape or at least part of a Southeast Asian television sphere. Yet there is little corroborating evidence for such identification. With a white population of largely European origin, the country can point to only a few regional political and military memberships such as those of SEATO, ASEAN and APEX. Since the early 1970s, trade with East Asia – particularly Japan, South Korea and the People's Republic of China – has grown enormously, effectively replacing older commercial ties with Britain. Yet geography and trade still only give Australia a nominal presence in the region. Not surprisingly, these links have fostered a desire for even greater political, economic and cultural integration with Asia in government, business and other circles.

In fact, among nations of the region, Australia and New Zealand are considered not to be part of Asia but to belong to Oceania, the island grouping of the South Pacific. By the same token, there have been few assertions that Australian television is part of an Asian regional mediascape. Amongst the few researchers to investigate such a claim have been Cunningham and Jacka (1996b). As part of their analysis of the global export of Australian film and television, these scholars have examined Australia's presence in Asian media beginning as early as 1939 with the establishment of Radio Australia. For the most part, their inquiry is confined to the presence of Australian-originated content in television services in the region. However, their major case study concerns the Australian Television satellite service into the region provided by the Australian Broadcasting Corporation (ABC). The latter has, until recently, practised a policy of 'reverse Orientalism' in its programming but is now moving towards a more robust and less apologetic engagement with subjects and sensitivities. Cunningham and Jacka endorse this broadcasting policy stance, noting that it would project 'some of the strengths of a relatively peaceful multicultural democracy' (1996b). In other words, as part of what they call Australia's 'paradigm shift' towards Asia, they suggest that Australian television might play a positive role not in turning a cultural outsider into an insider but at least changing its perception into that of a familiar foreigner. Nonetheless, despite this recent attempt at cultural 'enmeshment' noted by these scholars, Australia's media are joined to another formation that is linguistically unified, even as it is geographically dispersed. The territory's television service remains part of an Anglophone, Anglo-American television landscape – even if that is a changing and dynamic formation.

In this respect, it is worth noting a similar effort of regional cultural placement in the adjacent field of film studies. In his 1996 analysis of Australian national cinema, O'Regan offers a series of different lenses through which this cinema could be viewed. One of the perspectives he develops is that of language. As he puts it:

> As natural languages are the basis for cultural systems, communications corridors, markets, international trading systems and political alliances, they form cultural areas above the level of the nation. Australia and its national cinema is part of the larger family of English-language cinemas and cultures including the USA, English-speaking Canada, New Zealand, the UK and Ireland and to a lesser extent South Africa, Anglophone India and Singapore (O'Regan 1996: 82).

Although Hollywood is frequently seen in globally dominant terms (Olsson 1999; Miller et al. 2005), the fact is that it is first and foremost an English-language cinema. Although frequently said to reach a worldwide audience primarily through dubbing and subtitling, Hollywood communicates with approximately 600 million English-speaking people without the need for any kind of linguistic adjustment. O'Regan is concerned to chart the relationship of feature film markets within this Anglophone system. Australia is bracketed with English-language Canada so far as trade in international trade in symbolic goods is concerned. However, the United Kingdom is ignored in this arrangement when it might have been considered on a rung below the United States followed by Australia (and Canada) below that. Hollywood film exerts dominance over all other English-speaking markets, whereas others – including these three – are dominated as well as showing signs of minor domination of others in the Anglophone mediascape. This is not a fixed or immutable system for film, television or other cultural goods. O'Regan emphasizes that the commonality of language also means even Hollywood has historically been prone to market penetration by films from the different tiers of the Anglophone system as well as from elsewhere. When one considers the Anglophone television system, and especially Australia's place in this configuration, we discover particular variations on the film pattern. What this configuration underlines is the fact that any regional cultural system, including the English-speaking structure in audio-visual goods, is complex and dynamic. The passage of time reveals shifts and new arrangements in the system.

Anglophone television

As though any empirical testimony as to the existence of and English-language audio-visual landscape were necessary, we might recall the international linguistic circulation of the US remake of the Columbian program format *Yo soy Betty, la fea* outlined in Chapter 5. This was adapted for mainstream US network television as *Ugly Betty*. The United States constitutes the largest and wealthiest national English-language market in world television. As a result, the series carried the very high-quality production values that are a hallmark of that system, even if the language spoken on the soundtrack was American English. Following the historic export pattern for high-value US drama serials, the US remake of the telenovela could then be sold and shipped to other English-language markets in other territories. Additional Anglophone territories where *Ugly Betty* was subsequently screened are indicated in Table 9.1.

Table 9.1: *Ugly Betty* exports to English-language territories.

Country	Broadcaster	Potential audience
United States	ABC	Population
United Kingdom	Channel 4	Population
Canada	CityTV	Population
Australia	Seven	Population
Ireland	RTE2	Population
Hong Kong	TVB Pearl	Population

New Zealand, Singapore, Anglophone South Africa and Anglophone Zimbabwe were among a handful of other territories where English was spoken but sales not made. In total, *Ugly Betty* had a potential aggregate English-language viewership of 420 million. Mapping out the US remake's international distribution in this way makes it clear that this Anglophone linguistic region is a significant cultural and economic reality in global television industries. Historically, the domain has been shaped in the aftermath of the British Empire, even if one of the former set of colonies formed by that imperium, the United States, has become the dominant nation in the group. As Tunstall and Machin (1999) note, the United Kingdom occupies a second tier of importance and wealth while Canada and Australia belong to a subsequent tier. Mention of the British Empire as an important military and political forerunner to this linguistic disposition reminds one that the latter empire was not land based. Instead, it was held together by the waterways of the world and the British Navy. In other words, while the Anglophone region is a cultural continent marked by a good deal of historical, cultural and linguistic continuity, it is at the same time geographically dispersed and fragmented.

Australia in the Anglophone realm: Some past connections
As an outpost of world television in general and Anglophone television in particular, Australian broadcasting has a long history of interconnection with both US and UK television. A small sampling makes this relationship clear. The emphasis falls on the institution of a mixed system of television operation and its popular perception following Tunstall and Machin's (1999) observation above. In fact, the state as the instrument of political and business interests was a principal factor in the development of this dual system. Initially, though, the intention was to have Australia follow a more British type of broadcasting model so far as radio and then television were concerned. To this end, there were two concerted attempts to shape broadcasting as a public service monopoly (Inglis 1982; Moran 1985). Neither of these was successful Nevertheless, occasional attempts to blunt the perceived Americanization of broadcasting continued. Hence, between 1964 and 1972 the government allowed commercial television stations to count 50 per cent of UK program content time towards meeting their Australian programming time requirements (Moran 1985).

If this regressive attitude to a perceived US presence in television was evident in parts of the state apparatus, this was not the case elsewhere. In other early representations of just why Australian television had acquired a US/UK television mix, a different scenario was presented (McKay 1956; Horne 1965). This narrative claimed the outcome constituted a triumph of Australian imagination. The myth propounded was that Australia had deliberately delayed the introduction of service so that it could amalgamate the finest elements from both the UK and US television services, thereby achieving the very best system possible anywhere. The legend served several functions. It elided the repeated attempts to nationalize broadcasting as a public utility and the victory of commercial interests in that struggle. The postulated dualism ignored the fact that a good deal of the cultural and economic power lay with the commercial sector of the system. And, of course, it implied that UK television belonged on the first tier of English-language television when this was not the case.

Australian television still speaks English

If we shuffle forward to the present, it is clear that local media broadcasting remains just as firmly in the Anglophone realm. Australian television continues to occupy a third rung of this system, even if many elements and components of broadcasting have changed and there is much talk of media globalization. In this instance, it is necessary to adopt a different lens for viewing the current connection. The focus of attention, therefore, has to do with the provision of Australian program content. Until the mid-1960s, Australian television production was dominated by the television stations. These had been established on the model of the Hollywood film studio of the classical period. Under this regime, the broadcasting organizations not only distributed programs in the shape of broadcast transmission but were involved in the production of local programming on their own premises (Moran 1985).

After 1965, this situation changed. Following the example of US network television, outsourcing to independent program packagers became mainstream practice. There was a marked drop in the output of programs produced in house. Instead, a series of production companies emerged that became a permanent feature of the Australian television industry. These were local in origin and without international connection. They were small and under-capitalized, so that without an ongoing successful series in production they soon became extinct. With the notable exception of the game show packagers, they also lacked catalogues of successful program ideas that might be revived and remade in the future.

Three variations on this pattern are relevant. First, US program distributors such as FremantleMedia and Screen Gems briefly set up local production branches in the early 1960s only to soon close these. Additionally, ever since television began in Australia in 1956, program format adaptation and remake has occurred in low-cost genres, including game shows, talk and panel shows, current affairs, daytime drama, music, variety, and children's programs. The Australian remake of the US format *Romper Room* was mentioned in Chapter 1. The most consistent practitioner of adaptations has been the Australian Broadcasting Corporation (ABC). In the past, the ABC has had a close relationship with British broadcasting, most especially with the British Broadcasting Corporation (BBC), which it has looked to as mentor, mother and model. The ABC has enjoyed the first choice of canned BBC programming for Australian rebroadcast. It has also, over the years, adapted and remade very many BBC program formats for local broadcast. Licensing fees were rarely paid to the British originator, leading one executive with BBC Worldwide to complain about lost revenues (Jarvis 1996, 2006).

The third variation has to do with the brief surge of Australian program exports in the 1980s and early 1990s (Cunningham and Jacka 1996a). This boom saw a number of Australian program packagers enjoying good earnings, not only from the export of canned programs but also from the remake of Australian program formats elsewhere in the world (Moran 1998). Packagers that benefited from this trade included the Becker Group and Grundy World Wide. However, it was only the latter that achieved takeoff as a cross-border organization. In any case, this development was cut short in 1995 when Grundy World Wide was bought by Pearson Television in the United Kingdom and effectively Anglified (Moran 2006).

Transnationalization of Australian packaging

This development heralds a new era in Australian television program packaging. Many of the dominant local players are no longer Australian in origin but are instead national branches of large transnational communication organizations. These latter bodies are highly capitalized, with interests in program production, broadcasting outlets, new media, publishing, online and other media concerns in some of the world's wealthiest markets (Moran and Malbon 2006). Among their other capital assets, these organizations include extensive libraries of program formats. This ensures their ongoing importance in television program markets such as that of Australia, not only in terms of having access to successful, international program formats but also being involved in the adaptation and remaking of these for the Australian television broadcasting market. Three such organizations now dominate the local television program production landscape. Two are the result of joint-venture arrangements while the other represents a kind of transnationalization of an existing Australian company.

FremantleMedia Australia

Grundy was the latter production organisation. This entity was first established in Australia 50 years ago. Pearson Television had itself been set up in 1993 when the UK-based Pearson PLC bought Thames Television. The Grundy acquisition a few years later was part of an initial flurry of aggressive buyouts wherein Pearson Television acquired other companies in the United Kingdom, Italy, Germany and Finland in the area of production and distribution, and also obtained an important stake in Channel 5. Through Grundy, Pearson Television picked up a significant catalogue of program formats that it added to in 1997 when it acquired All-American International, whose format library included the properties owned by Goodson-Todman and Fremantle. In 2000, Pearson Television and CLT-Ufa merged as the Luxembourg-based RTL Group. A further name change was necessary. The following year, the content production division of RTL (Pearson, UFA and Grundy-UFA) was named FremantleMedia. The past decade has seen the group continuing to acquire smaller companies, with the German Bertelsman picking up a 30 per cent majority share in the RTL Group (Moran and Malbon 2006).

Grundy was unlikely to retain either its identity or even its name in this developing transnational conglomerate. In 1995, the company's operation in Australia was relabelled Grundy Television to preserve the existing brand name, but elsewhere the name disappeared in favour of first

Figure 9.1: FremantleMedia now uses its own brand image on programs formerly produced by Grundy Television.

Figure 9.2: Australian version of big international format produced by FremantleMedia.

Figure 9.3: Publicity image for FremantleMedia's Australian version of *The Biggest Loser*.

Pearson Television and later FremantleMedia. In 2003, the group acquired a second production company in Australia, Crackerjack Productions, and in 2006 it and Grundy Television were merged to become FremantleMedia Australia.

FremantleMedia is a transnational conglomerate of considerable proportions. Whether under the name of Grundy Television or FremantleMedia Australia, its Australian division is able to jointly dominate the Australian television program format market thanks to the commanding format library it has at its disposal. Among its most successful and recent remakes have been *Australian Idol, The Biggest Loser, The Con-Test, Quizmania, Temptation* and *The X-Factor*. It has also produced *Who Wants to Be a Millionaire?* and *Australian Idol* under licence from their UK owners. The company also continues to produce its long-running soap, *Neighbours*, which FremantleMedia distributes internationally and the cost of which is heavily underwritten by the BBC.

Southern Star-Endemol

Like FremantleMedia, Endemol has followed a path of deliberate and aggressive expansion in the global TV market. Easily the largest group operating in the field of TV program formats across the world, it has witnessed astonishing growth over the past 15 years. The organisation was founded in 1994 in The Netherlands by a merger of television production companies owned by Joop van den Ende and John de Mol, the name of the new group deriving from the combination of their surnames (Moran 1998). Endemol was floated on the Dutch stock exchange in 1996, sold at an inflated valuation to a Spanish telco in 2000, and recently repurchased for a more modest price by de Mol in partnership with Italian media mogul and politician, Silvio Berlusconi.

The onset of private commercial broadcasting, deregulation and production outsourcing in The Netherlands, Germany and elsewhere in Western Europe had given the two Dutch principals their start in the late 1980s and early 1990s. Realizing that the financial benefits of owning formats lay not only in the licence fees that they could attract, but also in the fees involved in their production, Endemol set about expanding its activities on a global scale.

Figure 9.4: Joint Venture Agreement (JVA) partners – Southern Star and Endemol.

Figure 9.5: Publicity image for the game show *Deal or No Deal*.

Following the merger and the new company's float on the Dutch stock exchange, the principals began setting up offices in the neighbouring territories of Germany, Portugal, Spain and Belgium. Endemol also acquired bases in other markets through company buyouts beginning in 2000 in France, Italy and the United Kingdom (Moran and Malbon 2006). By this time, Endemol had discovered its jewel in the crown in the shape of *Big Brother* (Bazalgette 2005). This show first went to air in The Netherlands in late 1999. Its overwhelming success there triggered adaptations in many other parts of the world. The format also enabled Endemol to further extend its global format production operation through joint-venture arrangements. One of the largest of these commercial marriages occurred in 2001 with the establishment of Endemol Globo in Brazil. Meanwhile, 1999 had seen the establishment of a joint venture agreement in the Australian market between Southern Star and Endemol.

Southern Star itself had been in existence for over a decade. Its origins lay in the early 1980s when US animator Hanna Barbera decided to set up an Australian production facility (Cunningham and Jacka 1996). In partnership with Australian businessman James Hardy, Taft-Hardy came into existence in 1983 with plans to operate both in the area of production and distribution. In 1988, there was a management buyout which led to the establishment of a public company, Southern Star. Southern Star operated both in the area of distribution of film and television, as well as acting as an umbrella company to several independent producers. The strategy was very successful and Southern Star became the largest and most profitable television packager with the exception of the Grundy Organization. When Endemol looked for a joint-venture partner for the Australian market, Southern Star proved to be the most attractive for its purposes.

Over the past decade, the partnership has proved to be very productive and formidable. Drawing on the Endemol international catalogue of format programs, the joint venture has produced a series of successful programs for the Australian television market including *Deal Or No Deal*, *Ground Force*, *Ready Steady Cook* and *Strictly Dancing*. Undoubtedly, though, its most valuable property has been the Australian series of *Big Brother*, which has had eight seasons on air.

BBC Australia
The original organisation, the BBC, is the body that provides the television, radio, online and other services to the United Kingdom (Cave, Collins and Crowther 2004; Rogers 2007). BBC

Worldwide is a commercial subsidiary that not only includes international merchandising but is also involved in the licensing of canned and format programs into other television territories of the world (BBC Worldwide 2002, the purpose of which is to license program formats for adaptation and remaking in other territories. Territories where the division has been active have included Australia, where licensing has led to local versions of such formats as *Ready Steady Cook, The Weakest Link, Dancing With the Stars* and *Just the Two of Us*. These and other formats were licensed on by BBC Worldwide so that the production of these series was undertaken by small locally based production companies, or production units of the television networks themselves (Jarvis 2006). Thereupon, BBC Worldwide shifted its policy in order to become a leading international content producer. Wayne Gardner, managing director of content and production at BBC Worldwide, explained this change:

> Historically, BBC Worldwide with television formats has licensed them. So if you take a show like *The Weakest Link* in North America, we licensed that format to a producer who went and made it for a broadcaster and that show lasted, it did quite well on NBC to begin with, and had a small window. With *Dancing With the Stars*, actually we produce the show in Los Angeles. We receive a format fee, we receive a production fee. And we make a profit, which is the difference between what the program costs and what the network is prepared to pay. On top of that we've been also able to manage the exploitation of the dancing format outside of the television arena (Media Report 2007).

With this end in view, BBC Worldwide in 2006–7 took a 25 per cent share in the ownership of local production company the Freehand Group. The Freehand Group was itself a relative newcomer although it had already successfully produced *The Great BBQ Challenge, Missing Persons' Unit* and *Joker Poker*. One of the partnership's first ventures was a remake of *Top Gear* for SBS Television (Freehand 2007). Meanwhile, the BBC also announced the formation of BBC World (Australia) Pty Limited, which was incorporated in Australia (BBC World 2007).

This last move was part of BBC Worldwide's strategy for international expansion. As a central component of this development, Gardner was particularly keen to stress the redevelopment of media connections based on Anglophone markets. The establishment of a production base in Australia was paralleled by comparable moves in the United States, Canada and India. In the United States, a production, distribution and marketing operation, BBC America, had come into existence in 2006. A BBC arm in Canada had followed in 2007. That year also saw the establishment of a production office in India following a successful partnership with *The Times of India* in publishing localized versions of *Top Gear* and *Hullo*. It was hoped BBC India would not only become a producer of pre-existing BBC formats, but would itself develop into a centre for their devising and circulation. As Gardner put it: 'We're hoping that by having a production

Figure 9.6: BBC logo.

Figure 9.7: Freehand logo.

Figure 9.8: *Top Gear* – the BBC's highly successful UK format.

company out there, will create properties that will have a value around the world for the Indian diaspora, and also for other people around the world.' (Media Report 2007)

Summary

This chapter has been concerned with the impact of global television trade in outlying television markets. At these production coalfaces, business deals first struck at the central global hubs constituted by such markets as NATPE and MIP come to fruition in the shape of programs adapted, remade and broadcast. The long distribution trail comes to an end. What is shown to local audiences with a format program is one that has been indigenized to seem familiar and nationally inclusive. Yet, even though the progress of individual television franchise properties may be no more, the fact is that the television corridors and pathways between centre and periphery remain intact, forming a complex ongoing network of the global television system. Many national television industries are clients of the major distributing organizations. This chapter has concentrated on one such market outpost as a means of focusing on the commercial and cultural links engendered in the format component of the global television system. As a case study of the local impact of the world TV format trade, Australian television is both unlike and like other industries. The region to which it belongs exhibits distinct characteristics in terms of geography, language, ethnicity, history and religion that are not repeated elsewhere. Yet what is striking is the continuing inverted power relationship between Australian television and global television companies.

Figure 9.9: Australian adaptation of the BBC's successful format *Dancing with the Stars*.

10

NEW FLOWS IN GLOBAL TV

Most people around the world prefer to be entertained by people who look the same, talk the same, joke the same, behave the same, play the same games, and have the same beliefs (and worldview) as themselves. They also overwhelmingly prefer their own national news, politics, weather, and football and other sports (Tunstall 2008: xiv).

New Flows in Global TV has been concerned to analyze the structure and dynamics of the global trading system of TV program formats. This is a relatively new and novel form of exchange in television industries and cultures. It appears to integrate television institutions into a trans-border, even perhaps worldwide, system of cultural business and finance. Yet, as I have also been at pains to point out, such an integration is by no means total or all-encompassing, especially when it comes to matters of language and culture.

Television formats may indeed be global in their flow, but they are usually local in their interaction with and resonance for national audiences. With that qualification in mind, the present study has been concerned to investigate the cultural organisation of world trade in television program formats. The system that has been analyzed determines exchange at levels ranging from the international through to the local. Television across the planet now circulates in very different ways, thanks in part to the emergence and maturing of this form of trade. Television flows along different commercial routes, as this study has sought to show. Geography is important in this movement, but so too is the social moulding that culture confers on such a geography.

New Flows has been structured according to this double focus. Chapter 2 analyzed the international television marketplaces where the trade comes together for business as well as cultural reasons. Social routines, customs and rituals are particularly important on such occasions, and this awareness framed the next three chapters. Taken together, these help amplify our sense of the world of international TV program format trade. The chapters examined the way that the trade speaks to itself, how and why particular traders are lionized, and how the trade operates in different linguistic worlds. This last analysis, contained in Chapter 5, is pivotal to the study as a whole, for it is poised between the global fact of the (international) TV program format industry and the customization of individual formats so that they can be understood and enjoyed by local and national audiences in particular parts of the world.

The second half of the book has been devoted to tracing this cultural geography in detail. Chapter 6 rehearsed this pattern with three market studies. The first looked at markets in general and the second at how companies divide territories for business purposes, while a third traced how one particular program has travelled internationally both as a canned program and as a format remade for particular audiences based on language and cultural fit. Customizing a program format for a particular audience is a difficult and delicate process. The next chapter analyzed the work of a kind of ambassador figure sent to help in this complex task of acclimatizing the program format. Some format remakes are sanctioned while others are not. Chapter 8 outlined the use of legal instruments in policing adaptations. Another partial means to the same end involves format owners and devisors entering into ongoing production arrangements with local production companies operating in particular territories. Chapter 9 rounded off the journey undertaken in the book by plotting the dynamics of this development in one particular broadcasting market.

Over and above the detail of how the television program format trade is organized across the world, this study also contributes to a larger debate concerning globalization or localization of media. When one talks about global television, is one talking about a complex, multi-layered system involving as many as five different tiers, ranging from the international to the local? Or is one referring to an increasingly uniform system of television across the world, where larger and larger audiences in different places are watching the same television content?

It is tempting to view the advent of the international television trade in program formats as evidence of the latter tendency (Tomlinson 1991). From a business viewpoint, 50 or 100 format versions of *Big Brother* or *Who Wants to Be a Millionaire?* have been adapted and remade in different territories across the world, and the globalization of television culture seems self-evident to the business sector. In fact, when a format program is adapted and remade in a particular territory, it takes on the kind of social hue and accent to which Tunstall refers at the beginning of this chapter.

This kind of customization can work just as easily and readily in Hollywood as in other parts of the world. Viewed from afar, Hollywood has been long regarded as a great producing and exporting centre. This is certainly the case. But it has also long been a great importing centre so far as audio-visual adaptation is concerned. This is affirmed by the long history of Hollywood remakes of film ideas first produced in other languages and cultures, such as those of France and Japan (Mazdon 2000). More recently, the same tendency is at work in television and in other sections of the culture industries (cf. Prestholdt 2008). As I have noted elsewhere in these pages, program formats originating in foreign parts, including *Millionaire*, *Pop Idol* and *Yo soy Betty, la fea*, have all found their way to Hollywood. There they received the 'Made in the USA' imprimatur. Although each was allocated more lavish production budgets than its counterparts elsewhere, nevertheless only *Ugly Betty* was distributed internationally. Even then, as I note in Chapter 6, this US remake was picked up only in Anglophone markets. In other words, in the case of these format remakes, Hollywood's capability was not so much global but more national, or even regional.

Tunstall (2008) explores this changing situation in his most recent book on media around the world. He writes:

> Many people have argued that the media have become globalized and Americanized. This book points to the resilience and (probably) increasing strength of national culture, national sentiment, and national media especially in the Asian and other countries where most of the world's people happen to live ... A global or world level of media certainly does exist. But world media, or American media, play a much smaller role than national media (Tunstall 2008: xiii–xiv).

Elsewhere, Tunstall returns to the same point, noting that worldwide trade in media – in this case, television programs – is quite ambiguous when it comes to 'TV format sales and piracy' (Tunstall 2008: 1). This incongruity is a significant point with which to end this book. Television everywhere continues to operate at the five different levels that it has always done, ranging from the local to the international – even though these levels are continuously shaped and remoulded by complex, multi-level forces. Nation-states appear to continue to matter, not only in domains such as finance and politics but also in culture (Morris and Waisbord 2001). New cross-border flows of TV formats certainly add a new dimension to global television. Paradoxically, though, these flows only happen because of the ongoing importance of the local and the national. Australian television executive Reg Grundy, himself an early proponent of this traffic, once referred to this cultural commerce as 'parochial internationalism'. After the intense use of the 'g' word over the past quarter-century by journalists, politicians and even media researchers, it is salutary and necessary to be reminded of the ongoing relevance of the nationally constructed local.

References

Acheson, K. and Maule, C. (1989), 'The Higgledy-Piggledy Trade Environment for Films and Programs: The Canadian Example', *World Competition*, 13, pp. 47–62.

Acheson, K., Maule, C. and Filleul, E. (1992), 'The Business Side of an International Television Festival', *Journal of Arts Management, Law and Society*, 22, pp. 118–33.

Acheson, K., Maule, C. and Filleul, E. (1996), 'Cultural Entrepreneurship and the Banff Television Festival', *Journal of Cultural Economics*, 20: 4, pp. 321–39.

Aksoy, A. and Robins, K. (2000), 'Thinking Across Spaces: Transnational Television from Turkey', *European Journal of Cultural Studies*, 3: 3, pp. 343–65.

Alvarado, M. (1996), 'Selling Television', in A. Moran (ed.), *Film Policy: International, National and Regional Perspectives*, London: Routledge, pp. 62–71.

Anderson, B. (1991), *Imagined Communities: Reflections on the Origin and Spread of Nationalism*, London: Verso.

Anon (2004a), 'Report on Mobile Phone TV', *The Moving Picture*, 1 April, p. 48.

Anon (2004b), 'Cannes Awaits MIPTV and MILIA', *Daily MIPTV and MILIA News*, 1 April, pp. 29–32.

Anon (2006a), Press releases, *Daily News*, 3–7 April.

Bagumet, J. and Schiller, R. (eds) (1990), *The Craft of Translation*, Chicago: University of Chicago Press.

Bakhtin, M. (1981), 'Discourse in the Novel', in M. Holquist (ed.), *The Dialectical Imagination: Four Essays by Mikhail Bakhtin*, Austin, TX: University of Texas Press.

Bakhtin, M. (1986), 'The Problem of Speech Genres', in C. Emerson and M. Holquist (eds), *Speech Genres and Other Late Essays*, Austin, TX: University of Texas Press.

Banerjee, I. (2002), 'The Locals Strike Back? Media Globalization and Localization in the New Asian Television Landscape', *Gazette: International Journal for Communication Studies*, 64: 6, pp. 515–35.

Barbera, E. (2004), 'Mexico', in H. Newcomb (ed.), *The Museum of Broadcast Communication Encyclopedia of Television*, Chicago: Fitzroy Dearborn, pp. 1483–87.

Barnouw, E. (1968), *The Golden Tower: A History of Broadcasting in the United States Volume 2 (1932–1953)*, New York: Oxford University Press.

Barnouw, E. (1970), *The Image Empire: A History of Broadcasting in the United States from 1953*, New York: Oxford University Press.

Barnouw, E. (1992), *Tube of Plenty: The Evolution of American Television*, 2nd ed., New York: Oxford University Press.

Bazalgette, P. (1987), *You Don't Have to Diet*, Harmondsworth: Penguin.

Bazalgette, P. (1989), *BBC Food Check*, London: BBC Books.

Bazalgette, P. (2001), 'Big Brother and Beyond', *Television*, October, pp. 20–23.

Bazalgette, P. (2005), *Billion Dollar Game: How Three Men Risked It All and Changed the Face of TV*, New York: Time Warner Books.

BBC (2007a), 'Part One: Annual Report and Accounts 2006/2007 – The BBC Trust's Review and Assessment', http://www.bbc.co.uk/annualreport/pdfs/bbctrust_eng.pdf. Accessed 20 February 2008.

BBC (2007b), 'Part Two: Annual Report and Accounts 2006/2007 – The BBC Executive's Review and Assessment', http://www.bbc.co.uk/annualreport/pdfs/bbcexeceng.pdf. Accessed 20 February 2008.

BBC News (2000), 'Blow for Mogul's *Big Brother* Claim', 24 August, http://news.bbc.co.uk/2/hi/entertainment/2284706.stm. Accessed 20 February 2008.

BBC News (2002), 'Geldof Takes Action Against "Celebrity"', 27 September, http://news.bbc.co.uk/2/hi/entertainment/2284706.stm. Accessed 20 February 2008.

BBC Worldwide (2002), http://www.bbcworldwide.com/aboutus/corpinfo/annualreps/annualreport2002/product/sales2.html downloaded 11/04/2003. Accessed 20 February 2008.

BBC Worldwide (2003), Annual Review, http://www.bbcworldwide.com/review/tvsales_and_formats.html. Accessed 11 April 2003.

BBC Worldwide (2007) Press Release, 'BBC World Wide to Take Stake in Australia's Freehand Group', 31 January, http://www.bbcgovernorsarchive.co.uk/annreport/subsidiaries.html. Accessed 10 February 2007.

Beauchamp, C. and Bohar, H. (1992), *Hollywood on the Riviera: The Inside Story of the Cannes Film Festival*, New York: William Morrow.

Bellamy, R.V. and Trott, P.L. (2000), 'Television Branding as Promotion', in S. Eastman (ed.), *Research in Media Promotion*, Mahwah, NJ: Lawrence Erlbaum, pp. 127–59.

Bellour, Raymond (2008), *The Analysis of Film*, Ed. Constance Penley, Bloomington, IN: Indiana University Press.

Berlin, I. (2007 [1927]), 'Blue Skies', Wikipedia entry, http://en.wikipedia.org/wiki/Blue_Skies_(song). Accessed 10 February 2008.

Bielby, W.T. and Bielby, D. (1994), 'All Hits are Flukes: Institutionalized Decision Making and the Rhetoric of Network Prime-time Program Development', *American Journal of Sociology* 99: 5, pp. 1287–1313.

Billig, M. (1995), *Banal Nationalism*. London: Sage.

Bodycombe, D. (2002), 'So You Want to Create a Game Show: A Guide for the Budding Quiz Devisor', http://www.tvformats.com/formatsexl2lained.htm.

Brunsdon, C., Johnson, C., Moseley, R. and Wheatley, H. (2001), 'Factual Entertainment on British Television: The Midlands Research Group 8-9 Project', *European Journal of Cultural Studies*, 4: 1, pp. 29–63.

Brunt, R. (1985), 'What's My Line?', in L. Masterman (ed.), *Television Mythologies*, London: Comedia, pp. 21–28.

Buneau, M.A. (2000), 'When is a Format Not a Format?', *Television Business International*, February, pp. 44–50.

Buneau, M.A. (2001), 'Up for the Prize', *Television Business International*, January/February, pp. 25–28.

Buonanno, M. (forthcoming), 'A Place in the Sun: Global Seriality and the Revival of Domestic Drama in Italy', in A. Moran (ed.), *Localising Global TV*, Bristol: Intellect.

Burnett, K. (2002), 'To Have and to Own', in *Television Asia's Guide to Formats*, Singapore: Television Asia, p. 9.

Burnett, M. (2000), *Survivor: The Ultimate Game*, New York: Ballantine.

Burnett, M. (2001), *Dare to Succeed: How to Survive and Thrive in the Game of Life*, New York: Hyperion.

Burnett, M. (2005), *Jump In! Even If You Don't Know How to Swim*, New York: Ballantine.

Burns, S. (1977), *The BBC: Public Service and Private World*, London: Macmillan.

Burston, J. (2000), 'Spectacle, Synergy and Megamusicals: The Global-industrialisation of the Live-entertainment Economy', in J. Curran (ed.), *Media Organisation and Society*, New York: Oxford University Press, pp. 44–63.

Burt, T. and Gautam, M. (2004), '*Pop Idol* Tycoons to Face Music in Legal Contest', *Financial Times*, London, 11 September, p. 1.

Camparesi, V. (2000), *Mass Culture & National Traditions: The BBC and American Broadcasting, 1922–1954*, Fuceccho, Italy: European Press Academic.

Carey, J. (1989), *Communications as Culture: Essays on Media and Society*, London: Routledge.

Carter, B. (2005), 'For Fox, *Idol* Success is Set on a Shaky Pedestal', *New York Times*, Late Edition (East Coast), 21 November, p. C.1.

Cauldry, N. (2003), *Media Rituals*, London: Routledge.

Cauldry, N. and McCarthy, A. (eds) (2004), *MediaSpace: Place, Scale, and Culture in a Media Age*, New York: Routledge.

Cave, M., Collins, R. and Crowther, P. (2004), 'Regulating the BBC', *Telecommunications Policy*, 28: 3–4, April–May, pp. 249–72.

Chalaby, J.K. (2003), 'Television for a New Global Order: Transnational Television Networks and the Formation of Global Systems', *International Communication Gazette*, 65: 6, pp. 457–72.

Chalaby, J.K. (ed.) (2005a), *Transnational Television Worldwide: Towards a New Media Order*, London: I.B. Tauris.

Chalaby, J.K. (2005b), 'Deconstructing the Transnational: A Typology of Cross-border Television Channels in Europe', *New Media & Society* 7: 2, pp. 155–75.

Charlemagne (2003), 'Europe: The Galling Rise of English', *The Economist* 366: 8313, p. 42.

Chausey, Sara (2006), Interview with Albert Moran, London.

Clark, D. (ed.) (1991), *The Cinematic City*, London: Routledge.

Clarke, S. (2005), 'Romance Abroad', Variety, 10–16 October, p. A1.

Clausen, L. (2004). 'Localizing the Global: "Domestication" Processes in International News Production', *Media, Culture & Society* 26: 1, pp. 25–44.

Clukas, T. (2002), Interview with Albert Moran, Sydney.

Coad, J. (2007), Interview with Manuel Alvarado, November, London.

Collins, R. (1989), 'The Language of Advantage: Satellite Television in Western Europe', *Media, Culture and Society*, 11: 3, pp. 351–71.

Coombe, R.J. (1998), *The Cultural Life of Intellectual Properties: Authorship, Appropriation, and the Law*, Durham, NC: Duke University Press, p. 60.

Cooper-Chen, A. (ed.) (2005), *Global Entertainment Media: Content, Audiences, Issues*, London: Routledge.

Couldry, N. (2000), *The Place of Media Power: Pilgrims and Witnesses of the Media Age*, London: Routledge.

Couldry, N. (2003) *Media Rituals*, London: Routledge.

Couldry, N. and McCarthy, A. (eds) (2004), *MediaSpace: Place, Scale, and Culture in a Media Age*, London: Routledge.

Cousin, B. (2006), Interview with Albert Moran, FremantleMedia, London.

Cowan, T. (2002), *Creative Destruction: How Globalisation is Changing the World's Culture*, Princeton, NJ: Princeton University Press.

Crisell, A. (1996), *Understanding Radio*, New York: Routledge.

Crystal, D. (2001), *Language and the Internet*, Cambridge: Cambridge University Press.

Crystal, D. (2003), *English as a World Language*, Oxford: Oxford University Press.

Cunningham, S. (2004), 'International Television Markets', in H. Newcomb (ed.), *The Museum of Broadcasting Communications Encyclopedia of Television*, New York: Fitzroy Dearborn, pp. 1183–84.

Cunningham, S. and Jacka, E. (1996a), *Australian Television And International Mediascapes*, Melbourne: Cambridge University Press.

Cunningham, S. and Jacka, E. (1996b), 'The Role of Television in Australia's "Paradigm Shift" to Asia', *Media Culture and Society*, 18: 4, pp. 619–37.

Currie, E. (2005), 'The Real Deal', *New Statesman*, 18 April, http://www.newstatesman.com/200504180044. Accessed 20 October 2005.

Curtin, M. (2003), 'Media Capital: Towards the Study of Spatial Flows', *International Journal of Cultural Studies*, 6: 2, pp. 202–28.

Curtin, M. (2004), 'Media Capitals: Cultural Geographies of Global TV', in L. Spigel and J. Olsson (eds), *Television After TV: Essays on a Medium in Transition*, Durham, NC: Duke University Press.

Czitron, D. (1982), *Media and the American Mind: From Morse to McLuhan*, Chapel Hill, NC: University of North Carolina Press.

Daihyhyanathan, S. (2002), *Copyright and Copy Wrong: The Rise of Intellectual Property and How It Threatens Creativity*, New York: New York University Press.

Daily News (2004a), 'Sony Adds New Dimension to Technological Future', 30 March, p. 19.

Daily News (2004b), 'Public Broadcasters Urged to Push Digital Boundaries', 1 April, p. 1.

Daily News (2004c), 'A Brand New Reality – Zone Vision Reality TV Channel', 30 March, p. 69.

Daily News (2004d), 'Mobile Operators Put Out Call for Content', 1 April, p. 36.

Daily News (2004e), 'Ben Silverma', 29 March, p. 10.

Daily News (2004f), 'Chinese Television', 31 March, p. 48.

Daily News (2004g), 'Chinese Open Window Shows Media Industry in Ascent: Panelists at the Window on the Chinese Market Conference', 2 April, pp. 10–11.

Daily News (2006a), 'It's Happening', 31 March, p. 48.

Daily News (2006b), 'Are Terrestial Bulletins Yesterday's News?', 4 April, p. 68.

Daily News (2006c), 'Welcome to Tomorrow's World', 3 April, p. 4.

Daily News (2006d), 'Today', 6 April, p. 1.

Daily News (2006e), 'Tough Acts to Follow', 3 April, p. 72.

Daily News (2006f), 'Korea's Recipe for Future', 5 April, p. 36.

Daswani, M. (2002), 'Managing Risk: Broadcasters are Betting on the Success of Affordable, Low-risk Formats, While Distributors are Looking for Novel Ideas to Keep the Genre Fresh', *World Screen*, July, http://www.worldscreen.com/featuresarchive.php?filename=managingrisk.txt.

Dawley, Heidi (1994), 'What's in a Format?' *Television Business International*, November, pp. 24–26.

de la Fuente, A.M. (2005) 'UB Grows into Swan Around the World', *Variety*, 27 June, pp. 28–29.

de Pablos, E. (2006), 'Telecinco Goes Local B', *Variety*, 13–19 February, p. 31.

de Cordova, R. (2006), 'The Discourse on Acting', in P.D. Marshall (ed.), *The Celebrity Culture Reader*, New York: Routledge, pp. 91–107.

DeSanto, B. and Petherbridge, J. (2002), 'Case 3, BBC America: How Britain Won the Colonies Back', in D. Moss and B. DeSanto (eds), *Public Relations Cases: International Perspectives*, New York: Routledge, pp. 39–50.

Dicke, T.S. (1992), *Franchising in America, 1840–1980*, Chapel Hill, NC: University of North Carolina Press.

DISCOP (2004), www.discop.com. Accessed 15 February 2005.

Drummond, M. (2000), Interview with Albert Moran, Sydney.

Dyer, R. (1979), *Stars*, London: British Film Institute.

Dyer, R. (1986), *Heavenly Bodies: Film Stars and Society*, New York: St Martin's Press.

Edmonds, M. (2004), 'Now You See It', *Daily News*, 3 April, p. 14.

Edmonds, M. (2006), 'Future Needs and Wants', *The News*, 4 April, p. 26.

Edwards, J. (1985), *Language, Society and Identity*, Oxford: Blackwell.

Ek, R. (2006), 'Media Studies, Geographical Imaginations and Relational Space', in J. Folkheimer and A. Jamson (eds.), *Geographies of Communication: The Spatial Turn in Media Studies*, Goteberg, Sweden: Nordicom, pp. 10–29.

EyeWorks 2004, 'Head-on Collision for French Driving Formats', http://www.eyeworks.tv. Accessed 22 November 2004.

Fairclough, N. (1995), *Critical Discourse Analysis*, London: Edward Arnold.

Falkheimer, Jasper and Jansson, Andre (eds) (2007), *Geographies of Communication: The Spatial Turn in Media Studies*, Nordicom: Goteborg.

Fang, I. (2004), 'Videotape', in H. Newcomb (ed.), *The Museum of Broadcast Communication Encyclopedia of Television*, Chicago: Fitzroy Dearborn, pp. 2438–40.

Farrer, G. (2005), 'Billion Dollar Game', *The Age*, 3 July, http://www.theage.com.au/news/reviews/billion-dollar-game/2005/07/02/1119724847136.html.

Federal Court of Australia (2005), *Nine Films & Television Pty Ltd v Ninox Television Limited* [2005] FCA 1404.

Ferguson, E. (2002), Interview with Albert Moran, Manchester.

Ferguson, E. (2005), Interview with Albert Moran, Manchester.

Fiddy, D. (1997), 'Format Sales, International', in H. Newcomb (ed.), *The Museum of Broadcast Communication Encyclopedia of Television*, Chicago: Fitzroy Dearborn, pp. 623–24.

Foucault, M. (1972), *The Archaeology of Knowledge*, London: Tavistock.

Franko, E. (2006), 'Marketing "Reality" to the World: *Survivor*, Post-Fordism, and Reality Television', in D.S. Escoffery (ed.), *How Real is Reality TV? Essays on Representation and Truth*, Jefferson, NC: McFarland & Co.

Frau-Meigs, D. (2006), '*Big Brother* and Reality TV in Europe', *European Journal of Communication*, 21: 1, pp. 33–56.

Freedman, D. (2003), 'Who Wants to Be a Millionaire? The Politics of Television Exports', *Information, Communication & Society*, 6: 1, pp. 24–41.

Freedman, S. (1996), Interview with Albert Moran, Los Angeles.

Freehand (2007), Press Release, http://www.bbc.co.uk/print/pressoffice/bbcworldwide/worldwide stories/pressreleases/2007/01_january/freehand_group1.shtml. Accessed 10 February 2008.

Frutkin, A.J. (2007), 'Burnett Rate: Reality TV Don's New Shows Go Flat as Genre Saturates', *Mediaweek*, 17: 25, 18 June, p. 6(2).

Fry, A. (2006), 'Hard Act to Follow', *The News*, 3 April, pp. 70–77.

Fung, A. (2004), 'Coping, Cloning and Copying: Hong Kong in the Global Television Format Business', in A. Moran and M. Keane (eds), *Television Across Asia*, London: Curzon/Routledge, pp. 74–86.

Fung, A. (2008), *Global Capital, Local Culture: Localization of Transnational Media Corporations in China*, New York: Peter Lang.

Ganson, J. (1994), *Claims to Fame: Celebrity in Contemporary America*, Berkeley, CA: University of California Press.

Garcia Canclini, N. (1995), *Hybrid Cultures: Strategies for Entering and Leaving Modernity*, Minneapolis: University of Minnesota Press.

Gibson, O. (2003), 'Granada Show Wins *Survivor* "Clone" Case', *Financial Times*, 14 January, p. 44, http://www.financialtimes.com/featuresarchive.php?filename=NOVELAS-ASIA-1203. Accessed 20 February 2008.

Gitlin, T. (1983), *Inside Television*, New York: Pantheon.

Gough, L. (2002), 'The Drama Over Format Rights', 'Managing Intellectual Property', 'Copyright Law', *Copyright World*, 127, pp. 21–24.

Grantham, B. (2003), Interview with Albert Moran, Brisbane.

Greenberg, L.A. (1992), 'The Art of Appropriation: Puppies, Piracy, and Post-modernism', *Cardozo Arts & Entertainment Law Journal*, 11, pp. 1–33.

Grego, M. (2005), 'Burnett's New Studio Model', *Television Week*, 24: 33, 15 August, pp. 1–3.

Griffin, J. (2005), 'The United Kingdom', in A. Cooper-Chen (ed.), *Global Entertainment Media: Content, Audiences, Issues*, London: Routledge.

Griffiths, A. (2003), *Digital Television: Business Challenges and Opportunities*, London: Palgrave.

Guider, E. (2007a), 'All Eyes on the Future at NATPE', *Variety*, 22 January.

Guider, E. (2007b), 'MIP Reflects Buoyant TV Business: Execs Stay Longer at Mart', *Variety*, 20 April.

Guider, E. (2007c), 'Virtually Vexed at MIP', *Variety*, 23 April.

Guider, E. and Dempsey, J. (2007), 'Confusion, Caution at Confab', *Variety*, 22 April.

Guider, E. and Foreman, L. (2007), 'Newbies Fuel a Hip MIP: Celebs, New Media Spice Up TV Sales', *Variety*, 23 April.

Hay, C. (2003), 'Simon Says…', *Billboard*, 115: 26, 28 June, p. 1, http://www.nbc.com/nbc/The_Apprentice/bios/Mark_Burnett.html. Accessed 10 February 2004.

Hay, J. (2001), 'Locating the Televisual', *Television and New Media*, 2: 3, pp. 205–34.

Hay, J. (2004), 'Geography and Television', in H. Newcomb (ed.), *The Museum of Broadcast Communication Encyclopedia of Television*, Chicago: Fitzroy Dearborn, pp. 974–99.

Heinkeilein, M. (2004), *Der Schutz der Urheber von Femsehshows und Femsehshowformaten*, Baden-Baden: Nomos Verlagsgesellschaft.

Hernandez, S. (2001), 'The Ugly Truth About Betty la fea', http://dir.salon.com/mwt/feature/2001/06/01/betty/index.html. Accessed 4 May 2009.

Hetsroni, A. (2005), 'Rule Britannia! Britannia Rules the Waves: A Cross-cultural Study of Five English-speaking Versions of a British Quiz Show Format', *Communications*, 30: 2, pp. 26–48.

Heylen, R. (1994), *Translation Poetics and the Stage: Six French Hamlets*, London: Routledge.

Hilmes, M. (2003a), 'British Quality, American Chaos: Historical Dualisms and What They Leave Out', *The Radio Journal*, 1: 1, pp. 42–65.

Hilmes, M. (2003b), 'Radio Nations: The Importance of Transnational Media Study', in *Atlantic Communications: Political, Social and Cultural Perspectives on Media and Media Technology in American and German History in the 20th Century* (Krefeld Symposium 2002), London: Berg.

Hjarvard, S. (2003a), 'A Mediated World: The Globalization of Society and the Role of Media', in S. Hjarvard (ed.), *Media in a Globalized Society*, Kobenhavn: Museum Tusculanum Press, pp. 75–97.

Hjarvard, S. (2003b), 'The Globalization of Language: How the Media Contribute to the Spread of English and the Emergence of Medialects', in S. Hjarvard (ed.), *Media in a Globalized Society*, Kobenhavn: Museum Tusculanum Press, pp. 29–49.

Hobley, A. (2002), 'Victor in a Global War of Words', *Financial Times*, 28 September, p. 38.

Hong, J. (2004), 'China', in H. Newcomb (ed.), *The Museum of Broadcast Communication Encyclopedia of Television*, Chicago: Fitzroy Dearborn, pp. 510–14.

Horne, D. (1965), *The Lucky Country*, Melbourne: Penguin.

Huettig, M.D. (1944), *Economic Control in the Motion Picture Industry: A Study in Industrial Organisation*, Philadelphia: University of Pennsylvania Press.

Huettig, M.D. (1944), *Economic Control in the Motion Picture Industry: A Study in Industrial Organisation*, Philadelphia: University of Pennsylvania Press.

Hyatt, W. (1997), *Encyclopedia of Daytime Television*, New York: Billboard Books.

Idato, M. (2004), 'Steal the Show', press clipping supplied by email by David Franken.

Inglis, K. (1982), *This is the ABC*, Melbourne: Melbourne University Press.

Innis, H. (1950), *Empire and Communications*, Toronto: University of Toronto Press.

Iwabuchi, K. (2002), *Recentering Globalization*, Durham, NC: Duke University Press.

Iwabuchi, K. (2004), 'Feeling Glocal: Japan in the Global Television Format Business', in A. Moran and M. Keane (eds), *Television Across Asia*, London: Curzon/Routledge, pp. 21–34.

James, J. (2002), 'Reinventing Reality', *Sunday Times*, 27 October, http://www.time.com/time/magazine/article/0,9171,901021104-384753,00.html. Accessed 10 February 2004.

Jarvis, C. (1996), Interview with Emma Sandon, London.

Jarvis, C. (2006), Interview with Albert Moran, London.

Jasper, N. (2003), 'Asia's Love Affair', Worldscreen.com, http://www.worldscreen.com\featuresearchive.plp?filename=NOVELAS-ASIA. Accessed 10 February 2004.

Jenkins, J. (2006), 'Global Intelligibility and Local Diversity: Possibility or Paradox?', in R. Rubdy and M. Saraceni (eds), *English in the World: Global Rules, Global Roles*, London: Continuum.

Jensen, K.B. (ed.) (2002), *A Handbook of Media and Communication Research: Qualitative and Quantitative Methodologies*, London: Routledge.

Junhao, H. (2005), 'China 2005', in H. Newcomb (ed.), *The Museum of Broadcast Communication Encyclopedia of Television*, Chicago: Fitzroy Dearborn, pp. 510–14.

Kachru, B. (1992), 'Teaching World Englishes', in B. Kachru (ed.), *The Other Tongue* (2nd ed.), Urbana, IL: University of Illinois Press, pp. 355–65.

Keane, M. (2004), 'A Revolution in Television and a Great Leap Forward for Innovation? China in the Global Television Format Business', in A. Moran and M. Keane (eds), *Television Across Asia*, London: Curzon/Routledge, pp. 88–104.

Kissell, R.V. (2006), 'ER at 13: Tourniquet Not Needed', *Variety*, 30 October–5 November, p. 30.

Kitley, P. (2004), 'Closing the Creativity Gap – Renting Intellectual Capital in the Name of Local Content: Indonesia in the Global Television Format Business', in A. Moran and M. Keane (eds), *Television Across Asia*, London: Curzon/Routledge, pp. 138–56.

Kolle, R. (1995), Interview with Albert Moran, Grundy Television, Sydney.

Krippendorff, K. (1980), *Content Analysis: An Introduction to its Methodology*, Beverley Hills, CA: Sage.

Lamont, D. (2003), 'Can a Television Format Be Owned?', *The Guardian*, 20 January, p. 28.

Lane, S. (1992),'Format Rights in Television Shows: Law and the Legislative Process', *Statute Law Review*,13: 1, pp. 24–49.

Lane, S. and Bridge, R.M. (1990a), 'The Protection of Formats under English Law – Part I', *Entertainment Law Review*, 11, pp. 96–102.

Lane, S. and Bridge, R.M. (1990b), 'The Protection of Formats under English Law – Part II', *Entertainment Law Review*, 11, pp. 131–42.

Laughlan, P. (1998), *Intellectual Property: Creative and Marketing Rights*, Sydney: Law Book Company.

Lee, D.H. (2004), 'A Local Mode of Programme Adaptation: South Korea in the Global Television Format Business', in A. Moran and M. Keane (eds), *Television Across Asia*, London: Curzon/Routledge, pp. 36–53.

Lee, L.T. (2004), 'Formats', in C.H. Sterling (ed.), *Encyclopedia of Radio*, Chicago: Fitzroy Dearborn, pp. 612–14.

Lee, P. (1991), 'The Absorption and Indigenization of Foreign Media Cultures: A Study on a Cultural Meeting Point of the East and West – Hong Kong', *Asian Journal of Communication*, 1: 2, pp. 52–72.

Lefevere, A. (1993), 'Introduction', in A. Lefevere (ed.), *Translation/History/Culture*, London: Routledge.

Leland, G. (2004), 'An Export/import Business: New Zealand in the Global Television Format Business', in A. Moran and M. Keane (eds), *Television Across Asia*, London: Curzon/Routledge, pp. 184–97.

Lessig, L. (2004), *Free Culture: How Big Media Uses Technology and the Law to Lock Down Culture and Control Creativity*, New York: Penguin.

Lewis, J. (2006), 'Profile: Peter Bazalgette', *MoneyWeek*, 3 February, http://www.moneyweek.com/file/8538/profile-peter-bazalgette.html. Accessed 20 February 2007.

Lim, T. and Keane, M. (2004), 'Let the Contests Begin! "Singapore Slings" into Action: Singapore in the Global Television Format Business', in A. Moran and M. Keane (eds), *Television Across Asia*, London: Curzon/Routledge, pp. 105–21.

Liu, Y.L. and Chen, Y.H. (2004), 'Cloning, Adaptation, Import and Originality: Taiwan in the Global Television Format Business', in A. Moran and M. Keane (eds), *Television Across Asia*, London: Curzon/Routledge, pp. 54–73.

Lotman, Y. (1990), *Universe of the Mind: A Semiotic Theory of Culture*, Bloomington, IN: Indiana University Press.

Lowry, B. (2007), 'Ahoy! Nets in Need of Burnett's Pirate Plunder: Television Producer Mark Burnett Fails to Attract Viewership', *Variety*, 407.1, 21 May, p. 21.

Magder, Ted (2004), 'The End of TV 101: Reality Programs, Formats and the Real Business of Television', in S. Murray and L. Ouellette (eds), *Reality TV: Remaking Television Culture*, New York: New York University Press, pp. 137–52.

Mangiron, C. and O'Hagan, M. (2006), 'Game Localisation: Unleashing Imagination with "Restricted" Translation', *The Journal of Specialised Translation*, 6, pp. 22–32.

Mann, C.C. (1998), 'Who Will Own Your Next Good Idea?', *Atlantic Monthly*, September, pp. 57–63.

Mar-Molinero, Clare (2000), *The Politics of Language in the Spanish-speaking World*, London: Routledge.

Marshall, P.D. (1997), *Celebrity and Power: Fame in Contemporary Culture*, Minneapolis, MN: University of Minnesota Press.

Marshall, P.D. (ed.) (2006), *The Celebrity Culture Reader*, New York: Routledge.

Mason, B. (1998), Interview with Albert Moran, Grundy Television, London.

Mattelart, A., Delacourt, X. and Mattelart, M. (1985), *International Image Markets: In Search of an Alternative Perspective*, London: Comedia.

Mazdon, L. (2000), *Encore: Hollywood Remaking French Cinema*, London: British Film Institute.

McCarthy, A. (2000), *Ambient Television: Visual Cultures and Public Space*, Durham, NC: Duke University Press.

McConnell, C. (2003), 'I'm a Production Company ... Get Me a Format Right: The International Distribution of Television Formats Raises Important Issues for Copyright Law', *Copyright World*, 127, pp. 21–24.

McDermott, M. (2004), 'Mark Goodson and Bill Todman', in H. Newcomb (ed.), *The Museum of Broadcast Communication Encyclopedia of Television*, Chicago: Fitzroy Dearborn, pp. 1183–84.

McKay, Ian (1956), *Broadcasting in Australia*, Melbourne: Melbourne University Press.

McLuhan, Marshall (1962), *The Guthenberg Galaxy*, Toronto: University of Toronto Press.

McTernan, S. (2005), 'Format Rights: Not So Simple for Simon', *Entertainment Law Review*, 16, pp. 32–34.

Medcalf v Martel (1988), Court of Appeal, Civil Division Panel: Morritt LJ. (Transcript: Smith Bernal).

Media Report (2007), 'The British are Coming', ABC (Australia) Radio National, 22 July.

MILIA (2004), http://www.milia.com. Accessed 7 November 2004.

Miller, J. (2000), *Something Completely Different: British Television and American Culture*, Minneapolis, MN: University of Minnesota Press.

Miller, T., Govil, N., McMurria, J. and Maxwell, R. (2005), *Global Hollywood*, London: British Film Institute.

MIPCOM (2003), http://www.mipcom.com. Accessed 7 November 2004.

MIPTV (2006a), MIPTV Press Release, Paris, 6 January, p. 1.

MIPTV Magazine (2004) 'Working the Platform', Preview Edition, 29 March, p. 22.

MITV Magazine (2006), 'Working the Platforms', Preview Edition, 4 April, p. 22.

Moore, A. (ed.) (1997), *Intellectual Property: Moral, Legal, and International Dilemmas*, Lanham, MD: Rowman & Littlefield.

Moran, A. (1985), *Image and Industry: Australian Television Drama Production*, Sydney: Currency Press.

Moran, A. (1998), *Copycat Television: Globalization, Program Formats and Cultural Identity*, Luton: University of Luton Press.

Moran, A. (2004a), 'Distantly European? Australia in the Global Television Format Business', in A. Moran and M. Keane (eds), *Television Across Asia*, London: Curzon/Routledge, pp. 168–84.

Moran, A. (2004b), 'Australia', in H. Newcomb (ed.), *The Museum of Broadcast Communication Encyclopedia of Television*, Chicago: Fitzroy Dearborn, pp. 173–80.

Moran, A. (2005), 'Configurations of the New Television Landscape', in Janet Wasko (ed.), *A Companion to Television*, Malden, MA: Blackwell, pp. 291–307.

Moran, A. (2006), 'The International Face of Australian Television', *Media International Australia*, 121, pp. 174–87.

Moran, A. (2007), 'Localizing Global Television', *Media International Australia*, 124, pp. 145–55.

Moran, A. (2008), 'Cultural Power in International TV Format Markets', in J. Wasko and M. Erickson (eds), *Trans-Border Cultural Production: Economic Runaway or Globalization?* New York: Cambria, pp. 333–58.

Moran, A. (2009a) 'Practicing Localization: Regimes of Television Production in the Era of Migrating Media', in G. Elmer (ed.), *Migrating Media: Space, Technology and Global Film and Television*, Langham, MD: Rowman and Littlefield.

Moran, A. and Keane, M. (eds) (2004), *Television Across Asia: Globalisation, Industry and Formats*, London: Curzon/Routledge.

Moran, A. and Keating, C. (2007), *Historical Dictionary of Australian Radio and Television*, Langham, MD: Scarecrow.

Moran, A. and Malbon, J. (2006), *Understanding the Global TV Format*, Bristol: Intellect.

Morley, D. (2000), *Home Territories: Media, Mobility and Identity*, London: Routledge.

Morley, D. and Robins, K. (1995), *Spaces of Identity: Global Media, Electronic Landscapes and Cultural Boundaries*, London: Routledge, pp. 10–25.

Morris, N. and Waisbord, S. (eds) (2001), *Media and Globalization: Why the State Matters*, Lanham, MD: Rowman & Littlefield.

Mosey, R. (2005). 'Everyone's a Winner?' *The Guardian*, 21 May, http://books.guardian.co.uk/review/story/0,,1487964,00.html. Accessed 20 February 2008.

Moving Picture, The (2006), 'The Mobile Phone Explosion', 30 March, p. 15.

Mules, T.J. (2004), 'Japan', in H. Newcomb (ed.), *The Museum of Broadcast Communication Encyclopedia of Television*, Chicago: Fitzroy Dearborn, pp. 1210–14.

Murdock, G. (2004), 'Silvio Berlusconi', in H. Newcomb (ed.), *The Museum of Broadcast Communication Encyclopedia of Television*, Chicago: Fitzroy Dearborn, pp. 243–45.

Murray, K. (2001), 'Surviving *Survivor*: Reading Mark Burnett's Field Guide and Denaturalizing Social Darwinism as Entertainment', *The Journal of American Culture*, 24: 3–4, p. 43.

NATPE (2004), http://www.natpe.org. Accessed 8 September 2004.

Neale, S. (1981), 'Art Cinema as Institution', *Screen*, 22: 1, pp. 11–39.

Newby, J. (2006), 'Ashley Highfield, BBC Responsible for New Media & Technology: Welcome to Tomorrow's World', *The News*, 1 April, p. 12.

Nine Films & Television Pty Ltd v Ninox Television Limited [2005] FCA 1404 (30 September 2005).

Nordenstreng, K. and Varis, T. (1974), 'Television Traffic: A One-way Street?', in *UNESCO Report and Papers on Mass Communications*, 70, Paris: United Nations Educational Scientific and Cultural Organisation, pp. 1263–64.

O'Dell, C. (2004), 'Kinescope', in H. Newcomb (ed.), *The Museum of Broadcast Communication Encyclopedia of Television*, Chicago: Fitzroy Dearborn, pp. 1263–64.

Olson, S.R. (1999), *Hollywood Planet*, Mahwah, NJ: LEA.

O'Regan, T, (1993), 'The Regional, the National and the Local: Hollywood's New and Declining Audiences', in E. Jacka (ed.), *Continental Shift: Culture and Globalisation*, Sydney: Local Consumption Publications.

O'Regan, T. (1996), *Australia's National Cinema*, London: Routledge.

Overett, M. (2002), Interview with Albert Moran, Brisbane.

Palais des Festivals (2006), 'Conference Program Gets Six of the Best', Palais des Festivals, Cannes, Press Release, 3–7 April, p. 1.

Parks, L. and Kumar, S. (eds) (2003), *Planet TV: A Global Television Reader*, New York: New York University Press.

Patterson, L.R. (1968), *Copyright in Historical Perspective*, Nashville, TN: Vanderbilt University Press.

Pelton, J. (1981), *Global Talk*, Boston: A.W. Sijthoff.

Penhaligon, L. (2002), 'In Brief – UK', *Copyright World* 19: 9, 28 August, pp. 14–29.

Pennycook, A. (1994), *The Cultural Politics of English as an International Language*, London: Longman.

Phillipson, R. (1993), *Linguistic Imperialism*, Oxford: Oxford University Press, pp. 74–97.

Prestholdt, J. (2008), *Domesticating the World: African Consumerism and the Genealogies of Globalization*, Berkeley, CA: University of California Press.

Purcell, C. (2001), 'To Import or to Format? That is the Question', *Electronic Media*, 15 January, p. 64.

Ranganathan, M. and Lobo, B. (2008), 'Localizing the Global: Analysis of Nationalist Ideologies in MNC Advertisements on Indian TV', *Nationalism & Ethnic Politics*, 14: 1: pp. 117–42.

Rhodes, P. (2006), Interview with Albert Moran, London.

Rice, L. (2007), 'Trouble "On the Lot": Fox's Much-hyped Reality Show is Desperate for Viewers', *Entertainment Weekly*, 939, 15 June, http://www.ew.com/ew/article/0,,20041696,00.html. Accessed 20 November 2007.

Ritzer, G. (1998), *The McDonaldization Thesis: Explorations and Extensions*, London: Sage.

Robertson, R. (1997), 'Glocalization: Time-space and Homogeneity-Heterogeneity', in M. Featherstone, S. Lash and R. Robertson (eds.), *Global Modernities*, London: Sage, pp. 25–44.

Rogers J. (2007), 'BBCW Format Factory Commission', *Broadcast*, 18 October, http://www.broadcastnow.co.uk/news/bbc_worldwide_format_factory_handed_first_us_commission.html. Accessed 11 November 2007.

Rubdy, R. and Saraceni, M. (2006), *English in the World: Global Rules, Global Roles*, London: Continuum.

Rydell, R. (1984), *All the World's a Fair: Visions of Empire at American International Expositions, 1876–1916*, Chicago, IL: University of Chicago Press, pp. 2–8.

Sanders, T. and Bazalgette, P. (1991), *The Food Revolution*, London: Bantam.

Sanghera, S. (2002), 'Where There's a Will', *The Financial Times*, 2 April, p. 28.

Santos, J.M.C. (2004), 'Reformatting the Format: Philippines in the Global Television Format Business', in A. Moran and M. Keane (eds), *Television Across Asia*, London: Curzon/Routledge, pp. 157–68.

Schmitt, D., Bisson, G. and Fey, C. (2005), *The Global Trade In Television Formats*, London: Screen Digest.

Schneider, M. (2006), '"Betty" Bops to Full Order: ABC Looks Pretty "Ugly"', *Variety*, 16 October.

Schroder, K.C. (2002), 'Discourses of Fact', in K.B. Jensen (ed.), *A Handbook of Media and Communication Research: Qualitative and Quantitative Methodologies*, London and New York: Routledge, pp. 98–116.

Scott, A. (2005), *On Hollywood: The Place, the Industry*, Princeton, NJ: Princeton University Press.

Shiel, M. and Fitzmaurice, T. (eds) (2001), *Cinema and the City: Film and Urban Societies in a Global Context*, Oxford: Blackwell.

Silj, A. (ed.) (1988), *East of Dallas: The European Challenge to American Television*, London: British Film Institute.

Sinclair, J. (1999), *Latin American Television: A Global View*, Oxford: Oxford University Press.

Sinclair, J. (2000), 'Geolinguistic Region as Global Space: The Case of Latin America', in G. Wang, J. Servaes and A. Goonasekera (eds), *The New Communications Landscape: Demystifying Media Globalization*, New York: Routledge, pp. 19–32.

Sinclair, J. (2004), 'Globalization, Supranational Institutions, and Media', in J.D.H. Downing (ed.), *The Sage Handbook of Media Studies*, Thousand Oaks, CA: Sage, pp. 65–82.

Sinclair, J., Jacka, E. and Cunningham, S. (1996), *New Patterns in Global Television: Peripheral Visions*, New York: Oxford University Press.

Skinner, T. (1995), Interview with Albert Moran, Singapore.

Smith, D. (2005), 'Are You Looking at Me?' *The Observer*, 8 May, http://books.guardian.co.uk/reviews/artsandentertainment/0,,1478794,00.html. Accessed 20 June 2005.

Smith, L.E. (1983), *Readings in English as an International Language*, Oxford: Pergamon.

Smith, L.E. and Forman, M.L. (eds) (2000), *World Englishes 2000: Selected Essays*, Honolulu: University of Hawaii and the EastWest Center.

Snoddy, R. (2005), 'Peter Bazalgette: Attack is the Best Form of Defence', *The Independent*, http:/news.independent.co.uk/media/article2472475.ecc. Accessed 12 January 2007.

Sonha, N. and Asthana, S. (2004), 'India', in H. Newcomb (ed.), *The Museum of Broadcast Communication Encyclopedia of Television*, Chicago: Fitzroy Dearborn, pp. 1172–77.

Spenser, G. (2006), Interview with Albert Moran, London.

Spiegel, L. and Olsson, J. (2004), *Television After TV: Essays on a Medium in Transition*, Durham, NC: Duke University Press.

Steemers, J. (2006a), 'Europe: Television in Transition', in L. Artz (ed.), *The Media Globe: Trends in International Mass Media*, Lanham, MD: Rowman & Littlefield.

Steemers, J. (2006b), *Selling Television: British Exports in a Global Marketplace*, London: British Film Institute.

Stober, B. (2006), 'Media Geography: From Pattern to the Complexity of Meanings', in Jasper Falkheimer and Andre Jansson (eds), *Geographies of Communication: The Spatial Turn in Media Studies*, Nordicom: Goteborg, pp. 29–44.

Storper, J. (2002), 'Globalization and Knowledge Flows: An Industrial Geographer's Perspective', in Mark Goodson and Bill Todman (eds), *Regions, Geography and the Knowledge Based Economy*, Oxford Subscriptions On Line.

Straubhaar, J. (1991), 'Beyond Media Imperialism: Asymmetrical Interdependence and Cultural Proximity', *Critical Studies in Mass Communication*, 8, pp. 39–59.

Straubhaar, J.D. (1997), 'Distinguishing the Global, Regional and National Levels of World Television', in A. Sreberny-Mohammadi, D. Winseck, J. McKenna and O. Boyd-Barrett (eds), *Media in Global Context*, London: Edward Arnold, pp. 284–98.

Straubhaar, J.D. (2003), 'Choosing National TV: Cultural Capital, Language, and Cultural Proximity in Brazil', in M.G. Elasmar (ed.), *The Impact of International Television: A Paradigm Shift*, Mahwah, NJ: Lawrence Erlbaum, pp. 77–110.

Straubhaar, J. (2007), *World Television: From Global to Local*, Thousand Oaks, CA: Sage.

Street, J. (2006), 'The Celebrity Politician: Political Style and Popular Culture', in P.D. Marshall (ed.), *The Celebrity Culture Reader*, London: Routledge, pp. 361–70.

Sutter, M. (2001), 'Latin America: Ugly Betty Turns Tables on Television Formula', *Variety*, 21 January, pp. 54–55.

Thomas, A.O. and Kumar, K.J. (2004), 'Copied from Without and Cloned from Within: India in the Global Television Format Business', in A. Moran and M. Keane (eds), *Television Across Asia*, London: Curzon/Routledge, pp. 122–37.

Thompson, K. (2003), *Storytelling in Film and Television*, New Haven, MA: Harvard University Press.

Thorburn, D. and Jenkins, H. (2003), 'Introduction: Towards an Aesthetic of Transition', in D. Thorburn and H. Jenkins (eds), *Rethinking Media Change: The Aesthetics of Transition*, Cambridge, MA: MIT Press.

Thussu, D. (ed.) (2007), *Media on the Move: Global Flow and Contra-flow*. New York: Routledge.

Tomlinson, John (1991), *Cultural Imperialism: A Critical Introduction*, Baltimore, MD: John Hopkins University Press.

Tunstall, J. (ed.) (1973), *Media Sociology*, London: Constable.

Tunstall, J. (2008), *The Media Were American: US Mass Media in Decline*, New York: Oxford University Press.

Tunstall, J. and Machin, D. (1999), *The Anglo-American Media Connection*, Oxford: Oxford University Press.

Turan, K. (2000), *Sundance to Sarajevo: Film Festivals and the World They Make*, Berkeley, CA: University of California Press.

Turner, G. and Tay, J. (eds.) (2009), *Television Studies After TV*, London: Routledge.

Vaidhyanathan, Sida (2001), *Copyrights and Copywrongs*, New York: New York University Press.

Vaidhyanathan, Sida (2004), *The Anarchist in the Library: How the Clash Between Freedom and Control is Hacking the Real World and Crashing the System*, New York: Basic Books.

van Leeuwen, T. (2006), 'Translation, Adaptation, Globalization: The Vietnam News', *Journalism*, 7: 2, pp. 217–37.

Van Manen, J.R. (1994), *Televiseformats: en-iden naar Netherlands Recht*, Amsterdam: Otto Cramwinckle Uitgever.

Van Manen, J.R. (2003), Interview with Albert Moran, Amsterdam.

Venuti, L. (1995), *The Translator's Invisibility: A History of Translation*, London: Routledge.

Waisbord, S. (2004), 'McTV? Understanding the Global Popularity of Television Formats', *Television and New Media* 5: 4, pp. 359–83.

Waisbord, S. and Jalfin, S. (forthcoming), 'Imagining the National: Television Gatekeepers and the Adaptation of Global Franchises in Argentina', in A. Moran (ed.), *Localizing Global TV*, Bristol: Intellect.

Wallraff, S. (2002), 'What Global Language?', *Atlantic Monthly*, November, Online. http://www.theatlantic.com. Accessed 20 February 2005.

Wang, G. and Yeh, E. (2005), 'Globalization and Hybridization in Cultural Products: The Cases of *Mulan* and *Crouching Tiger, Hidden Dragon*', *International Journal of Cultural Studies*, 8: 2, pp. 175–93.

Wasko, J. and Erickson, M. (eds) (2008), *Trans-Border Cultural Production: Economic Runaway or Globalization?* New York: Cambria.

Wikipedia (2007), Simon Fuller http://en.wikipedia.org/wiki/Simon_Fuller. Accessed 20 July 2008.

Wikipedia (2008a), Mark Burnett IMDB.com. Accessed 20 July 2008.

Wikipedia (2008b) *Ugly Betty*, http://www.univision.net/corp/en/pr/New_York_14052003-2.html. Accessed 20 July 2008.

Williams, R. (1974), *Television: Technology and Cultural Form*, London: Fontana.

Wollen, P. (1968), *Signs and Meaning in the Cinema*, London: British Film Institute.

Wright, C. (2006), 'Welcome to the Jungle of the Real: Simulation, Commoditization, and *Survivor*', *Journal of American Culture*, 29: 2, pp. 170–84.

Wright, D. (2005), 'Mediating Production and Consumption: Cultural Capital and Cultural Workers', *British Journal of Sociology*, 56: 1, pp. 101–21.

INDEX